Games

THINKING ART

Series Editors
Noël Carroll and Jesse Prinz, CUNY Graduate Center

Thinking Art fills an important gap in contemporary philosophy of art, focusing on cutting edge ideas and approaches to the subject.

PUBLISHED IN THE SERIES:

Attentional Agency:
A Perceptual Theory of the Arts
William P. Seeley

Games

Agency As Art

C. THI NGUYEN

OXFORD
UNIVERSITY PRESS

OXFORD
UNIVERSITY PRESS

Oxford University Press is a department of the University of Oxford. It furthers the University's objective of excellence in research, scholarship, and education by publishing worldwide. Oxford is a registered trade mark of Oxford University Press in the UK and certain other countries.

Published in the United States of America by Oxford University Press
198 Madison Avenue, New York, NY 10016, United States of America.

Library of Congress Cataloging-in-Publication Data
Names: Nguyen, C. Thi, author.
Title: Games : agency as art / C. Thi Nguyen.
Description: New York, NY : Oxford University Press, 2020. |
Series: Thinking art | Includes bibliographical references and index.
Identifiers: LCCN 2019035272 (print) | LCCN 2019035273 (ebook) |
ISBN 9780190052089 (hardback) | ISBN 9780190052102 (epub) |
ISBN 9780190052096 (updf) | ISBN 9780190052119 (online)
Subjects: LCSH: Games—Psychological aspects. | Agent (Philosophy)
Classification: LCC GV1201.37.N48 2020 (print) |
LCC GV1201.37 (ebook) | DDC 793.01—dc23
LC record available at https://lccn.loc.gov/2019035272
LC ebook record available at https://lccn.loc.gov/2019035273

5 7 9 8 6

Printed by Integrated Books International, United States of America

Contents

Games

1

Agency as Art

Games can seem like an utterly silly way to spend one's time. We struggle and strain and sweat—and for what? The goals of games seem so arbitrary. Game players burn energy and effort, not on curing cancer or saving the environment, but on trying to beat each other at some unnecessary, invented activity. Why not spend that time on something real?

But the goals of a game aren't actually arbitrary at all. They only seem arbitrary when we look in the wrong place. In the rest of life, we are used to justifying our goals by looking at the value of the goals themselves or by looking forward, to what follows from those goals. But with the goals of games, we often need to look *backward*. We need to look at the value of the activity of pursuing those goals. In ordinary practical life, we usually take the means for the sake of the ends. But in games, we can take up an end for the sake of the means. Playing games can be a *motivational inversion* of ordinary life.

Seeing this motivational structure will also help us to understand the essential nature of games. A game tells us to take up a particular goal. It designates abilities for us to use in pursuing that goal. It packages all that up with a set of obstacles, crafted to fit those goals and abilities. A game uses all these elements to sculpt a form of activity. And when we play games, we take on an alternate form of agency. We take on new goals and accept different sets of abilities. We give ourselves over to different—and focused—ways of inhabiting our own agency. Goals, ability, and environment: these are the means by which game designers practice their art. And we experience the game designer's art by flexing our own agency to fit.

Games, then, are a unique social technology. They are a method for inscribing forms of agency into artifactual vessels: for recording them, preserving them, and passing them around. And we possess a special ability: we can be fluid with our agency; we can submerge ourselves in alternate agencies designed by another. In other words, we can use games to communicate forms of agency.

Games turn out to be part of the human practices of inscription. Painting lets us record sights, music lets us record sounds, stories let us record

Games. C. Thi Nguyen, Oxford University Press (2020). © Oxford University Press.
DOI: 10.1093/oso/9780190052089.001.0001

narratives, and games let us record agencies. That can be useful as part of our development. Just as novels let us experiences lives we have not lived, games let us experience forms of agency we might not have discovered on our own. But those shaped experiences of agency can be valuable in themselves, as art.

Consider *Sign*, a product of the avant-garde wing of role-playing games, by designers Kathryn Hymes and Hakan Seyalioglu. It's a live-action role-playing game about inventing language. The game is based on a true story. In the 1970s, Nicaragua had no sign language; deaf children were deeply isolated. Eventually, the government brought together deaf children from across the country to form an experimental school, whose goal was to teach those children to lip-read. Instead, the children collectively and spontaneously invented their own sign language. In the game *Sign*, the players take up the roles of those children. The game assigns every player a backstory and an inner truth each has always wanted to communicate. For example, "I'm afraid one day I'll be like my parents," and "I'm afraid [my cat] Whiskers thinks I've left her."

The game is played in total silence. The only way to communicate is through a new sign language, which the players must invent during the game. There are three rounds. In every round, each player invents a single sign and teaches it to the other players. Then all the players attempt to have a free-form conversation, desperately struggling to communicate through their tiny inventory of signs. Invented signs get used and modified; new signs evolve spontaneously from old signs. Communication happens painfully and slowly, with the occasional rare and luminous breakthrough. And every time you feel that you are misunderstood, or do not understand somebody else, you must take a marker and make a "compromise mark" on your hand.

The experience of the game is utterly marvelous. It is intense, absorbing, frustrating, and surprisingly emotional. But to have that experience, the players must commit, temporarily, to the goal of communicating their particular inner truths. And that commitment, combined with the particular rules of the game, leads to a very concentrated practical experience. To play *Sign* is to become entirely absorbed in the practical details of inventing language and stabilizing meanings.

Here, then, is the particular motivational state of game playing which I wish to investigate. The rules of the game tell us to care about something and we start caring about it. A board game instructs us to care about collecting one color of token. A video game tells us to care about stomping on little mushroom people. A sport tells us to get a ball in a net. In order to achieve that cherished state of absorbed play, we let that goal occupy our conscious-ness, for a while. And the fact that the game designer specifies goals and abil-ities for the player to take on—that is precisely what makes games distinctive as an art form.[1]

Frameworks and Approaches

My interest here is in uncovering the unique potential and the special value of games. There have been, in recent years, many arguments for the value and importance of games. In many cases, however, these arguments tend to avoid looking at some of the more unique qualities of games. Instead, they assimilate games into some other, more respectable category of human prac-tice. We've seen arguments that games are art because they are a type of fic-tion (Tavinor 2009). We've seen arguments that games are a type of cinema, one that adds a new technique—interactivity—to the familiar lexicon of cin-ematic techniques (Gaut 2010). We've seen arguments that games are a kind of conceptual art, which is valuable when it offers social critique (Flanagan 2013). We've seen arguments that games can be a special way of making arguments, which can criticize economic and political systems by simulating them (Frasca 2003; Bogost 2010). And surely, games can function in these ways. Many modern video games are, indeed, a kind of fiction and a kind of interactive cinema. And games can, as Ian Bogost puts it, function as a kind of procedural rhetoric, making arguments by modeling causal systems in the world. But I worry that overemphasizing these sorts of approaches may also suppress our appreciation and understanding of the truly unique potential of games.[2,3]

Over in the philosophy of sport, the value of game playing is usually spelled out in terms of skills, excellences, and achievements. But notice that this also cashes out the value of games in some very familiar currency. For example, Tom Hurka argues that games are valuable because they enable

---

[1] For simplicity's sake, I will speak as if there is a single game designer, when in actuality, games are often designed in large teams.

[2] My account is moderately aligned, in spirit, with those scholars who call themselves *ludologists*, who argue that games are a unique category and should be studied as such. For surveys of ludology, and of the debate between narratology and ludology, see Nguyen (2017c) and Kirkpatrick (2011, 48–86). For key texts of ludology, see Aarseth (1997); Frasca (1999); and Eskelinen (2001). I differ from some of the classic positions in ludology in many of the details. In particular, see Chapters 3–6.

[3] Much of the remainder of this chapter has been adapted from material that originally appeared in Nguyen (2019d).

difficult achievements. But difficult achievements are, obviously, not confined to games. Curing cancer and inventing a better mousetrap would also
be difficult achievements, and they would give us something useful besides.
This leads Hurka to conclude that playing games is generally less valuable
than engaging in more useful non-game activities. Science and philosophy
are valuable in the same way as games in offering difficult achievements, but
they are also valuable in other ways. They give us truth and understanding,
or at least some useful tools, as well as difficulty. Games can offer us only difficulty (Hurka 2006). Games might truly come into their own, says Hurka,
once we've solved all our practical problems and entered some sort of
techno-futurist Utopia. But in the meantime, we're probably better off doing
something more useful with our lives. Notice that Hurka's conclusion arises
precisely because he thinks games are valuable in virtue of something rather
commonplace—difficulty—rather than in virtue of something unique. Thus,
the value of games is easily superseded by the value of other, equally difficult
but more practical activities.

All these approaches miss much of what's special about games. Games,
I will argue, are a distinctive art form. They offer us access to a unique artistic horizon and a distinctive set of social goods. They are special as an art
because they engage with human practicality—with our ability to decide and
to do. And they are special as a practical activity precisely because they are
an art. In ordinary life, we have to struggle to deal with whatever the world
throws at us, with whatever means we happen to have lying around. In ordinary life, the form of our struggle is usually forced on us by an indifferent and
arbitrary world. In games, on the other hand, the form of our practical engagement is intentionally and creatively configured by the game's designers.
In ordinary life, we have to desperately fit ourselves to the practical demands
of the world. In games, we can engineer the world of the game, and the agency
we will occupy, to fit us and our desires. Struggles in games can be carefully
shaped in order to be interesting, fun, or even beautiful for the struggler.

This is enabled, in significant part, by the peculiar nature of our in-game
ends. Games ends are extremely different from the sorts of ends we stand
behind in ordinary life. Our values, in ordinary life, are largely recalcitrant. Much of what we value seems universal and immoveable. We value
life, freedom, and happiness. Even with our personal values, there's typically
little short-term flex. I care about art, creativity, and philosophy. Changing
my core values would take, at the very least, significant time and effort. My
core values are thick and recalcitrant. But game activity is different. We can

change our in-game ends easily and fluidly. We can adopt new ends, which will guide our actions for the duration of the game, and then drop them in an instant. When we play games, we take on temporary agencies—temporary sets of abilities and constraints, along with temporary ends. We have a significant capacity for agential fluidity, and games make full use of that capacity.

Suits and Striving

Why think we have this strange capacity for agential fluidity? The best place to start is Bernard Suits's analysis of games. Let's start with what Suits calls the "portable version" of his definition:

> Playing a game is the voluntary attempt to overcome unnecessary obstacles. (Suits [1978] 2014, 43)

In a marathon, the point isn't simply to get to the finish line. Usually, we don't actually care about being at that particular spot, in and of itself. We know because we don't try to get there as efficiently as possible. We don't take shortcuts, and we don't take a taxi. The whole point is to get there within certain limitations. Suits contrasts game playing with what he calls "technical activity." In technical activity, there is some end that we value, and we pursue it because of the value of that end. Since that end is genuinely valuable, we try to pursue it as efficiently as we can. But in games, we don't take the most efficient route to our in-game ends. In game playing, we try to achieve some specified end under certain specified inefficiencies. The end is largely valuable only when achieved inside those constraints. We can tell that this is our motivational structure, precisely because we are willing to set up blockades to that end. By itself, getting a ball through a stupid little basket has no independent value on its own. I don't go to the basketball court late at night with a ladder and spend hours passing the ball through the hoop; nor do I pull out my *Monopoly* set by myself, and roll myself around in heaps of *Monopoly* money, glorying in all that I command. Getting the ball through the hoop or holding *Monopoly* money in my hand is worthless outside of the constraints and structure of the game.

We must distinguish carefully here between the *goals* of a game and our *purpose* in playing a game. The goal of a game is the target we aim at during the game: getting to the finish line first, making more baskets, maximizing points. Our purpose with a game, on the other hand, is our reason for playing the game in the first place. Our purpose in playing a game might be to have some fun, to get some exercise, to de-stress, to develop our skills, to vanquish our opponents, to achieve some difficult task, or even to experience the beauty of our own skilled action.

For some game players, goal and purpose can be one and the same. A professional poker player is just in it for the money; an Olympic sprinter just wants to win, period—for these players, the goal is the purpose. Winning is genuinely valuable for them. For other game players, the goal and purpose are distinct, but achieving the purpose follows from achieving the goal in a straightforward way. This basketball player wants to win for the sake of fame and status; this *Starcraft 2* professional wants to win the tournament for the prize money. For these types of players, winning is only a means to their true purpose, but winning is still genuinely valuable to them.

What Suits exposes, however, is another, entirely different motivational structure: that our goal and purpose in a game might be entirely skew to one another. When I play a party game with my friends, my goal is to win, but my purpose is to have fun. The way to have fun is to try, during the game, to win. But I don't really care if I win or not—not in any lasting way. I have to *chase* the goal of winning to fulfill my purpose, but I don't actually need to win in order to have fun. Winning, in this case, is rather incidental to my true purpose. In fact, if I start up a game of Charades for the sake of having a little fun, but I am so aggressive and competitive that I make everybody else miserable, then I may have succeeded in achieving the goals of the game, but I have failed entirely in my purpose.

Suits took himself to be offering a complete account of games and game playing. For this he has been roundly criticized. There are, as many have pointed out, aspects of game playing that do not conform to Suits's theory. Some games involve no real struggle against obstacles at all, such as certain children's games of make-believe. Certain narratively oriented tabletop role-playing games, like *Fiasco*, and narrative computer games, like *The Stanley Parable*, also don't seem oriented around struggles and obstacles. I agree with these criticisms. I do not think Suits has provided a complete account of all forms of game playing.[4] But we should not throw away Suits's analysis entirely, just because he failed in his stated goal. Let us adapt Suits's analysis and

---

[4] Criticism of Suits on this point is a common refrain; see Upton (2015, 2016) for a representative example. I provide an extended analysis of the relationship between make-believe play and striving play, and an argument against Suits's account of games being a complete one, in Nguyen (2019b).

treat it, instead, as an exceedingly insightful description of one particular—but very important—form of game play. For the remainder of this book, I will focus on understanding those games and playings that fit the Suitsian definition.[5] For the sake of brevity, whenever I simply use the bare term *game*, I can be taken to be referring to Suitsian games.

A more significant worry is that Suitsian play is necessarily immature and unworthy of serious attention. Suitsian games always involve practical struggles. We become absorbed in the instrumental activity of overcoming obstacles and achieving seemingly arbitrary goals. And it is precisely these aspects that can make game playing seem like a lesser activity. For example, media critic Andrew Darley condemns video games for offering only "surface play" and "direct sensorial stimulation." Says Darley: "Computer games are machine-like: they solicit intense concentration from the player who is caught up in their mechanisms . . . leaving little room for reflection other than an instrumental type of thinking that is more or less commensurate with their own workings" (Darley 2000; as quoted in Lopes 2010, 117). The same worry recurs in the new wave of games scholarship, even among some of games' most ardent defenders. These scholars often argue for the worth of games by pointing out how games can offer us rich content, beyond mere instrumental challenges. Such arguments often proceed by highlighting the capacity of games to represent. For example, Ian Bogost argues for the value of games by showing that games can be a form of rhetoric, making arguments via their ability to simulate the world. Bogost points to games like *McDonald's Video Game*. In that game, you run the McDonald's corporation. Your goal is to maximize profits while protecting the environment. But when you play the game, you quickly discover that you actually pull off both of these goals. The game argues, through its simulation, that the goals of capitalism and the goals of environmentalism are essentially at odds (Bogost 2010, 28–31). John Sharp reserves his highest praise for those games that move beyond the "hermetically sealed" experiences of merely solving the game, and instead represent and comment on the world. Sharp highlights Mary Flanagan's game *Career Moves*, which resembles that old family game *The Game of Life*, but

---

[5] Some readers may agree with me that Suitsian games are only one type of game; others might think that all games are Suitsian games. My argument should be palatable to both. Even those Wittgensteinians who maintain that the term *game* is essentially indefinable should be able to find my analysis somewhat palatable, by treating the category of "Suitsian games" as an artificial stipulation. I am not interested in debating whether or not the category of Suitsian games does or does not match up with some bit of natural language; I am interested in the fact that the category is clearly specified and useful, and applies to a broad range of human activities.

forces players to make stereotypically gendered career choices for their female character in order to cause them to reflect on gender biases in the workplace (Sharp 2015, 77–97). Flanagan herself praises Gonzolo Frasca's game *September 12th: A Toy World*, a pointedly political game in which one plays the United States, dropping bombs by drone on an unnamed Middle Eastern locale, attempting to kill terrorists, only to find that all their efforts only destroy innocent civilians and increase the number of terrorists (Flanagan 2013, 239–240).

Notice that these sorts of accountings pick out a very particular type of game as genuinely respectable. *September 12th*, *Career Moves*, and *McDonald's Video Game* may not present very interesting instrumental challenges, but that lack is unimportant by these lights. These games are good in virtue of what they represent. Underneath all these approaches seems to be the presumption that Suitsian play—the play of skills and clearly defined goals—cannot be valuable in any really deep or fulfilling way. These accounts seem motivated by the need to find some other footing from which to establish the value of games.

But I think we ought not dismiss instrumental play so quickly. That dismissal arises, I think, from misunderstanding the richly varied motivational structures involved in game playing. Let's return to the distinction between goals and purposes. This distinction helps us see that there are two very different modes of play. First, you might be playing for the sake of winning. You want the win either for its own sake or for the sake of something that follows from winning, such as goods and money.[6] Let's call this *achievement play*. Professional poker players who play for money, Olympic athletes who play for honor, and people who simply play to win are all achievement players. In achievement play, goal and purpose are aligned. Alternately, you might be pursuing the win for the sake of the struggle.

---

[6] It should be noted that the term *winning* here is slightly imprecise. There are many other sorts of states we can pursue in games. For example, one might have lost the opportunity to actually win in particular chess match, but one can still play on, aiming to achieve a stalemate rather than an outright loss. For another, as Suits points out, many games don't have victory condition, but only loss conditions. For example: a ping-pong volley, where we try to keep the ball going as long as possible, has no win condition, only a loss condition, and the goal of the activity is to stave off the loss for as long as possible. Technically, what I should be discussing here is not "winning" but the pursuit of the lusory goal, in its various shades and forms. However, I will use the term *winning* loosely, from here on out, to refer to the larger notion of the pursuits of lusory goals, and use the terms *achieving a victory* and *winning proper* to refer to the narrower notion. I do not use the term *success* because I think its natural use is ambiguous between win-related concepts and our larger purposes for playing a game. My spouse will say that our playing of a party game was "successful" if it was fun for all involved, regardless of whether she did well by the internal standard of the game.

Let's call that *striving play*. In striving play, goal and purpose are skew. An achievement player plays to win. A striving player acquires, temporarily, an interest in winning for the sake of the struggle. Thus, striving play involves a motivational inversion from ordinary life. In ordinary practical life, we pursue the means for the sake of the ends. But in striving play, we pursue the ends for the sake of the means. We take up a goal for the sake of the activity of struggling for it.

This motivational inversion is, in my eyes, the most interesting possibility raised by the Suitsian analysis. I will largely focus my analysis on striving play, not because I think it is the superior form of play, but because I think it is the more convoluted, more fascinating, and most frequently misunderstood form of play. Thinking about striving play will teach us something remarkable about ourselves, as rational agents who are capable of entering into such motivational inversions.

But first, let's take a step back. Does striving play really exist? I think it is quite commonplace, in fact. For example: my spouse and I took up racquetball in order to keep fit in a moderately entertaining way. When we play racquetball, I try with all my might to win. And my *trying* to win—my actually *caring* about winning, during the course of the game—is quite useful. Wanting to win helps my fitness by getting me to try harder during the game; it also helps the process to be engaging and compelling. In order to obtain those benefits, I need to induce in myself an interest in winning. But that interest is only temporary, and disconnected from my larger and more enduring ends.

We can see how disconnected and short-term that interest is by looking at how I strategically manipulate my ability to win in the long term. Suppose somebody were to offer me free racquetball lessons. Taking these lessons would cause me to jump far ahead of my spouse in skill. If I were an achievement player, I should certainly take them. But, as a matter of fact, I wouldn't actually take those lessons. If either my spouse or myself pulled substantially ahead of the other in skill, the game would turn quite unpleasant for both of us. Our matches would lose their interest and sparkle. We'd probably end up giving up racquetball altogether. In other words: in my long-term life, I make strategic decisions that keep my skill in check and prevent me from winning too many games. I manipulate my capacity to win, with an eye toward maintaining a desirable sort of struggle. But during the game itself, I play all out to win. If my decision to forego those lessons is comprehensible, then striving play is a real motivational possibility.

Consider, also, what we might call "stupid games." Stupid games have the following characteristics: first, they are only fun if you try to win; and second, the fun part is when you fail. There are a great many stupid games, including many drinking games and party games. Take the game *Twister*, in which you try to keep in balance as long as you can, but the funniest part is when everybody collapses on top of each other. My own favorite stupid game is Bag on Your Head, a ludicrous party game in which everybody puts a brown paper grocery bag on their head. The goal of the game is to try to take the bags off other people's heads. When somebody takes the bag off your head, you're out, and you have to go to the side of the room and leave play. The game, of course, involves lots of stumbling and tripping and flailing around by people with bags on their heads. And the best vantage point from to watch all this is that of the losers, watching from the side. And, at some point, there will be only one person still stumbling blindly around the room with a bag on their head, fumbling around for the other nonexistent opponents, while everybody else gets to watch, desperately trying not to laugh. That last person is the winner, and the very best part of the game is seeing how long it takes them to figure out that they have, in fact, won.

The children's game of Telephone is also a stupid game. You may remember the game from your childhood. To play, everybody sits in a circle. The starting player thinks of a message and then whispers it to the next person in the circle. Each player passes the message on, whispering it to the next player, until the message makes its way all around the circle. Then the players compare the original version with the circulated version. The circulated version is, inevitably, wildly distorted, much to everybody's amusement. We play the game because it's funny, and the funny part is failing, but it's only funny if our attempts to communicate really are failures. And that failure is real only if the players really did earnestly try to communicate clearly. Imagine if we played Telephone, but we intentionally tried to distort the message. There would be no actual failure, and thus no hilarity. In *Twister* and Telephone, to have the desired experience—a funny failure—the players must pursue success. But success isn't the point. Stupid games cannot be properly played by achievement players, only by striving players. Stupid games make sense only if striving play is possible.

And if striving play is possible, it must also be that we have a further capacity. We must be able to *submerge* ourselves in the temporary agency of the game. In order to engage in striving play, I must be able to take on a *disposable end*. That is, I must be able to bring myself to temporarily care about an end, and for that end to appear to me *as final*. But I also must be able to dispose of that end afterward. Why must submersion in a temporary agency be possible? Why must we be able to take on disposable ends?

Imagine what it would be like if we could not submerge ourselves in this way. Imagine a striving player who can only pursue game ends in the normal, transparently instrumental fashion—who cannot become submerged in an alternate agency. The purpose of such players in play is having a struggle, and that purpose is perpetually before their minds and active in their reasoning. This striving player, then, can't really pursue the game end wholeheartedly. If we are always constantly aware of, and fully motivated by, our broader purpose in striving play, then our struggles to achieve victory would curiously be undercut. In any game without a time limit, if victory were in our grasp, it would be entirely reasonable to delay the victory in order to have more of the activity of striving.[7] But this would be very odd behavior, and would defeat much of the point of striving play.

A friend of mine relates the following story: his ten-year-old son was beating my friend badly at *Monopoly*. The son was very much enjoying the experience. My friend discovered that every time he was about to lose, his son would sneak him some extra cash just to keep the game going. The son just wanted to extend the experience, to keep on beating his father forever. The story is funny precisely because the son is missing something crucial about how game playing works. In order to be absorbed in a game, we must behave as if winning were a final end. That end must phenomenally engulf us, if we are to be gripped by the game and if its thrills and threats are to have emotional punch for us. We must pursue the goals of the game wholeheartedly, putting our larger purpose out of mind. In other words, we must submerge ourselves in a temporary agency.

Aesthetic Experiences of One's Own Activity

Stupid games are not the point of our inquiry; they are merely a blunt example to show the possibility of striving play. I'm interested in showing that games can be an art form. So, let's start by thinking about how games can support aesthetic experiences. (I do not mean to imply that aim of art is exclusively to provide aesthetic experiences, but only that it is one of the characteristic

---

[7] This excellent point was originally raised to me by Christopher Yorke.

functions of art to do so.) The recent discussion of game aesthetics has largely focused on thinking about games as a form of fiction (Tavinor 2017, 2009; Robson and Meskin 2016). What we lack is an aesthetics of Suitsian play.

So: consider the category of *aesthetic striving play*—that is, game play engaged in for the sake of the aesthetic quality of the struggle. Can striving really give rise to aesthetic qualities, and what would those be like? Let's start with some paradigmatically aesthetic qualities: those of gracefulness and elegance. We obviously attribute such aesthetic qualities to particular playings of games, especially from the spectators' perspective. Sports spectatorship, for example, is full of talk of the beauty and elegance of athletic motion. But the spectator's perspective is not the end of the story. There are distinctive aesthetic qualities available primarily to the causally active game player. These are aesthetic qualities of acting, deciding, and solving.

And those aesthetic qualities can arise, not just for our actions in isolation, but also for our actions as practically functional. Some actions are beautiful because of what they get done. Consider the difference between two superficially similar activities: dancing freely and rock climbing. Dancing freely—as I do by myself with my headphones on—can be an aesthetic experience. My own movements can feel to me expressive, dramatic, and, once in a rare while, even a bit graceful. I also rock climb, and rock climbing is full of aesthetic experiences. Climbers praise particular climbs for having interesting movement or beautiful flow. But, unlike many traditional forms of dance, climbing aims at overcoming obstacles. The climbing experiences that linger most potently in my mind are experiences of movement *as the solution to a problem*—of my deliberateness and gracefulness that got me through a delicate sequence of holds (Nguyen 2017a). Dancing may occasionally be a game, but climbing is essentially a game. It is unnecessary obstacles, taken on for the activity of trying to overcome them.

Take another paradigmatically aesthetic property: harmony. When chess players discover a move that elegantly escapes a trap, the harmony of the move—the lovely fit between the challenge and the solution—is available both to themselves and to outsiders. But something more is available especially to players: a special experience of harmony between their abilities and the challenges of the world. When your abilities are pushed to their maximum, when your mind or body is just barely able to do what's required, when your abilities are just barely enough to cope with the situation at hand—that is an experience of harmony available primarily to the players themselves. It is a harmony between self and challenge, between the practical self and the obstacles of its world. It is a harmony of a practical fit between your whole self and the world.

This, it seems to me, is a paradigmatic aesthetic experience of playing games. Once we've seen it, we can see that aesthetic experiences with this character exist outside of games. I value philosophy because I value truth, but I also savor the feel of that beautiful moment of epiphany, when I finally find that argument that I was groping for. Games can provide consciously sculpted versions of those everyday experiences. There is a natural aesthetic pleasure to working through a difficult math proof; chess seems designed, at least in part, to concentrate and refine that pleasure for its own sake. In ordinary practical life, we catch momentary glimpses, when we are lucky, of harmony between our abilities and our tasks. But often, there is no such harmony. Our abilities fall far short of the tasks; or, the tasks are horribly dull.

But we can design games for the sake of this harmony of practical fit. In our games, the obstacles are designed to be solved by the human mind and the human body— unlike, say, the tasks of curing cancer or grading. John Dewey suggested that many of the arts are crystallizations of ordinary human experience (Dewey [1934] 2005). Fiction is the crystallization of telling people about what happened; visual arts are the crystallization of looking around and seeing; music is the crystallization of listening. Games, I claim, are the crystallization of practicality. Aesthetic experiences of action are natural and occur outside of games all the time. Fixing a broken car engine, figuring out a math proof, managing a corporation, even getting into a bar fight—each can have its own particular interest and beauty. These include the satisfaction of finding an elegant solution to an administrative problem, of dodging perfectly around an unexpected obstacle. These experiences are wonderful—but in the wild, they are far too rare. Games can concentrate those experiences. When we design games, we can sculpt the shape of the activity to make beautiful action more likely. And games can intensify and refine those aesthetic qualities, just as a painting can intensify and refine the aesthetic qualities we find in the natural sights and sounds of the world.

Aesthetic striving games, then, are games designed primarily for the purpose of providing aesthetic experiences of practicality to their players. Notice that the categories of aesthetic striving games and aesthetic striving players do not quite always align. A game could have been originally designed to promote achievement, but certain players might take it up for aesthetic striving. Or an achievement player could take up an aesthetic striving game simply because they wanted to win, but be led by the game's design into having aesthetic experiences along the way. But, in most cases, aesthetic striving games seem made for aesthetic striving players.

Let's return to *Sign. Sign* is distinctive in several ways. In many other role-playing games, such as *Fiasco*, the relationship of player to character is theatrical. Players may choose to have their characters act counterproductively—against that character's goals—because it would be narratively meaningful. In such a game, I might choose to act out how my character, a sad-sack con man, unwisely confesses his crimes to a pretty stranger in a bar. It is an idiotic choice for my character, and works against all his goals, but I made the choice because I thought it would make for a satisfying narrative arc. *Sign*, on the other hand, is a striving game. Each player must take up the goal of communicating their inner truth, pursuing it wholeheartedly in order to have the desired experience. But the players themselves aren't really interested in winning in any enduring sense. Their larger purpose is to experience the precise texture of struggling, flailing, and barely managing to communicate. But one will only be gripped by these experiences if one genuinely tries to win during the game.

The fact that *Sign* is an aesthetic striving game is particularly clear to me now that I have added my own house rule. I have decreed that, at the end of the game, nobody will explain what their inner truth was; nor will they say what they thought anybody else's truth was. Nobody ever gets to find out if, in fact, we have successfully communicated with each other, even though we pursued that goal during the game. My players and I all agree that this house rule improves the strange potency of the game, and that it is very much in the spirit of the thing. This house rule would be absurd if we actually cared about winning in any enduring way. But it is perfectly comprehensible if winning is only a temporarily adopted interest, taken up for the aesthetic qualities of the pursuit.

The Artistic Medium of Games

So how do game designers fashion these aesthetically rich struggles? It will be useful here to think in terms of the *artistic medium* of games. Let's follow Joseph Margolis's suggestion and distinguish between a physical medium and an artistic medium (Margolis 1980, 1–42; Davies 2003, 183). Or, as Dominic Lopes puts it, an artistic medium is not merely a certain set of materials, but a set of "technical resources" (Lopes 2014, 133–139). For example, in paintings, the physical medium consists of pigments applied to a surface, while the artistic medium includes various techniques, including brushstrokes.

So: is there some sort of artistic medium in common to all aesthetic striving games? What is the medium of games? The medium, whatever it is, must be quite abstract if it is to cover the wide variety of Suitsian games—which includes video games, board games, role-playing games, card games, sports, and party games. The medium couldn't be something as specific as, say, software, interactive video, or boards and pieces.[8]

First, it is tempting to say that the medium of games is constraints and obstacles. Certainly, that's part of the story, but it doesn't capture the full richness of the game designer's efforts. That view might seem plausible if we narrowly focus on only physical games, such as traditional sports. Traditional sports are played in the physical world with our actual bodies. Thus, the rules of a sport usually start with our physical bodies, with our full range of abilities, and then selectively restricts our use of those abilities. For example, we might disallow the use of hands in soccer, or the use of punching and kicking in basketball. But game designers actually create new sorts of actions and possibilities all the time.[9] This is clearest in video games such as *Portal*, where I am given a gun that can shoot the ends of a wormhole into the world to create space-bending passageways. But we need not focus solely on such radically new abilities. Most games create new actions. "Taking a piece" in Chess and "a home run" in baseball are new actions that arise only within the context of a particular rule set.

In that case, we might be tempted to say, instead, that the artistic medium of games is rules. And perhaps this is right, if we have a sufficiently loose notion of "rule." But under most standard uses of the term, this proposal doesn't work either. Say that you mean by "rule" an explicit, stated principle for action that is mentally upheld by the players. First, as many computer-game scholars have pointed out, much of what computer-game designers do is design the virtual environment through software manipulations. The software environment is not a set of rules consciously held by a player; it has some independent existence (Leino 2012). Of course, you might think that the software

---

[8] If the reader has a particular theory of medium here that forbids such abstraction, please substitute the term "artistic resource," as borrowed from Riggle (2010). For a useful discussion of how abstract a medium might be, see Elisabeth Schellekens's discussion of ideas as the medium of conceptual art (Schellekens 2007).

[9] Cardona-Rivera and Young (2014) offer a useful survey of work on game *affordances*.

code itself is a set of rules, just rules that run on a computer rather than on a human brain. But even so, there's more to game design than rules. The case is clearest with physical games. Think, for example, about obstacle courses and artificial rock climbs. What fills out the experience are the physical details of the material object, and how that particular physicality interacts with the specified rules and the goals of the game. The physicality of games extends even to video games. A rule might tell you to use a particular game-console controller, but the physicality of the controller itself partially conditions the gaming experience.[10] The video game *PewPewPewPewPewPewPewPewPew* illustrates this quite nicely. In the game, two people together control a single avatar, who has a jetpack and a ray gun. Both players have microphones. One player controls the jetpack by shouting "Shhhh!" into the microphone; the other player controls the gun by shouting "Pew! Pew! Pew!" into the microphone. Imagine the different texture of practical experience if the game were played with buttons instead. And even when played with microphones, so much depends on the physical details—the sensitivity of the microphones, the acoustics of the room. These aren't just rules—they are environmental features. What unites software environments and physical environments is their relationship to challenge. We might say, then, that part of the medium is the *practical environment*—the environment conceived of in its opposition to our goals and abilities.

This points us toward the last key element of game design—the goal. Reiner Knizia, elder statesman of German board-game design, has said that the central tool in his game-design arsenal is the scoring system. The scoring system creates the motivation, says Knizia (Knizia, quoted in Chalkey 2008). The scoring system tells you whether you need to collaborate or compete with the other players. And the scoring system helps shape how that interaction will go. The goals, combined with the game's mechanics, tell us whether we are to manipulate our opponents or bargain with them, whether we are to cleverly profit off their actions or simply attack them. A game's goals tell us what to care about during the game. When we play a game, we simply take on the goals it indicates, and acquire the motivations that the game wishes us to acquire.

Think about a board-game night between friends. We sit around the table and pull out a new board game that has just arrived in the mail, taking off the

---

[10] For a study of the aesthetics of our physical interaction with video-game controllers, see Kirkpatrick (2011, 87–116).

shrink wrap. We pop out the cardboard tokens into a great heap on the table and begin to sort them into neat piles of green tokens, blue tokens, and gold tokens. We don't know what these tokens will represent; the physical tokens themselves have no particular importance. If, for instance, my dog eats all the blue tokens, we can replace them with pennies and still be able to play the game. Now we open the rule book, which tells us that the gold tokens are money, and that they are useful for buying various resources during the game but don't count toward victory at the end. The winner will be the person who has collected the most green tokens. Notice that before the game starts, we have no interest in collecting green tokens. But during the game, we acquire a hearty interest in the green tokens, to the point where an insufficiency of tokens may inspire armpit sweats, jitters, and a surge of adrenaline at the prospect of pulling off a last-ditch plan to get more. And once the game is finished, we lose our interest in the green tokens entirely, shove all of them into a messy pile, and scoop them into a Ziploc plastic bag.

What the Suitsian analysis suggests is that games are structures of practical reason, practical action, and practical possibility, conjoined with a particular world in which that practicality will operate. A game designer designates *this* as the goal of the game player, and *those* as the permitted abilities, and *that* as the landscape of obstacles. The designer creates, not only the world in which players will act, but the skeleton of the players' practical agency within that world. The designer designates players' abilities and goals in the game. The designer's control over the nature of the players' agency is part of how the game designer sculpts the game's activity. Games can offer us more finely tuned practical harmonies because the designers have control over both world and agent.

We now have an answer to the question of artistic medium. The common artistic medium of aesthetic striving games—the technical resources by which the game designer sculpts practical experience—are the goals, the rules, and the environment that these various parts animate into a system of constraints. The game designer crafts for players a very particular form of struggle, and does so by crafting both a temporary practical agency for us to inhabit and a practical environment for us to struggle against. In other words, the medium of the game designer is agency. If you want a slogan, try this one: games are the art of agency.

Note that I haven't offered anything like a definition of agency. This is intentional. I do not take there to be a settled account of agency in general, and that literature is currently undergoing a number of upheavals. Much of this change is due to challenges regarding the possible existence of group agents and collective agents, such as companies and corporations, and other edge cases, including animal agency, robot agency, and the agency of algorithms (Barandiaran, Di Paolo, and Rohde 2009; List and Pettit 2011; Gilbert 2013). When I speak of agency, I am generally thinking in terms of a fairly traditional conception—in which agency involves intentional action, or action for a reason. I am in no way presuming that this is a complete account of agency. I don't think we need a full definition or metaphysical account of "paper" to usefully say that origami uses the medium of paper folding, and I don't think we need to settle on a particular philosophical account of "agency" to usefully say that games use the medium of agency. In fact, I think that investigating how games work in the medium of agency will actually teach us something about the nature of our agency.

But this basic idea—that games work in the medium of agency—reveals something quite profound about the role games can play in human life, especially in our social lives. Games turn out to be a way of *writing down* forms of agency, of inscribing them in an artifact. Games are one of our techniques for inscribing and recording bits of human experience. We have developed methods for recording stories: novels, poetry, film, and other kinds of narrative. We have developed methods for capturing sights: drawing, painting, photography, and film. We have developed methods for capturing sounds: written music, recording technologies, and wooden duck calls. We have even developed methods for capturing sequences of action to be performed—cookbook directions, dance choreography, and stage directions. Games are a method for capturing forms of agency. And these techniques and technologies enable all sorts of interactions and modifications. Once we can write something down, that enables us to more easily study and refine it.

And this suggests another possibility: that games can be a way that we *collaborate* in the project of developing our agency and autonomy. If games can record and transmit forms of agency, then I can learn new modes of agency from a game. And you may write down a useful form of agency and pass it to me through a game. This may, in the abstract, seem slightly insane. But I think it is, in fact, quite plausible, especially when we think of what we actually learn from games. I am not alone in thinking that I acquired a certain focused, logical, and tactical mindset from playing chess. Rock climbing taught me to focus precisely on my balance and precision of motion. *Tetris* gave me the mental state required to pack my trunk optimally for a trip. My suggestion here is more than the familiar old saw that games teach us skills and develop our abilities. My claim is that games can teach us the agential mindsets behind those skills—the pairings of a particular kind of interest with a focus on a particular set of abilities. And the practice of striving play itself teaches us how to be flexible with our agency—how to pick up and set aside interests for a moment. That flexibility is of great use outside of game. We use our agential flexibility when we switch between our various roles, such as parent, professional, and friend, and adopt the different frames of mind that go with such roles.

As it turns out, the development of our agency and autonomy is not a solitary project. As with many of our other aspects—our scientific understanding, our logical capacities, our morality—we can help each other in the project of personal self-development, and we often do so, not just in person, but through artifactual vessels. And games are an artifactual vessel with which we can communicate modes of agency. The games that we have made constitute a vast library of agency, in which we have recorded a wide variety of different forms of agencies and which we can use to explore different ways of being an agent. And it is our capacity to submerge ourselves in alternate agencies that makes it possible for us to use this library.

Games and Artificiality

But games also offer one more promise. They can function as a refuge from the inhospitality of ordinary life. In practical life, the world is mostly fixed, and our values, relatively inflexible. Most of us cannot help but desire company, food, success. The recalcitrant world and our inflexible values generate certain obstacles. These are not the obstacles we wanted to struggle against, but they are the ones we must overcome in order to get what we want. So we must try to sculpt ourselves and our abilities to fit the needs of the world. The world tells us we must eat, so we must find a job and pretend to ourselves that we enjoy it. The world tells us that we must find romantic partners, so we learn to be witty, or at least to make to make a decent online dating profile. The world tells us that if we wish to be professional philosophers, we must grade an endless sea of student papers, no matter how mind-numbing we find the task. So we put nose to grindstone and force our way through.

In games, on the other hand, we sculpt for ourselves exactly the kind of practical activity we wish to engage in. We pick the goals, abilities, and the world. In games, our abilities can precisely suit the challenges we are presented with. In *Super Mario Brothers*, we are given the ability to run and jump, and a world full of chasms to jump over and monsters to jump upon. What's more, our jumping abilities and speed in *Super Mario Brothers* are just barely enough to cope with the chasms and monsters we face. The chess knight's strange leaping movement is just what we need to break through our opponent's defenses. In games, we are given the right kinds of abilities, but just barely enough of them—which creates drama and interest. And not only do the abilities fit, but their exercise is often pleasurable and interesting and exciting, at least when we've found the right game for our tastes.

How unlike our own dreary world this is! Our abilities sometimes fit our goals in the world, but so often they do not. We want to invent a cure for cancer, but lack the capacities to do it. We wish to help students learn to write better, but the process is boring and mind-numbing and provokes occasional thoughts of suicide—or at least of throwing it all in and becoming a lawyer instead. We do not fit this world comfortably. The obstacles in our path are often intractable, exhausting, or miserable. Games can be an existential balm for our practical unease with the world. In games, the problems can be right-sized for our capacities; our in-game selves can be right-sized for the problems; and the arrangement of self and world can make solving the problems pleasurable, satisfying, interesting, and beautiful.

Even with our opponents, there is a harmony. In a good game, our opponent's attempts to harm us may, in the right circumstances, actually be channeled so as to create experiences we value. In ordinary life, social attacks and financial attacks are usually painful and unpleasant. They can be survived and gotten over, but rarely can they be enjoyed. But games are often designed such that your attacks on me are channeled into interesting obstacles for me to overcome. Even our motivations can be curiously harmonized, even if we are at each other's throats. Outside of games, much of the pain and difficulty of social life with others arises from the dizzying plurality of values. Each of us cares about different things; trying to mesh the plurality of disparate values into livable communities is incredibly difficult.

In games, values are usually singular and shared. In games, each person is a simplified agent. And in most cases, competing agents are pursuing the same goal. When we are playing tennis, I do not have to cope with subtle differences between your and my view of the good. You and I are after exactly the same thing: points and victory. It is not that we are cooperating, exactly—but we are motivationally coherent to one another. In some sense, the motivational world described by traditional economics—one in which identically motivated rational actors compete with one another—is false in the actual world, but true in game worlds. When games work, they can sometimes present us with the world as we wish it could be. The worlds of games are harmonious and interesting worlds, where even our worst impulses are transformed into the pleasure of others. In ordinary life, we must build practical activities and relationships from gears that were never made to fit. But in games, we can machine all the gears to fit from the start.

And this, I suspect, is both the great promise and the great threat of games. Games can offer us a clarifying balm against the vast, complicated, ever-shifting social world of pluralistic values, and an existential balm against our internal sense that our values are slippery and unclear. In games, values are clear, well-delineated, and typically uniform among all agents. But this also creates a significant moral danger—not just from graphically violent games, but from all games. This is the danger of exporting back to the world a false expectation: that values should be clear, well-delineated, and uniform in all circumstances. Games threaten us with a fantasy of moral clarity.

The positive part of my view might seem rather familiar. Jane McGonigal makes a similar point in her argument for making our lives more game-like. The world wasn't made to fit us, she says, but games can be made to fit. Playing games is far more pleasurable; our motivations in games are more potent. Thus, concludes McGonigal, we should try to make life more like a game, by gamifying our work, our chores, and our education. We should fill our lives with leaderboards, rankings, and badges, and fill our work with carefully engineered gamified systems, in order to make our work and educational lives more pleasant (McGonigal 2011).

But this mistakes how peculiar game values are. We can tailor our struggles in games precisely because our game ends are disposable. But when we try to make the rest of life like a game, we will need to adapt our enduring ends to make the struggle more pleasurable and satisfying. When we do that—when we instrumentalize our enduring ends as if our lives are a game—we court disaster. When we gamify our ordinary lives, we will be tempted to shift and simplify our ends for the sake of the struggle—but then we are no longer be aiming at the same target. Games can be safely tailored precisely because they are games.

Games involve taking on temporary ends and submerging ourselves in alternate agencies. And, like any other form of art, exactly the features that make games potentially valuable also make them potentially dangerous.

Games are the art form of agency, and it is in their use of agency where we will find both a great promise and a significant threat.

I have sketched here the broad strokes of my view. The rest of the book will explore, in greater detail, these arguments and possibilities.

In Part I, I focus on the motivational structure of game play. First, in Chapter 2, I defend the possibility of striving play against skeptics. In Chapter 3, I explore our capacity for submerging ourselves in alternate agencies and our ability to forget our enduring ends for the span of the game. And I draw lessons for philosophical agency and practical reasoning from the fact that we can play games. Together, these two chapters are the core of my theoretical account of the motivational structure of game play. They are the philosophically densest chapters, but also the heart of the story.

In Chapter 4, I argue that games can play a special role in the development of our own agency and autonomy. Games can communicate modes of agency. And when we play games, we can learn new modes of agency. Games can constitute a *library of agencies*, and we can use that library to grow.

In Part II, I focus on games as an art form. In Chapter 5, I explore the aesthetics of agency. Beauty is not just confined to sunsets and symphonies; our own actions, choices, and decisions can also have their own kind of beauty. I also defend the aesthetics of agency against the worries that aesthetic experience is essentially incompatible with practical and instrumental states of mind.

In Chapter 6, I argue that games are like traditional art works in some very significant ways. Most importantly, games involve socially maintained prescriptions for attention—they are a way of framing certain parts of the world for our appreciation. Games are a way of aesthetically framing our own practical activity.

In Chapter 7, I look at how games are distinctive as an art form. Unlike most traditional arts, the aesthetic qualities of a game arise, not in the artifact itself, but in the activity of the player. Thus, the aesthetic qualities of games are significantly distanced from the designer and the game itself. Game designers must cope with a distinctive artistic difficulty: they must achieve their aesthetic effects through the agency of the player.

In Part III, I focus the social and moral consequences of the agential manipulations of games. In Chapter 8, I argue that games work not only in the medium of agency but also in the medium of sociality. Games arrange social relationships and create social patterns through their use of the agential medium. And in doing so, they can achieve some very remarkable effects, such as transforming competition into cooperation.

In Chapter 9, I worry about a distinctive danger of the agential medium. Games might threaten our autonomy if we do not properly manage the transition back to non-game life. Games may foster the expectation that values be clear, simple, and easily stated—that our goals be obvious and measurable. Games may present a fantasy of moral clarity. And in Chapter 10, I argue that aesthetic striving play might offer us some protection against the fantasy of moral clarity.

One last word of warning: my discussion involves a fairly large number of in-depth case studies of particular games—far more than one might usually find in a work of academic philosophy, even one in aesthetics. This is due, in part, to the relative novelty of trying to present a unified account of the art form across a broad range of games. My account will include computer games, team sports, solo sports, board games, card games, party games, tabletop role-playing games, and live-action role-playing games. Much of the recent discussion of games as an art form has focused fairly narrowly on a very small set of games: computer games, and mostly single-player computer games, often with a strong narrative component. I wish to broaden the focus. Unfortunately, there is no established canon of games that I can depend on the reader to be familiar with. My case for depends on the reader seeing the extraordinary variety of ways that games make use of the medium of agency. So, if you'll bear with me, I think it very important to describe, in loving detail, a fair number of games. And I hope that the reader, if sufficiently interested, will also seek out and play some of these games. I have played all of the games I mention and have chosen to discuss those I think are exemplars of game design, with a few exceptions as noted. My hope is to develop, through both argument and examples, a compelling picture of games as a very special type of human artifact and as a unique art form.

PART I
GAMES AND AGENCY

2

The Possibility of Striving Play

Here's the picture so far: games are the art form of agency. When playing games, we can adopt alternate agencies, and we can do so for aesthetic reasons. We can take up goals temporarily, not because we actually care about achieving them in an enduring way, but because we want to have a certain kind of struggle. And we can do so for the sake of aesthetic experiences of striving—of our own gracefulness, of the delicious perfection of an intellectual epiphany, of the intensity of the struggle, or of the dramatic arc of the whole thing. This is, to be clear, only one form of game-play among many. Not all striving play is oriented toward the aesthetic. There are plenty of other reasons to engage in striving play, including fun, relaxation, fitness, and social lubrication. But I think that a significant amount of game play is, in fact, aesthetic striving play.

Striving play involves an inverted motivational state. We take on ends for the sake of the means they force us through. And this picture of the inverted motivational state will help to show why gaming activity isn't a waste of time. The worry arose because many in-game ends appear worthless. But, in striving play, the purpose of the activity isn't actually to attain those in-game ends. In-game ends are taken up, temporarily and disposably, for the sake of sculpting the activity of their pursuit. Thus, the structure of justification for game goals is inverted from the norm. In most of life, we justify our goals in terms of their intrinsic value or in terms of the valuable things will follow from them. In games, we justify our goals by showing what kind of activity they will inspire. The justification of game goals has a backward-looking, rather than forward-looking, direction. And those backward-looking explanations can point us to valuable aesthetic qualities. Those who condemn striving play as useless or arbitrary crucially misunderstand its inverted value structure.

But one might doubt that striving play is actually possible. Perhaps the tangled motivational structure of striving play seems impossible to occupy. Crucially, I've claimed that Suits's account implies the existence of *disposable ends*. Disposable ends are ends that we take on temporarily, that aren't

Games. C. Thi Nguyen, Oxford University Press (2020). © Oxford University Press.
DOI: 10.1093/oso/9780190052089.001.0001

attached in the usual way to our enduring ends. The particular goals in a game are always disposable in a quite trivial way. I care about collecting yellow tokens only during this board game; afterward, I don't care at all about those yellow tokens. This is trivial disposability holds for both striving players and achievement players. But if I am right that striving play exists, then we have run across a very deep form of disposable end. For striving players, the interest in winning itself is a disposable end. It is an interest they take on for the sake of the struggle and then discard after the game is through.

But is striving play really possible? And can we really have disposable ends? A skeptic might deny the possibility of striving play. Instead, the skeptic would claim, achievement play is the only possible motivational mode. In other words, the only way to play a game is to genuinely and enduringly care about winning. Such a skeptic thus rejects the possibility of the motivational inversion I've described, preferring to impute to all game players a more straightforward motivational structure.

In this chapter, I respond to this skepticism and argue for the genuine possibility of striving play. I will argue that we are capable of entering into a *motivationally inverted state*—that we can take up disposable ends and temporarily care about winning for the sake of the ensuing activity. To start, I provide a more careful analysis of Suits's account, which will help us fill out the motivational picture of striving play. I then argue that many familiar phenomena from our lives with games only make sense if we really can engage in striving play and take on disposable ends. In order to account for many of the basic phenomena of game playing, we must admit that our agency is moderately fluid.

The next three chapters will be a careful look at the structure of motivation and agency involved in game playing, and what we can learn about our own agential capacities from the fact that we can play games. I largely set aside questions of aesthetics and art for now, returning to those topics in Chapter 5, where our investigations into the fluidity of our own agency will bear some artistic fruit.

Getting Clear about Practical Inversions

In the Chapter 1, in a bit of admittedly loose brushwork, I characterized game playing as a motivational inversion of practical activity. In normal practical activity, we pursue the means for the sake of the ends. In games, we invert that relationship: we take up the ends for the sake of the means. The arguments I offered were quick and admitted of many objections. It is now time to refine them.

In this chapter, I offer a more careful version of the argument for the possibility of striving play. Next, in Chapter 3, I take a more careful look at what the experience of striving play is like. There, I examine the psychological mechanisms and the structures of motivational consciousness that we must be able to deploy in order to genuinely engage in striving play.

The best place to start is by focusing on the Suitsian account. How deep is the motivational inversion of striving play? So far, we have only been working with what he called the "portable version." Suits has been unfairly dismissed, I think, by some scholars, who have found problems with the portable version of the definition. His full account is much more robust. Let's upload the full technical version of Suits's analysis.

When we are playing games, says Suits, we are pursuing *pre-lusory goals*. These are the states of affairs we are trying to bring about during game play, described without reference to any particular means of achieving them. For example, the pre-lusory goal of basketball is getting the ball through the hoop. Then there are the *constitutive rules* of a game, which prohibit more-efficient means in favor of less-efficient means. In basketball, these include various rules constraining how the ball may be moved, along with rules that create opposition. To achieve the pre-lusory goal within the means permitted by the game is to achieve the *lusory goal* (Suits [1978] 2015, 24–43). The lusory goal of basketball is "making baskets." The all-important difference is between the pre-lusory goal—getting the ball through the hoop—and the lusory goal of making baskets. What it is to make a basket is to get the ball through the hoop while obeying the rules.

For Suits, the truly distinctive feature of game playing is a particular motivational and valuational state in the player. In games, says Suits, we do not pursue the pre-lusory goal for its independent value. Otherwise, we would simply show up after hours with a ladder and pass the ball through the basket as many times as possible. Nor do we accept the constitutive rules because they are the most efficient way to achieve the pre-lusory goal. Rather, game playing is marked by the *lusory attitude*: we adopt the pre-lusory goal and the constitutive rules for the sake of the activity they make possible. We adopt unnecessary obstacles in order to make possible the activity of trying to overcome them.

Notice, crucially, that the constraints of game playing only place obstacles and create inefficiencies between the player and the pre-lusory goal. These constraints do not impede our progress toward the lusory goal, since they actually help constitute the lusory goal. If you want to win at basketball, you have to follow the rules. The requirement to dribble the ball while moving doesn't interfere with making baskets—it makes them possible.

Pre-lusory goals, then, aren't significantly valuable for their own sakes. Otherwise, we would pursue them as efficiently as possible. The very fact that we are willing to impose inefficiencies on our path to the pre-lusory goals shows that we value these pre-lusory goals less than we value the activity of struggling for them under certain inefficiencies. Otherwise, we wouldn't be willing to abandon the most efficient path to those pre-lusory goals for the sake of bringing about some ludicrous activity of struggle. What we value is either the lusory goal—in other words, winning within the constraints of the game—or the process of struggling within those constraints.

How thorough, then, must the practical inversion be to meet the minimum standards of Suits's definition, and how thorough might it be at its maximum? One possible view is that all games are complete and thorough-going inversions of practical activity—it's impractical turtles all the way down. Under such a view, to count as playing a game, one must always be playing for the sake of the playing itself. Let's call this the requirement for *game purism*: that we take up the game activity entirely for the intrinsic value of the activity of play itself, rather than for any sort of practical outcome that might follow from playing the game. Notice that game purism excludes all sorts of activities that we might ordinarily take to be playing a game, including playing a game for money, fame, education, personal development, or fitness. So, is Suits a game purist?

The answer is no. Under the Suitsian definition, if you adopt the rules of sprinting in order to win the Olympic gold medal for sprinting and thereby gain fame and glory, you are still playing a Suitsian game. Here is how Suits would describe the activity: you take up the rules in order to make possible the activity of sprinting. You are doing so in order to win fame and money through victory at the game. But this still counts as a Suitsian game because of the first step: you are still taking up the rules to make possible the activity. As Suits puts it, the professional game player is trying to win money by winning *at the game*.

Crucially, Suits's definition leaves unspecified whether one makes possible the activity for some further purpose or for the intrinsic value of the activity itself. But Suits is often misread on this point. Some writers have attributed to Suits such a purity requirement.[1] Under such a purist reading of Suits, only amateur game players can be truly playing a game. Those who read Suits as a purist usually reject him on these grounds, by pointing to the many external reasons there can be for playing a game—fitness, social status, money, etc. But the purist reading of Suits is entirely mistaken. For Suits, the professional game player is still playing a game. Suits's definition doesn't draw a line between intrinsically valuable and extrinsically valuable game playing; it draws a line between purely instrumental activity and game activity.

Imagine three people climbing a mountain. The Medical Climber is climbing the mountain because there is a rare herb at the top that will cure kidney infections. The Professional Climber is climbing the mountain to set a mountain-climbing record for the fame, glory, and money. And the Amateur Climber is climbing the mountain for the pure joy of climbing it. By Suits's account, both the Professional Climber and the Amateur Climber are playing a game, because they are taking up a pre-lusory goal and constraints on that goal for the sake of making possible a particular activity—the game of mountain climbing. We know it's a Suitsian game because getting to the top won't count as a victory for them unless it is done within the specified constraints. If both or either of them takes a helicopter, they will not have climbed the mountain. The Amateur Climber wants to be engaged in the *activity* of mountain climbing. The Professional Climber wants the glory that comes from *winning* at mountain climbing. But what makes it a game for the both of them is the fact that the activity they are engaged in is partially constituted by the obstacles. They are both playing a game, albeit for very different reasons. The Professional Climber would not achieve glory by taking a helicopter to get to the top, because glory only follows from the achievement of the lusory goal, and not the pre-lusory goal. Glory will only come from climbing the mountain within those constraints, and not from getting to the top by any efficient available means (Suits [1978] 2014, 90–92). The Medical Climber, on the other hand, is not playing a game at all. They are climbing the mountain because it happens to be the best way to get that valuable herb. If the conditions of the world change, so that they could get the herb more efficiently in some other way—if a helicopter became available

---

[1] For example, Kevin Kee imputes a purity requirement to Suits when he treats the existence of educational games and Bogost-style rhetorical games as a counterexample to Suits's definition (Rockwell and Kee 2011).

or the herb is suddenly available online—they would use one of those other methods instead. The victory that both the Amateur and the Professional seek is partially constituted by the specified constraints. What it is to climb a mountain is to do so by certain specified means: yes to hands, feet, and rope; no to helicopters, jet-packs, and magic carpets. The Amateur is interested in the game itself, and the Professional is using the game for some other end, but both have an interest that can only be achieved by playing the game. The Professional wants to win at the game to attain something else that will follow from winning—but still wants to win *at the game*. The Medical Climber, on the other hand, is not interested in the activity of the game at all. Thus, Suits's theory does not demand that all game playing be done solely for the intrinsic value of the game play.

By "Suitsian play," I refer to the kind of play specified in Suits's full definition. What I hope to have made clear is that Suitsian play is compatible with differing motivations for game playing. Suitsian play includes playing for the sake of some value intrinsic to the game itself—intrinsic play. It also includes playing for extrinsic purposes—what Suits calls "instrumental game playing." Playing a game in order to gain fame and glory through victory or to increase fitness through the effort—these are all forms of extrinsic play.

Crucially, the intrinsic/extrinsic play distinction is entirely different from the achievement/striving play distinction. Achievement play is Suitsian play done for the sake of winning; striving play is Suitsian play done for the sake of the struggle to win. The achievement/striving distinction concerns the *location* in game playing to which value adheres; the intrinsic/extrinsic distinction concerns the *type* of value that adheres. Achievement play can be done for intrinsic reasons—for the value of winning itself. Achievement play can also be done for extrinsic reasons—for the value of something that follows from winning, like the prize money. Similarly, striving play can be done for intrinsic reasons, such as the value of the struggle itself, or for extrinsic reasons, such as the physical fitness that follows from the struggle.

This gives us four categories of game play:

Intrinsic achievement play is play for the sake of winning in and of itself. Purely competitive players fit here.

Extrinsic achievement play is play for the sake of what winning brings instrumentally. This includes the professional poker player in it for the money and the Olympic athlete in it for the personal and national glory.

Intrinsic striving play is play for the sake of the intrinsic value of engagement in the activity of play. Players who play simply for the value of the struggle fit here.

Extrinsic striving play is play for the sake of what engagement in the activity of play brings ones instrumentally. Playing sports for the sake of physical fitness, running races for mental health, or playing Chess for the "brain training" fit here.

These categories are not exclusive. One can play out of a mixed interest in both achievement and activity; and one can play both for the intrinsic value of the game and for some extrinsic consequences. The point here is that there are two very different dimensions by which we may locate where a player finds value in a game.

I emphasize this distinction by way of a clarification. Most of the philosophical work on Suits, and on the value of games in general, has focused on the intrinsic value/extrinsic value distinction. But to my mind, what Suits's account illuminates most clearly is in thinking about the difference between achievement play and striving play. In particular, I make the distinction to ward off a common error. It is easy to slip into thinking that all striving play must be performed for the intrinsic value of the play itself. But this confuses the issue of striving play with the issue of intrinsic value. Playing a game for the sake of fitness or for the sake of learning skills—both of these are forms of striving play. I only need to pursue the win to get those benefits; actually, winning is entirely unnecessary.

Achievement play is quite motivationally straightforward. One is interested in winning, so one pursues the win by the best means available. In order to win at a game, one must obey its rules, so the value of obeying the rules derives from the value of winning, whether that value be intrinsic or extrinsic. Striving play involves a much more convoluted motivational structure. Striving players do not play to win; they acquire a disposable interest in winning in order to have the activity or experience of struggling for the win.

The Reality of Disposable Ends

What makes striving play possible is the existence of *disposable ends*. A disposable end is an end that is not directly attached to one's other enduring ends. It is an end that one takes up voluntarily and that one can rid oneself of without doing significant damage to one's enduring value system or core practical identity.

The possibility of disposable ends is inherent in Suits's description of games. What it is to play a game is not simply to take on restrictions, but to take on an interest an achieving the goals of the game. Games, in other words, aren't simply constraints; they are constraints and goals in a package. When we play games, we take on goals and obstacles voluntarily. The voluntary acquisition of goals may have been elided in Suits's portable version of the definition. The portable version, again, is that playing a game is taking on voluntary obstacles for the sake of the activity of trying to overcome them. The portable version makes no explicit reference to voluntary goals. Is this simply an omission in the portable version, to be repaired in the full version? I suspect, rather, that Suits has quietly packaged the notion of voluntary goals inside the notion of voluntary obstacles. It is useful here to unpack what he means by an "obstacle." An obstacle is something that gets in the way of a goal; it isn't an obstacle unless it interferes with a goal. Various features on a rock wall are just that—features—until a rock climber sets for themselves the goal of climbing that wall. Only then do some of those features become difficult obstacles, and other features become tools to get around those obstacles. An obstacle's nature as such is thus partially constituted by the goal with which it interferes.

We can see this by noting that various features of the world become obstacles only when they are considered in relation to certain goals. In other motivational contexts, those same features are neutral or actively helpful. The fact that I have a pan of delicious fresh-baked cookies in front of me is only an obstacle if I am trying to diet; if I am trying to have a Christmas party or trying to up my weight for an upcoming sumo training camp, they are a help. The walls of this maze are only an obstacle if I wish to get out. But if I am a misanthropic hermit who wishes only to be left alone and to tend my garden in peace, then the maze walls that surround my hovel are a comfort and a sinecure. Thus to take up something as a voluntary obstacle, I must also have taken up some voluntary goal that runs me into that obstacle. We can thus say that *a goal is partially constitutive of an obstacle as such*.

This is clearest for games that make use of natural features. Mountain climbing, again, is a Suitsian game. The obstacles are natural in some sense, but we also know that they are voluntary, because we know that a mountain climber would forego, say, hiring a helicopter or taking an escalator up the back of the mountain. They are interested in negotiating the difficulties of the mountain using their own bodies. Note that the various features of the mountain are not obstacles for me if I am, say, a sightseer armed with a telescope, out to admire some scenic vistas. In that case, the steep ice walls and vast crevasses are simply beautiful features of nature to be admired. They could even be useful instruments in my pursuit of watercolor painting. The walls and crevasses become obstacles for me only if I acquire the goal of climbing the mountain. And different goals will turn the same feature into very different sorts of obstacle. A grey and shadowy crevasse on a mountain is one sort of obstacle for the mountain climber, and a very different sort of obstacle for the landscape painter.

I often think of Suits's work here as an extension of some long-standing ideas about the voluntary nature of play. In *Homo Ludens*—a foundational text in the academic study of games—Johan Huizinga says that play is irrational. But, says Huizinga, the fact that we play games shows, not that we are defective, but that we are capable of transcending rationality. Play, not rationality, is the characteristic activity of humans. We are *homo lumens*, not *homo sapiens*. For Huizinga, games are a descendent of other human activities, such as religious ritual and theater. In all of them, we set aside a special time and space apart from ordinary life. When we enter that space, we suspend the normal relationships and practices and take up alternate roles and relationships. The significance of our actions in that space is kept segregated from ordinary practices. When I strike my fellow actor on stage, or brutally decimate my opponent's forces in Chess, I am not held morally responsible for such actions when we return to ordinary life (Huizinga 1955).

There are many problems, I think, with collapsing fiction, theater, and game playing, which I will discuss in Chapters 6 and 7. But Suits rescues one key part of Huizinga's view: the claim that when we step inside the magic circle of a game, we acquire new motivations, which we dispense with when we leave the circle. Suits's theory can be treated here as a rigorous working out of Huizinga's insight. Games specify the goals that their players will pursue. In so doing, they shape the players' in-game motivations, and thus their in-game practical reasoning. Games are temporary structures of practical reasoning.

As I argued in the last section, Suits's theory only requires that the *prelusory* goal be disposable; it is silent on whether the *lusory* goals are disposable. In other words, Suits's theory requires that the pursued in-game state, like getting the ball through the hoop, is disposable; the theory says nothing about whether we care disposably or enduringly about *winning*. Which is as it should be, since Suits's account is intended to capture all sorts of game play, including professional play.

Imagine a player who is interested in winning any game, simply for the sake of winning. They are an achievement player—an intrinsic achievement player, in fact. Their interest in winning isn't disposable in any way. Winning is, in fact, their purpose. What is disposable is only how that winning is cashed out in each particular game. Our achievement player disposably acquires a temporary interest in making baskets or capturing kings during the course of the game, in order to achieve their true purpose of winning. But their motivations still have a straightforward structure. They are interested in making baskets because it is the way to win in this context, and they are interested in winning. But Suits's theory leaves the door open for a second and much more far-reaching form of disposable end. In striving play, the player adopts an interest in winning for the sake of playing the game.

Let's take a step back and think about our relationship to winning in games. Playing games would be very odd business if we didn't care about winning at all. We might be able to go through it as an exercise, but it's hard to imagine that it would be very pleasurable, satisfying, or fun. The paradigmatic experience of game playing isn't one of being at some sort of intellectual remove; it is one of becoming utterly absorbed in trying hard, of trying to get something you really want. In fact, a certain kind of person doesn't seem to be able to care about winning in any form at all; such a person typically complains that games are silly and that points are just arbitrary. Such a person can never really become absorbed in game play at all. For games to provide any sort of engagement, for their challenges to have any grip on us, it must be that we can come to care, in some way, about winning. But how deep and lasting is our interest in winning?

Achievement players care about winning all the way down. But striving players need only to temporarily acquire an interest in winning, in order to sustain the experience of engagement. That doesn't require a thoroughgoing commitment to the value of winning; it only requires that we acquire an interest in winning for the course of the game. And this, I suspect, is the actual mode of play for many game players. I myself usually have very little enduring interest in winning or beating my opponent. In fact, my usual opponent is my spouse. From a perspective outside a particular session of game playing, I am just as happy when she thoroughly trounces me with a clever tactic as when I beat her. My preference, in fact, is that we both will win in about equal proportions in the long run. I will actually put in a fair amount of work into researching which games we are likely to both be good at, in order to ensure this balance. But during a game itself, we each must care about winning for the game to really grip us. In fact, when one of us gets so good at a particular game that they start winning consistently and easily, the game loses its interest for us and, with a sigh, we retire it. I am not interested in winning globally, or I wouldn't manipulate our life with games in such way, but I must be interested in winning locally for the game to have its grip. Thus, I must have the ability to take up an interest in winning disposably, for the sake of being engaged in the processes of the game

But a certain kind of skeptic will doubt the possibility of striving play, and doubt this motivational story. They will claim that achievement play is the only possible sort of play. They will claim that the reconstruction of my motivations here is flawed—that, deep down, the only reason to play a game is an enduring interest in winning. I will argue otherwise. I am not claiming that all game-play is striving play. It seems plain that some players are achievement players; for them, there is very little in the way of significant practical inversion. But I do want to deny that achievement play is the only possible motivational structure for game playing. Striving play, I argue, is a genuine possibility.

Skepticism about Striving Play

In order to show that striving play is possible, I must show that players can, not only treat pre-lusory goals disposably, but also treat lusory goal disposably. On the face of it, it seems that if we have the psychic flexibility to take on pre-lusory goals disposably, then we should have the psychic flexibility to take on the goal of winning disposably. But this might not seem plausible to some readers. When I have described striving play in talks, some audiences have responded with overt skepticism. What is the point of playing, they say, if not winning? To turn this into a fully formed skepticism about the possibility of striving play, we must interpret it not as an individual statement of psychology ("I only play to win"), but as a skepticism about the possibility of striving play in general. That is, the skeptic here must deny the possibility that anybody can engage in striving play.

How could such a denial go? The most plausible route for the skeptic here is to argue that the disposability of ends is a rather shallow and easily explained phenomenon. Winning, says the striving skeptic, is always the point. We only care about the pre-lusory goal only insofar as it helps us win. The skeptic is offering here a simple deflationary account of our ability to suddenly invest the specified goals of a game with great importance. According to the skeptic, all players come into a game with an enduring interest in winning. During the game, the rules specify that to win, the player must collect green tokens. Thus, the player cares about green tokens only insofar as they contribute to victory—in short, only during the game itself. As soon as the game ends, the green tokens no longer contribute to winning, and so the player will lose interest in them. Nothing special about game motivations is going on here, says the skeptic. Rather, this is like any other kind of contextually valuable object, like currency. I have no interest in collecting copper discs, until a certain country comes into being and declares copper discs to be "money." And when that country collapses, those copper discs become valueless once again. The skeptic thus denies the deep disposability of ends in game play. All players care enduringly about winning, they say; it is merely that what constitutes a win varies from game to game.

One shallow response to the skeptic would be to point out that, obviously, we don't only value winning, because then we would just seek out lousy opponents and beat them all day long. But the skeptic has a ready response for that, too: mature achievement players factor the difficulty of the win into its value. As long as achievement players value, not just any kind of winning, but winning over significant challenges, then they will want decent opponents. We need a more delicate response to the skeptic.

Here's a first pass: if the skeptic is right and the only available motivation for playing is winning, then why would anybody ever play a game that they were unlikely to win? But people often play games that they probably won't win. My circle of board gamers includes players with very different skills sets. I myself am not particularly good at precise numerical calculation, but quite good at psychological manipulation and managing wildly chaotic situations. My circle includes my spouse, who is not great at psychological manipulation, but very good at numerical and geometrical calculation. We also play with Andrew, who is extremely good at fine-tuning and managing very precise plans in well-controlled circumstances, but less good at coping with more chaotic game situations. As it turns out, for any particular game, given the skills involved, there is one of us is who is pretty likely to win, and one of us who doesn't have a chance in hell. But we all continue to play these various games anyway, including the ones that we are congenitally bad at. Why? If

I am only in it for achievement, then trying a game I am relatively unsuited for seems like a bad bet. If I value a challenge only when I actually manage to beat it, then I should only seek manageable opposition and never overwhelming opposition.

A skeptic might attempt to save their position with the following explanation of my board-gaming circle's behavior. The skeptic could say that my fellow board gamers and I are involved in some sort of exchange. I agree to suffer through a game that I will almost certainly lose, so that the others will later consent to play a different game that I will most likely win. According to this skeptical response, then, the only reason I can have for playing a game that I will lose is as a sacrifice for a later gain. But this explanation rings false when we consider the actual experience of play. If it were true, then no players, engaged in a game they will probably lose, could enjoy themselves or think fondly of the experience. They would only be grinning and bearing it, in order to get something else in return down the line. But plenty of players adore playing games when the win itself is unlikely or impossible, because the process of struggling to win is interesting, engaging, or satisfying. If, for instance, players only played for the sake of winning, then when a Chess grandmaster showed up the local Chess club, all the local Chess players should flee. But, as a matter of fact, they do not; often, they line up for the experience of trying their damned best and losing beautifully.

The skeptic might then respond that even when a player loses to a Chess grandmaster, they are learning something, thus making future wins down the road likely. This is also an unsatisfying response. First, I might be utterly happy to play and lose to a Chess master, even were it to be the last Chess game of my life. It is easy to imagine that a devoted basketball player might, say, make a dying wish to have a one-on-one game with Kobe Bryant. The skeptic might then respond that what's important is not winning per se, but achievement. And playing well against Kobe Bryant or a Chess master is something of an achievement, even if we lose the game. In these cases, the player is best described as pursuing different and limited sorts of achievement in various contexts. For example, perhaps, in the case of my spouse and myself, I might be said to be "pursuing the achievement of winning without help." Perhaps, in the case of playing the grandmaster, I know that I can't win in the proper sense, but I can pursue the achievement of doing as well as I can against a grandmaster. And, in any case, by playing against one of the greats, we are developing our actual skills and excellences—even if we won't get to apply them later.

But even thinking in terms of achievement won't work, nor will thinking in terms of developing our excellences. Gwen Bradford offers us a plausible account of achievement: to achieve is to engage in a difficult process, and so competently bring about some product. The greater the skill, the greater the achievement (Bradford 2015). But that can't be the right explanation, because we don't always pursue achievements, even limited ones. We aren't always making choices to increase our skill. Consider the following case: I play many boardgames with my spouse. We have just acquired an exciting new board game—*High Frontier*, a game of space colonization, in which each player takes on the role of a national government, racing to colonize the inner solar system. The game board involves a carefully researched map of the various flight paths possible throughout the inner solar system, including Lagrange points and possibilities for slingshot maneuvers, along with an actual physical spreadsheet by which one ascertains how much fuel one must burn in order to make a particular maneuver. The game involves making an enormous number of very complex calculations. Players have to bid on different technologies, including more efficient engines, automated mining vessels, and landing rovers. The game permits various wildly differing paths to victory, including firing off many cheap, disposable automated exploratory drones on slow solar sails, or trying for a much larger manned vessel that can refuel in the asteroid belt. The decision space is massive, and the calculations brutal. For example, each time one fires one's rockets, one burns up fuel and one's vessel becomes lighter, which changes the fuel cost for the next maneuver.

When we acquired the game, my spouse and I discovered that we were precisely matched. We each won about half the time, and every game was a breakneck competition, which one of us would win by the skin of our teeth. The learning process was utterly delightful, as one of us would discover an entirely new possibility implied by the game rules—for example, creating automated drones in the early game and sending them to the asteroid belt to create fuel dumps for future manned missions. One of us would invent a new strategy and win the game, and in the next game the other would steal that strategy and try to push it even further. The thrill, the challenge, and the fight were all mesmerizing.

Now suppose I see a chance to leap ahead of my spouse in skill. I could read an online strategy guide, or perhaps play a few rounds with a much more experienced player, which would develop my skills much more quickly. In that case, I could return to the games with my spouse and begin to win all our matches handily. Now, my spouse is quite a good sport and would happily continue to play even if she mostly lost. If I were solely an achievement player, I would have no reason to hold back from developing my skills. As Bradford notes, what makes something an achievement is not subjective effort, but actual difficulty. The violin master who plays a Brahms violin concerto effortlessly has more of an achievement, rather than less, because of this effortlessness. So becoming able to beat my spouse effortlessly should be attractive to me, if I was an achievement player.

But in truth, I do hold back in situations like this, and I don't think I am insane to do so. The reason I hold back is not to keep from offending my spouse—she doesn't mind. Nor am I trying to create the possibility of more games—she'd keep playing regardless. I hold back precisely because our games are wonderfully challenging, and if I were to advance past her in skill, they would become boring. In short, I hold back from developing my skill outside the game, and so consciously forego the possibility of winning more of our games and achieving greater degrees of excellence, precisely for experiential qualities of the struggle. And this can only be a reasonable choice if striving play is a legitimate possibility. Our relationship to skill acquisition in games is significantly more complicated than what the skeptical position allows. If it were the case that we were only playing to maximize worthwhile wins in the long run, then we should always be interested in increasing our skills. But we are not always motivated that way.

Of course, here a skeptic might point to the fact that I have picked a very peculiar context: social game playing in a familial context. But what is so peculiar about that? I've noticed, in reading the various literatures about games and play, that different literatures tend to focus on different paradigms of play. There is a tradition that focuses on children's play and creative play and that treats the seriousness of professional play as something of an aberration. The philosophy of sports, on the other hand, tends to take professional and Olympic sports as its paradigm and rarely considers, say, children's sports or a basketball match between friends (Nguyen 2017c). Notably, that focus tends to lead to explanations in terms of excellence and skills development to cash out the value of games. But I see no reason to take professional and elite play as the primary focus for theorizing about games. It seems just as important—if not more important—to understand everyday play: board games with families, drinking games with friends, or a quick after work session on an online shooter.

Recall again the category of stupid games—games that one has to try to win to really experience the game, but where the most enjoyable experience is one of failure. Stupid games are only possible if striving play is possible. Notice, though, that stupid games are inimical to professionalization or elite play. There are no serious *Twister* tournaments, no Bag on Your Head leagues. These games seem essentially silly. They are usually designed to entertain a large number of people, many of whom might have never played such a game before. Consider a drinking game, such as the one that when it's your turn, you have to name a real candy bar that hasn't yet been named by anybody else in the game. The best part, of course, is when one is sufficiently drunk that one cannot even perform the simplest task, much to the joy of all involved. (Importantly, for this sort of drinking game, there is no victory condition, only a loss condition.) When one recalls great sessions of such drinking games with one's friends, one doesn't recall those skilled moments when one managed to remember *yet another candy bar name*. One remembers the stunning failures, the sputtering, and the glorious moments when players groan at their own idiocy and drink up. Imagine, also, what it would be like if somebody trained to get good at such a game—memorizing long lists of candy bar names and practicing recalling their names while drunk. Such a player is missing the point. The game, in fact, is designed to make evident how much skill isn't the point. The task is inherently stupid and valueless. It is designed, as Quintin Smith has pointed out, to accentuate the silliness of the failure by making the task at which we fail obviously trivial (Smith 2014). And this is why players of such games usually have a vast store of them. The very point is to prevent the emergence of skill; we want them to be played rarely, so that nobody can get particularly good at them.

The academic literature on games has rarely discussed stupid games and their ilk. Academics—especially philosophers—tend to devote their theoretical energies to the serious side of human, and tend to ignore the humorous, the playful, and the ridiculous. There is, for example, a great inequity between the rather great amount of philosophy that has been written on tragedy, and the paltry bit of work on comedy. This suggests an explanation for the philosophy of sports' focus on elite sports. Elite sports are valuable in the way that many other serious activities are valuable, and so are more amenable to theorizing with pre-established conceptual tools. The discussion in the philosophy of sports has, for this reason, largely been couched in terms of such familiar values as difficulty, achievement, winning, skill development, and the production and display of personal excellence. The philosophical work on games has largely ignored stupid games, silly games, and funny games. This is, I suggest, because such games are exemplars of the motivationally unfamiliar category of striving games, and do not fit well with our standard accounts of justification and value.

The skeptic might finally attempt a last-ditch variation of their last response: with stupid games, they might say, the point is achievement within a certain context. Stupid games, they might insist, are games where we try to win without any skill development. Similarly, they might say that, in playing against my spouse, I am trying to win without any outside assistance. But this seems rather to be missing the point. Here, remember that I'm not trying to argue that achievement play is impossible in certain contexts; I'm simply trying to argue for the possibility of striving play. And the possibility of striving play is to be found, not in the bare explicit rules of stupid games, but the spirit in which so many of us play them. In stupid games, we enjoy the failure itself. If I had to step back and choose, I might reasonably prefer the sequence of events where I lost dramatically and hysterically at *Twister*, to the one where I played carefully and won. But again: I cannot have that experience if I actually seek the loss in the moment-to-moment course of play. I must be guided, in each of my particular actions in the game, by the goal of winning. The cherished experience in *Twister* is one in which I am actually trying to win but failing abjectly. I have to be trying to win, at least enough for that failure to make sense *as a failure*. For it is only funny as a failure, and it is only a failure if I was trying to win. And the best way to make sense of this strange motivational state is as a form of striving play. The interest in winning is not an enduring one, but one confined to a particular temporary agency, adopted for experiential motives. Similarly, I might easily prefer a session of Go where I screw up an early sequence, but which leads us into to an utterly new and fascinating situation that I end up losing, over the session where I play perfectly and eke out a dull win.

More importantly, the skeptic has little to offer as an explanation for why an achievement player might prefer such limited skill achievement. Why would an achievement player want to "win without consulting another guidebook" or "win without any skill development"? If the value of winning were to be cashed out solely in terms of achievement—in terms of ability, success, or skill development—then these seem like arbitrary limitations. But if we think that we can pursue the win for the sake of the quality of striving, then such limitations make perfect sense. In fact, we can expand this point to one about how we choose games in general. If we were all only achievement players, then we might have a hard time explaining why we would choose the limitations of one game over the limitations of another. Either that choice would be entirely arbitrary or the choice would have to track the development of human excellences that are valuable outside the game. But that is not at all like how so many players talk. Their choices are soaked in talk of interestingness, fun, fascination, beauty, and other experiential qualities of play. Striving play makes sense of many of our decisions about *which* game to play.

Thus, attention to the spirit in which many games are played, and the source of our enjoyments and valued experiences, weighs heavily against the skeptic about striving play. But for those who are not convinced, perhaps another tack will help. Here it will be useful to switch approaches and consider a slightly different form of skepticism about striving play.

It May Be Disposable, but Is It an End?

Are disposable ends really any sort of end at all? Suppose I am a striving player, and I adopt an interest in winning for the sake of playing the game. In what sense is my interest in winning an actual end? One might think that pre-lusory and lusory goals do not rise to the status of genuine ends, even disposable ones. Perhaps they are only pretend ends. That is, perhaps when I am playing a game, I am play-acting as if something is my end, rather than taking it on as an actual end.

This supposition, however, erodes the difference between theatrical acting and game playing. Suppose I am in an improvisational theater troupe, playing the character of a bank robber. My fellow players might weave a story and a set of challenges for my character. They might create a scenario, say, where I am trapped in a bank vault with only one bullet, a bottle of bleach, and a rope to my name. In this case, I might think through what somebody who did care about getting out would try to do, and how my character might think through those challenges. But I myself, the actor, wouldn't share any of those interests. And I, the actor, make the decisions about how my character will act. I, the actor, might decide that my character will act stupidly and against his interests for the sake of an interesting narrative or an interesting death. I, the actor, do not adopt the desires of my character in a practically decisive way.[2]

But in games, a player usually does genuinely desire to win during the course of the game. This desire is what powers the thrill, the absorption, the

---

[2] In Suitsian lingo: These aren't games, because I'm guided by the pursuit of an independently valuable end—artistic expression. Nothing plays the role of a pre-lusory goal in most traditional theater.

anxiety, and the danger. Only if a player genuinely desire to win the game will it be horrifying when their position erodes, terrifying when they see, in a multiplayer online shooter, an enemy pop out with an assault rifle. And that desire to win guides their actions and grounds the intensity of their motivations. Such actors are engaged in a very different way. They may be thrilled about whether the story is going well for the audience, but they aren't engaged and absorbed in whether or not their character's actions come off well or badly as practical endeavors. Even method actors, who try to partially remake their own psyches in the shape of the psyche of the characters they play, don't actually do whatever it takes to achieve their characters' ends. A method actor's choices about how their character will behave are still regulated by the actor's own artistic ends, and not the specified ends of the character. Otherwise, actors would never guide their characters to act non-optimally toward the character's goals. They would, say, never guide their tragic character toward his or her inevitable doom.[3]

But the relationship of players to their in-game roles is quite different. In the paradigmatic cases of game play, the players do take on an alternate agency. I'm not claiming that this is the case for all game play. Some players do, in fact, only act as if winning is an end. Some game players are just in it for socializing and merely go through the motions of attempting to win. However, it seems that for many players, the interest in winning is a genuine end—though a disposable one. It is genuine because it functions as their primary guide to practical reasoning and decision-making within the context of the game. Only that can explain the psychological absorption, excitement, and drama that is the paradigmatically desirable phenomenology of game play.

This is, I take it, the central peculiarity of game playing. The relationship between the interest in winning and the activity of playing cannot be explained with a straightforward means-end story. A striving player does, in fact, take

---

Of course, there are some theatrical games, such as improv comedy games, in which teams compete for some sort of judged points. But this is precisely why just this small set of theatrical activity is called a game, and most theatrical performances are not.

[3] A much more careful version of the argument of this paragraph can be found in Andrew Kania's discussion of why gamers are not performers (Kania 2018). Kania criticizes, to my mind quite successfully, Berys Gaut's game-play-as-performance account. Kania's argument might plausibly be extended to provide a criticism of other play-as-performance accounts, such as Graeme Kirkpatrick's view that video-game playing is something akin to dance performance (Kirkpatrick 2011). See also Stear (2017) for further discussion.

up an interest in winning in order to make the activity of striving possible. But the striving player's motivational structure is not simply reversed. That is, the striving player does not take up an interest in winning as a simple means to the activity of striving. In order to actually sustain practical engagement in the activity, the interest in winning has to temporarily take the phenomenal position of being something like a final end.

Outside the game, I can have a normally instrumental attitude toward my taking up an interest in winning. I can explain it straightforwardly: "I'm trying to capture the king here, because Chess calculations are interesting." But in the game itself, to be fully in the mental attitude of striving, I need to adopt a mental posture in which a disposable end illuminates my practical consciousness much like a final end—in which I pursue that goal single-mindedly, without thinking of some other purpose beyond it. I need to *immerse* myself in this temporary agency. Playing a game in this way, then, involves not only taking on an alternate practical agency, but subsuming ourselves within it. It involves making that agency temporarily dominant in the phenomenology and practice of reasoning and acting. The disposable ends of games cannot appear to us as straightforward and transparent means to some other end. They need to function for us, temporarily, like final ends.

Why? Imagine, instead, a striving player who pursues game ends in a transparently instrumental way. Instead of subsuming themselves to a temporary practical agency that is wholly devoted to the win, the player pursues the end of winning simply as a means to the end of having a struggle, and they keep this relationship active in their reasoning process. Since they took up the desire to win as a mere means, their interest in maintaining that desire would be transparently subservient to their desire for the struggle. But it would be impossible for such a striving player to be wholehearted in their game play in any non-timed game. If I were playing Chess and the win was in my grasp, I should see that winning would terminate the struggle. In that case, it would be reasonable for me to throw the game in order to prolong the struggle. Or, suppose that I am interested in Chess for the experience of a desperate struggle. If I am in the middle of a game of Chess and I see a particularly devastating move that would make the rest of the game easy for me, it would be reasonable for me to avoid that move in order to maintain the desperate struggle. Such a player would have to maintain a perpetually anxious secondary consciousness, worrying not only about losing, but also about winning. They should be taking care to avoid winning, at the same time as they are trying to win. Taking up disposable ends as transparently instrumental makes it impossible to enter a fully absorbed experience of striving play. In order for a player to become fully absorbed in play, the disposable ends must occupy a central place in their consciousness. Thus, disposable ends are genuine ends in the following ways: they ground reasoning; they guide action; and for a period of time, they occupy the forefront of the agent's mental awareness.

But one may take all this motivational complexity as yet another reason to be skeptical about striving play. One might think that achievement play is much more motivationally simple, and that it would be more explanatorily elegant to confine our explanations entirely to achievement play. What might impel us to accept the motivational complexity of striving play as a real possibility? In particular, why think that we can perform this very peculiar self-manipulation of taking up a disposable end for instrumental reasons, and then submerging ourselves in it, making it loom in our consciousness, for a time, as something like a final end?

Let's think more about what the picture of disposable ends says that game playing is *like*. If we accept that disposable ends are a real possibility, then we must take ourselves to have a very odd psychological capacity. In order to be immersed in the activity of striving, we have to take on something that feels like a final end, that guides our activity and attention the way a final end does. In the next chapter, I will argue that this is best described, not as a change in our agency, but as the construction of a temporary agency layered within our overall agency. The ends of the overall agency continue to function to regulate our choices and to maintain temporary agencies, and can intercede to cancel the game if, say, nobody is having any fun.

But why go through all this rigmarole of creating, sustaining, and submerging ourselves in temporary agencies? For many of us, the desirable experiences are ones of single-minded, wholehearted immersion. A significant part of the appeal of games is that we do not have to deal with the complex fluidity of the world and its shady, ambiguous, and pluralistic values. In Chess, in football, and in *Settlers of Catan*, there is a single goal, clear and measurable, and we can be wholehearted and unswerving in pursuit of that goal. Insofar as the activity or experience of wholehearted pursuit is what a game player desires, they must let the goals of the game occupy their consciousness with the weight of a final end.

But notice that these observations also weigh in favor of the story about agential fluidity and disposable ends. Suppose we desire game experiences of single-mindedness and wholehearted immersion. We surely do find these sorts of experiences in games. But the very fact that game playing does, in fact, seems to us to be motivationally clearer than ordinary life shows something crucial. It shows that, in the transition into game playing, we have actually changed our motivational structure to some significant degree. If we didn't accept the possibility of some degree of agential layering and immersion in alternative agencies, we would have a hard time explaining the psychological shift between the motivationally scattered experience of ordinary life—full of its thousand competing purposes—and the pleasing single-minded motivational clarity of game life. That change is well-explained by ascribing to ourselves an ability to set up an alternative agency and temporarily submerging ourselves within it. The experience of single-mindedness in games is a reason to believe in agential fluidity.

In this case, a skeptic might respond by saying that the experience of game playing is merely an experience of narrowed motivation, rather than changed motivation. That is, a skeptic might claim that players are simply picking out one of their ends and focusing on it for a time, excluding others ends from their attention for a while. But that strikes me as already invoking a fairly significant degree of agential fluidity—of immersing oneself inside an alternate agency. Of course, the skeptic still has some wiggle room here. A skeptic can claim that it is possible to exclude from one's current awareness enduring ends that one has, but not possible to take up new ends temporarily. But this is an odd position to take. Why ascribe to agents a power for negative fluidity, but not for positive fluidity? Why think that we could phenomenally suppress an enduring end for a time, but not phenomenally take up a new end for a time? If we can manipulate our phenomenal experience of our own ends in one direction, why not the other?

Perhaps the skeptic thinks that we have some evidence that we could temporarily suppress our awareness of an end we already have, but no reason to think that we can acquire new ends. Agential fluidity, the skeptic could say, is restricted to momentarily narrowing our focus—and this process doesn't involve bringing in anything so odd as disposable ends. But that skeptical position, too, seems to ignore a wide variety of phenomena. The fact that we play stupid games is evidence that we can take on a temporary end that has nothing to do with our enduring ends.

Think about how fluidly we can take up and abandon our interests in winning. Suppose I have a party of awkward people. I propose a game, which might be a pleasant icebreaker. Perhaps it is Charades. We break into teams, and acquire an interest in winning. We acquire, in fact, an interest in cooperating with one arbitrarily assigned set of people, in order to beat another arbitrarily assigned set of people. We play the game for a while; we invest ourselves in it. But if the game is failing to serve its purpose—if it is, for example, making people anxious and causing them to bicker, we can simply pivot. We can decide that the game isn't fun and give it up—and then our interest in winning simply fades. If I set up the game of Charades for the sake of social ease and fun, and we're not getting any of those payoffs, I don't grudgingly give in because the genuine value of winning is overweighted by other considerations. Instead, winning just comes to seem pointless. The phenomenal experience of exiting a game is, in many cases, not simply one of the game's ends rejoining the constellation of one's other ends; it is one where the game's ends fade out of sight.

Consider, too, Eljiah Millgram's account of the fluidity of final ends in his discussion of the moral psychology of boredom, which contains an intriguing parallel to our present discussion. Millgram takes on Harry Frankfurt's view that we need to have final ends to avoid being bored. On the contrary, says Millgram, merely having final ends is no insurance against being bored. In fact, having the same final ends day after day will leave me open to the corrosive effects of routine, boredom, and the humdrum. Instead, remaining interested in the world requires fluidly changing one's interests. I explore one topic of interest, and discover something else interesting that I had no prior concern with. But now, understanding this second topic suddenly becomes a new final end for me. Ends and interests change all the time. We can lose them pretty easily. When an academic starts to become bored with the process of academic research, for example, the associated goals just start to fade. They will lose interest in scoring publications, pumping up their CVs, getting more prestigious jobs. And we can gain ends and interests easily, too. An unathletic, uncompetitive person who takes up an interest in bicycling, for example, will suddenly gain a wide panoply of new interests—in getting fitter, stronger, and faster; in acquiring lighter bikes; and getting better times. So, says Millgram, we can acquire new ends in the long term because they are associated with interesting processes and activities. Engaging in an activity is valuable to me, and the activity's goals become more important to me. I acquire my ends from my experiences of value in an activity (Millgram 2004). So, it turns out, we already have a significant degree of agential fluidity, and the capacity to pick up new ends. All that is required to make room for striving play is to impute to ourselves the short-term capacity to acquire temporary ends.

What reason is left to prefer the skeptic's position? The skeptic must attribute to us a power to temporarily reduce our phenomenal involvement with some of our ends, but not a power to temporarily increase our phenomenal involvement in a disposable end. The experience of game play, I've argued, gives us a rich panoply of experiences that all suggest that we have that latter power. A picture that includes the possibility of striving play, disposable ends, and temporary agencies fits the wide variety of orientations we have around games—the way we pick them up, change between then, and abandon them.

Fluidity, Both Great and Small

We have learned from the discussion of disposable ends, not only something interesting about games, but also something about our capacity for agential fluidity. This shows that the process of end acquisition is more voluntary that we might have thought. This is will be, I suspect, surprising to some theorists of agency. Let me illustrate by showing how the existence of striving play brings pressure to bear on at least one picture of agency: Millgram's account, which we've just discussed.

Millgram's target in his discussion of boredom and the fluidity of ends is Frankfurt's view that we need final ends to avoid boredom. Millgram's picture of fluidity resembles mine in some very important respects. For Millgram, we enter into new roles, taking on new interests and focusing on new capacities. We try on the role of "academic" and care for a while about advancing knowledge and publishing papers, focusing on our intellectual capacities. When we try on that role and its concomitant interests and it goes well for us, our interest naturally strengthens. Millgram's view differs from mine, however, in his claim that the process of changing ends is slow and largely involuntary. In his view, our experiences of interest and boredom are what tighten or weaken our grip on our ends. Since the experiences of interest and boredom are out of our control, our shedding of ends is also largely out of our control. Interest and boredom are involuntary, says Millgram, because "their function is not to stabilize the self, but to push you past the structures of final ends that you might have taken for your own personal that-without-which-not" (Millgram 2004, 180–183). In other words, the changes in our ends can't be voluntary, because the changes don't come from decisions we ourselves make—these changes constitute changes in our selves and in the basic structures by which we make voluntary decisions.

For Millgram, boredom and interest are functional guides to finding the best-fitting ends and roles for oneself. But I've suggested that boredom and interest can serve another, less globally transformative function. For Millgram, the primary function of both boredom and interest is to alter the enduring self by signaling that the self's current interests and ends won't do to sustain its psychic health. In Millgram's view, boredom and interest are instrumentally useful—they are guides for the gradual transformation of oneself into something better. But in games, we can transform ourselves just for the sake of alleviating boredom and having interesting experiences. If a game is boring, I will drop the particular agencies involved. In other words, what is strictly instrumental for Millgram becomes the whole point in striving play. Boredom and interest don't only serve to push our whole self past its present structure of final ends; they guide the choice of temporary agencies with regard to their disposable ends. Sometimes, as Millgram suggests, we use boredom and interest as a guide to changing our enduring self. But sometimes we play around with a toy version of our self for the sake of avoiding boredom and having interesting experiences.

The existence of striving play, as it is found in games, shows that our fluidity of agency is not slow and involuntary, but something rather nimbler. In striving play, temporary ends can be adopted at will. Again: I am told to value green tokens, as acquired through a system of trading resources. For a couple of hours, they become my primary and overriding interest. I am told to try to beat the other players in this game, or to cooperate with the other players to beat randomly generated challenges in another game. In both cases, I simply take on the specified interest. This is not to say that we have such instantaneous and voluntary control over our enduring ends. Disposable ends have a very different phenomenology and embeddedness in our psyche. And, of course, the act of taking on these disposable ends is embedded in a structure of more stable final ends. I am willing to take up whatever pre-lusory goals the game rules tell me to, because I have an abiding interest in striving experiences. But it is to say that, in games, we are fluidly playing around with parts of our own agency.

3

Layers of Agency

So far, I've argued that we have the capacity to engage in striving play. We can take up an interest in winning for the sake of the struggle. What's more, game designers have an extraordinary degree of control over the nature of that struggle. They shape the obstacles, and they shape the skeleton of the practical agent who will face those obstacles. That agential sculpting includes the designation of abilities and goals.

The designation of goals plays a crucial role in shaping the activity of play. Consider the vastly cynical board game *Imperial*, in which the six major powers of World War I duke it out. Crucially, the players do not play as the countries. They play as the shadowy investors behind those countries, buying bonds and taking temporary control over countries through investment. Many of the actions that are available in the game are very much like those in more conventional war games, such as *Risk*. Any country you have the most stock in, you have control of. So long as you retain a majority of stock, you can direct that nation's military: buying armies, paying for them out of the national treasury, and marching them around to attack other armies and destroy other countries' factories and infrastructure. But the game's goals are set up in a peculiar way. The game tells you to care not one whit about the fates of the countries or their victories in war, but only about the total amount of cash that you have at the end of the game. And the structure of investments can shift radically during the game as players move around their investments and pass around control of the countries, and as the players vie for profits. The game experience here is vastly different from that of *Risk*. Here, players may engage in such stratagems as losing a war on purpose and then selling their investments in the country at just the right moment to make a tidy profit. You can force a country you control to pay out its treasury to its stockholders, even if that would cripple the country. It can sometimes even be profitable for a player to stage a war between two countries that they control. The game becomes one of financial manipulation—of controlling the structure of shared incentives between the various players and of arranging profitable alliances through careful co-investment. And the designer of *Imperial*, Mac

Games. C. Thi Nguyen, Oxford University Press (2020). © Oxford University Press.
DOI: 10.1093/oso/9780190052089.001.0001

Gerdts, shaped this very specific form of practical activity, in significant part, by setting the goals. The goal is not victory in war but profit. That goal is achieved, not through beating other countries, but through stock payouts.

Game designers shape a struggle by designating goals, along with setting the abilities and creating the practical environment. And players become absorbed in that struggle by taking on those goals, temporarily. In Chapter 2, I argued for the bare possibility of striving play. In this chapter, I put some flesh on those bones. I fill out a picture of the psychological mechanisms involved in striving play, and talk more about the structure of practical rationality required to engage in striving play. At the center of this picture is our capacity for submersion—for losing ourselves in a temporary agency, and momentarily blotting out our connection with our enduring values and ends. And I start to think about why it might be important for us to have this capacity, and how our ability to play games may relate to other practical needs and abilities we may have.

Agential Submersion and Agential Layering

Striving play involves a fairly complicated motivational structure. Suppose I am a pure striving player. From the perspective of my enduring practical identity, I intrinsically value the experiences of striving and don't value winning at all. But in order to have those experiences, I must be able to do something fairly odd. In the last chapter, I focused on one facet of that oddity: our capacity to take up a new disposable end. But merely adding an end isn't enough to explain our *absorption* in striving play. I must also submerge myself in that new end—to phenomenally make that temporary end dominant in my reasoning, my motivation, and my practical consciousness. I not only need to add to my usual structure of ends, but also to temporarily subtract from my motivational structure, sealing myself off from many of my normal interests and ends. But are we really capable of such submersion and layering? And would our capacity for submersion and layering play any real function in our lives, other than solving some abstruse technical puzzles about aesthetics and games?

This submersion and layering might seem quite odd. It is something of a motivational two-step. But the more one reflects on the nature of game play, the more it seems that such a motivational two-step must be possible. If one values the experience of single-minded absorption in a practical task, one cannot pursue that experience directly. Rather, one must submerge oneself in the pursuit of some other end. This is a relative of what Henry Sidgwick called the *paradox of hedonism*—that one cannot achieve pleasure by pursuing it directly, but only by devoting oneself to some other end (Sidgwick 1907, 136–137). For example, the pleasures of being a devoted parent aren't available to the selfish hedonist; it is only available to parents who are genuinely and wholeheartedly devoted to their child. Moral theories with this quality have been called "self-effacing" (Pettigrove 2011, 192–193).[1] Loosely following Sidgwick's formulation, let's call something a *self-effacing end* if it is an end that cannot be achieved through direct pursuit, but only through pursuit of some other end. As Sidgwick says, the rational method of attaining such an end requires that "we should to some extent put it out of sight and not directly aim at it."

Self-effacing ends turn out to be fairly common. Several different yoga teachers I've had have said that yoga asks us to focus on physical movement, but achieving flexibility and physical fitness isn't the point. Concentrating on the physical goals is just a way to sneak up on certain mental and spiritual effects that are too subtle to be grasped directly. To translate into our terms: yoga has self-effacing ends. You can't achieve relaxation by pursuing it directly. Instead, you must set your mind to little tasks of balance and posture, from which relaxation will un-self-consciously arise. Similarly, you cannot achieve a calm and blank state of mind by directly aiming at it. (Have you ever tried?) Such a state usually arises out of the pursuit of some other goal, like getting to the end of a hike or counting your breath for ten minutes.

Notice that the game-playing is full of such self-effacing ends. If you wish to have an experience of single-minded practical absorption, then you must be able to temporarily put your aesthetic interest out mind. You must acquire, for the moment, a single-minded interest in winning. You cannot achieve absorption in a rock climb by aiming at the mental state of absorption. You achieve absorption when you aim, with all your heart, at getting to the top. Thus, the end of becoming absorbed in a practical struggle is a self-effacing end.

We know it's possible to engage in these motivational two-steps outside of games. We do it all the time, in little ways. I can think to myself, "I need to relax this weekend and clear my head of all this work stress." But I can't

---

[1] The language of "self-effacement" was introduced by Derek Parfit (1984, 23–24). Further discussion in Railton (1984); Hurka (2000); Keller (2007); and Annas (2008).

actually clear my head just by directly willing myself to clear my head. What I need to do is set my mind to some other task, like hiking to the top of a mountain. And I need to exclude from my awareness, for a little while, the reasons and considerations that brought me to this activity. Suppose that I am a ball of stress because of my work and family responsibilities. Those responsibilities are, in fact, the very reason that I'm trying to de-stress in the first place. I need to fix my head in order to get back to work and do what needs to get done. But in order to de-stress, I must put all those considerations out of mind. De-stressing involves forgetting for a while about my responsibilities, but I won't be able to do that if I hold constantly before my mind the fact that I desperately need to de-stress in order to take care of all those damn responsibilities.

But, miraculously, I can often pull off this mental manipulation. I can go on a hike to clear my head, and put my reasons for doing so out of mind. My ability to do this isn't perfect; sometimes, the larger world of reasons breaks through. But often, I can get most of the way there. I can throw myself into the sheer physical effort of getting to the top and let all my other practical worries fall away. And that success involves managing, for a little while, to put my larger purposes out of mind. So we do, in fact, have this capacity. Manipulating our interest in temporary ends to achieve self-effacing ones is actually a familiar technique, and one which we use regularly. Games simply formalize it.

Submersion is also crucial for getting many of the key experiences of games. What we want out of many games is an experience of practical absorption in a task. Take one of the characteristically desirable experiences of game play: *flow-state*. To achieve flow-state, you cannot take flow-state as your constant and conscious end; the very nature of flow-state is of being unself-consciously absorbed in the details of the task. We want to be absorbed in the practical moment, and not worried about whether we are in fact absorbed in the practical moment.

Recall our friend from Chapter 1, the ten-year-old *Monopoly* player. I argued that when we engage in striving play, it must be that we do not take up the game's goals as internally transparent instruments to achieve the activity of striving. If the striving player recalls their reason for playing—the joys of the struggle—then they won't be able to achieve it. Instead, they will be caught in a curious form of double-consciousness. Since they are trying to win for the sake of the struggle, they could find themselves in positions where, whenever the win is within their grasp, it would be rational for them to throw the game and deny themselves that win in order to keep on playing. Admittedly, there may be other reasonable choices. A player might take the win, thinking that another game was following. But even with that on the table, the instrumentally transparent striving player must consider the relationship between winning and the continuation of the striving experience. Such a player must worry about whether winning the game too handily might, say, reduce the possibility of future games. But those sorts of considerations need to be off the table in order to achieve practical absorption. We need to be able to submerge and layer, in order to really get into the game.

This picture of agential layering also helps to explain the complex relationship that striving players have to winning. It is only during the game itself that I need to maintain a dominant interest in winning—in which winning must appear to me, phenomenally, as something like a final end. But recall that, outside the game, we do often push away the win. We do it by changing games or refusing to improve our skill. An interest in winning is, for the striving player, only a temporary feature of the inner agent, which they set up and submerge themselves in for the sake of the struggle. The outer agent sets up the inner agent with a particular motivational structure for the sake of the outer agent's enduring interests—say in the beautiful experience of struggling. The inner agent tries to win. The outer agent has no reason to help the inner agent, and may manipulate their overall ability to win, in order to get the right degree of struggle.

We have, then, the capacity to submerge ourselves in a temporary agency, and thereby create layers of motivational states. In striving play, the inner layer involves taking on motivations to succeed in the game's terms—to win, and to win by achieving whatever the game specifies as the goals. The outer layer involves those motivations which brought us to play the game in the first place—an interest in aesthetics, fun, fitness, or whatever. These motivations of the inner layer are *justified* by the motivations of the outer layer, but that justification isn't phenomenally active during the game. We do not hold both layers in the forefront of our consciousness. We hide our larger reasons from ourselves for a time, submerging ourselves in the inner layer.

There are, then, several ways in which the striving player might err in their attempt at psychological self-manipulation. The first is by being what we might call the diffident player, who can't bring themselves to actually care about the game. "What's the point? It's just a game," they say. The second is by getting stuck in the game agency. Such a player, once they take up the goal of winning, is incapable of putting it away again afterwards. Such a player is often called "excessively competitive" in contexts where the attitude of striving play would be more appropriate, for losses hurt them terribly, and wins give them great pride. Having set up a temporary agency to pursue some self-effacing purpose, and absorbed themselves in the temporary goal, they neglect, after the game is through to dispose of that temporary agency, and restore to their sight their larger purpose. But the successful striving player can both submerge themselves in an alternative agency and pull themselves back from it.

Striving play demands that we momentarily silence some of our ends, but practical conditions may make this psychologically impossible. I cannot submerge myself in play if I am starving or if I fear for my life. There, my enduring ends may ring so loudly for me that I cannot submerge myself in the more delicate temporary agency. This is not an iron-clad rule, of course. As Suits points out, some games, like mountaineering, integrate physical extremes into their activity. A hobbyist mountaineer continues in pursuit of their lusory goal, even in the face of hunger and possible death. Such is the case with many extreme sports, depending on which physical extremes are part of the desired experience. And the cases may be subject to psychological variation. One game-loving friend of mine was going through a terrible divorce, constantly beset by worries about his finances, his love life, and caring for his son. The only thing that cheered him up was a nice, absorbing board game. For the moment, he could adopt another practical identity and another set of concerns, and experience a temporary relief from the pressures of his ordinary life. Similarly, when a group of progressive activists were sitting at my dinner table waiting for the Clinton-Trump election results to come in, the only way they managed to distract themselves from gnawing sorrow and dread was by playing the children's competitive storytelling game *Dixit*.

Of course, our submersion in temporary agency can also be quite fragile. This is as it should be. If my house begins to burn down during a game, or another player begins having a heart attack, then my enduring values should re-assert themselves and pierce the temporary agency. If, during a friendly board game night between ordinarily competitive friends, one of the players, who has just been been dumped by a partner, breaks down crying mid-game, good-hearted people ought to abandon their submersion. To maintain the temporary agency, with its single-minded interest in winning, in such a situation is to be something of an asshole.[2]

---

[2] I mean here to invoke Aaron James's technical account of an "asshole" (James 2014).

The possibility of cancellation also helps to better illuminate the structure of our layered agencies. How are these layers arranged and separated? One simple account is that the layering is *chronological*: our agential layers are separated strictly in time. Before the game, we occupy our full agency. During the game, we submerge ourselves in the gaming agency and forget about our full agency. When the game ends, we return to our full agency. The agential layers would exist, by this sort of account, merely from the mind's capacity to temporarily alter itself. But I do not think that can be the complete story. At least to some degree, we must have the psychological capacity to maintain these layers simultaneously—to run the outer layer in the background, as it were. This is because, as we've seen, we are usually capable of cancelling the inner layer when necessary. For this to occur, we must retain some contact with our full agency, even as we are mostly submerged in the inner agency.

Perhaps readers will find this all so unlikely that they would rather reject the possibility of striving play than accept the possibility of agential layering. But striving play and agential layering are, I think, very plausible—especially when considered together. Take a certain kind of experience often described by various players of games. You can be caught in the throes of the game, desperate to win, doing whatever you can. But you can also, in the middle of such a game, step back and see what a beautiful game you're involved in, how dramatic and elegant all the moves have been. You can be about to lose a game, in agonies over the failure of your plans, but also love it—even though you have lost—precisely because the moves played were so wondrous. The skeptic who rejects the possibility of striving play and agential layering cannot explain these experiences; they can't explain the peculiar phenomenal duality of our gaming experience. But in my view, that experience is easily explained: you are moving between your temporary adopted practical agency and your more lasting agency. If you are losing in the most interesting game of your life, the temporary practical agency should be miserable, but the enduring agency—the one that only put on that temporary agency for the sake of a good and interesting struggle—should be in raptures.

Love and Games

But perhaps this motivational layering, though possible, is a bad idea. Perhaps, we might worry, such layering counts as a problematic sort of agential dis-integration. Michael Stocker had something very similar in mind when he accused modern ethical theories of schizophrenia. Imagine, says Stocker, an egoistic hedonist who wishes to love for all the pleasures that love brings. They will inevitably fail—because when love is pursued for such transparently narcissistic ends, it isn't actually love. The true lover must primarily value the beloved, and not, say the state of being in love. Thus, the egoist is too narcissistic to reap the benefits of love.

Of course, says Stocker, that egoist could try to forget their egoism, to submerge themselves temporarily in the mentality of a genuine lover.

> It is, of course, essential to the transformation of the person from egoistical motivation to caring for others that the person-as-egoist lose conscious control of him/herself. This raises the question of whether such people will be able to check up and see how their transformed selves are getting on in achieving egoistically approved goals. Will they have a mental alarm clock which wakes them up from their nonegoistical transforms every once in a while, to allow them to reshape these transforms if they are not getting enough personal pleasure—or, more generally, enough good? I suppose that this would not be impossible. But it hardly seems an ideal, or even a very satisfactory, life. It is bad enough to have a private personality, which you must hide from others; but imagine having a personality that you must hide from (the other parts of) yourself. Still, perhaps this is possible. If it is, then it seems that egoists may be able to meet this second criticism. But this does not touch my criticism: that they will not be able to embody their reason in their motives; that they will have to lead a bifurcated, schizophrenic life to achieve what is good. (Stocker 1976, 457–458)

Stocker, then, is critical of any theory that asks us to temporarily hide parts of ourselves from ourselves—that asks us to temporarily disconnect ourselves, internally, from our own ends. That, says Stocker, is a terrible life to have; it is motivational schizophrenia. Note that the schizophrenic life Stocker worries about is exactly one where one's purpose in taking up an activity is distinct from the goal one consciously pursues during that activity, and where the conscious pursuit of the purpose makes its achievement impossible. That is why schizophrenics must temporarily forget their true purpose, in order to achieve it.

But such a disconnect between purpose and goal is precisely the motivational structure of striving play. One plays such a game for the sake of, say, aesthetic experiences that arise from practical absorption, but one cannot pursue those aesthetic experiences directly, since they are experiences of the wholehearted pursuit of the in-game goal. One must, instead, forget one's aesthetic interests and submerge oneself in an alternate agency interested solely in achieving the in-game goals. And, in fact, we do have something like Stocker's interrupting clock. It is exactly that moment when we shake ourselves out of absorption in a game, and ask ourselves, "Wait. Are we really having any fun here?" that is the interrupting clock in action. Striving players are, in a crucial sense, Stockerian schizophrenics. We take up and discard temporary agencies whose commitments and ends do not match up with those of our full selves. But in the context of games, such schizophrenia starts to seem less repellent.

So where does that leave us? Have we discovered that the schizophrenic life is fine, and that philosophers worry too much about internal consistency? Not exactly. When we think of many of the grand plans and relationships of our lives, Stocker seems entirely right. There would be something very odd about setting the alarm clock, of setting up temporary agencies and checking in on them. We hope, in that context, for a fuller sort of integration across our ends. But when we think of games, setting up the alarm clock and popping in and out of hierarchical agencies seem far less repellent. A moderate amount of dis-integration seems fine when we move from thinking about love and life projects to thinking about games. Why this difference?

Consider Stocker's next point, that the same problem arises, not just for egoists, but for utilitarians who are told to love for the sake of the greater good. Again, this isn't really love, because it's not motivated by concern for the beloved. The problem isn't narcissism or egoism, says Stocker; it's that modern ethical theories are too impersonal. For such a theory, "any other person who would elicit as much of this good would be as proper an object of love as the beloved," says Stocker (459). If the point of love is simply to *be in love*, then one's love will be strangely detached from its object, and one should be willing to consider any other target of affection that could sustain similar love. And this, once again, isn't really love. But that strange detachment is, in fact, characteristic of genuine game playing. Playing striving games is precisely the act of taking on artificial goals and being willing, when one changes games, to change out one set of goals for an entirely new set. Any goal will do, as long as it sustains worthwhile activity. The difference is that love demands genuine commitment to its end. To love is to think of the beloved as genuinely and finally valuable. One does not love instrumentally, for the sake of the feeling. But striving play does not demand such genuine commitment to its goals. In fact, many of its peculiar virtues are enabled precisely by the very artificiality of its temporary goals, and by the fluid capacity of human agency to temporarily embrace those goals.

What we have learned here is that, in a certain sense, game playing is the opposite of love. Love requires a direct and nonfungible commitment to its object. But the aesthetic striving player, though capable of great local commitment to the in-game goals, ought be globally noncommittal toward those in-game goals. (This may be why we say: "Don't play games with my heart.") To love noncommittally is to be something of a terrible lover. But with games, the real problem is too much commitment to game goals. This is the problem of being "too competitive"—that is, of failing to properly dispose of the game ends after the game is finished, when such disposal is appropriate. Love gives us a reason to be steadfast and loyal in certain contexts. But the aesthetics of agency gives us a good reason to value a certain fluidity of agency, and to maintain the capacity for a certain fickleness and disloyalty toward a special class of ends. Stockerian schizophrenia, in short, is only a problem for the class of ends that demand wholehearted commitment. But the ends of striving play, I suggest, demand only a temporary form of commitment. Globally, they demand a certain fickleness toward their goals.

I think we are also starting to see why thinking about games and play might be important for other parts of philosophy. Various philosophical accounts of agency have tended to think, in various ways, that unity is an ideal for all agents. And the way they have presumed this involves assuming that a unified agent is always motivated by all of their ends. Millgram, for example, puts it this way: an agent's ends are subject to a *unity constraint*. What makes a value, end, or other consideration belong to a particular agent is that it can weigh with or against other such considerations in any other chain of practical reasoning by that same agent. What it is to be unified as an agent is for all your ends to be live for you, and present themselves whenever relevant. And to the degree that your ends aren't unified in this way, you are an agential failure—you are absentminded or unable to bring a relevant consideration to mind, or something else along those lines (Millgram 1997, 50–56).

But striving play and submersion make it obvious that there are also many forms of desirable disunity in our agency. They make it easy to see how structurally complicated our agency can be over time, how many nooks and crannies it might have. Our agency is not one that needs to be perpetually bathed in the light of its guiding core. We can alter ourselves, create layers, become absorbed in them, seal ourselves off from our central ends, and flit between modes of agency. Such a playful and compartmentalized agency is still unified, in that all these maneuvers are, in the long run, justificationally guided by the same set of enduring values and ends. But that is a fairly high-order and abstracted form of internal consistency. Striving play teaches us that the agential unity we really want is complex, many-layered, and distributed over time. If we only look at shorter snapshots, a playful agency can appear quite inconsistent with itself.

Agential Layers and Maieutic Ends

Let's put all the pieces together. I am attributing to game players the power to take up disposable ends. Disposable ends are the animating center of the temporary agencies we take up in games. Our agential structure becomes crucially nested. The disposable ends of striving play aren't integrated into our usual network of ends. They are justified in a backward-looking, rather than an intrinsic or forward-looking, manner. The disposable ends of game play are justified, not by their intrinsic value, or by the value of what what will follow from them, but by the form of activity their pursuit inspires. But to achieve full absorption in game play, we must forget this justification, at least from the perspective of our practical consciousness. We must submerge ourselves within an alternative agency, making it, for the moment, phenom-enally like our standard agency. That is the only way we can have experiences of practical absorption in the pursuit of a disposable end.

Now that we have the account of agential submersion and layering, it will be useful to compare it to some neighboring, but distinct, phenomena. Consider David Schmidtz's discussion of choosing ends. There is, says, Schmidtz, a special class of end that has been largely overlooked: the ends of acquiring other ends. Suppose that, as a teenager, Kate has no idea of what she wants to do with her life. She knows that she wants to do something, but she just doesn't know what it is yet. She wants to find goals to pursue, a career to settle on. She has what Schmidtz calls a *maieutic end*—"an end achieved through a process of coming to have other ends." Her end, says Schmidtz, was to settle on some other end as final. Let's say that she eventually settles on becoming a doctor, acquiring the final end of helping other people to be healthy. It is crucial to recognize that in doing so, Kate's end of helping people isn't merely taken on as a means to some further end—say, of self-definition.

She isn't helping people in order to have a goal. Helping people is now a final end for her; once chosen, it stands on its own. This is what it's like to successfully settle on a life pursuit.

Perhaps a bit of etymology here will be illuminating. Nowadays, the term *maieutic* usually alludes to the Socratic method of bringing understanding through questions and answers, but Socrates originally selected the term as a metaphor. *Maieutic* originally meant something having to do with midwifery. Schmidtz explicitly selects the term for both of these meanings—maieutic ends, he suggests, give birth to further ends with their own independent life (Schmidtz 2001, 239–244).

Consider, also, that many of us have a maieutic end of falling in love. What it is to fall in love is to come to become devoted to somebody else—to take on their well-being as an intrinsically valuable, final end. We don't love somebody as means to having somebody to love. We simply love them, full stop. When we want to fall in love, what we want is to create a new end for ourselves, one that stands alone. In other words, says Schmidtz, we first *choose* the final end for the sake of the maieutic end. But once we have that new final end, we don't *continue to pursue* the final end for the sake of the maieutic end. When we fulfill the maieutic end of settling on a career or falling in love, that maieutic end disappears, replaced by the newly acquired final end. Consider what it would be like if it were otherwise. Imagine that I have a maieutic end of being completely and lovingly devoted to somebody. Suppose that leads me to fall in love with Jessie. If my love for Jessie were merely a means to my being completely and lovingly devoted to *somebody*, then I ought to strategically manipulate that love. For example, if Jessie becomes sick with an incurable cancer and has only six months to live, my maieutic end should direct me to switch my love to somebody healthier at the first available opportunity. But, once again, this isn't love. Loving somebody involves, among other things acquiring their well-being as a final end. And what it is to want to fall in love is to have the end of acquiring another's well-being as a distinct and final end.

Though maieutic ends may seem strange from the perspective of philosophical theorizing about reasoning, they surely exist, says Schmidtz:

> Maieutic ends are not merely a theoretical postulate. They are real. The drive to find a career or a spouse can be powerful, even painful, and such drives are drives to settle on a particular career or a particular person. Recall what it was like to choose a major subject in college or to choose a

career. One way or another, we had to choose something, and, for some of us, not having done so yet was an occasion for considerable anxiety. Some of us had hardly any idea of what we really wanted, but it felt better to settle on some end or other than to let that part of our lives remain a vacuum. (Schmidtz 2001, 244)

This might seem a lot like how I've described the process of taking up disposable ends in game playing, and there are some compelling similarities. We might now be tempted toward a tidy conclusion: that what happens when we pick a game for the evening is a small-scale model of what happens when we settle on a life project. Our lives are empty until we settle on a career and a goal and somebody to love. And our evenings might be empty until we settle on a goal of, say, inventing a language in a game of *Sign*. Settling on a game, we might think, is a playful miniature of the long-term project of self-construction.

But though Schmidtz's description of Kate and my description of the game-player may seem similar, their motivational structures are actually quite different. In fact, the difference will help to highlight the peculiarity of striving play. In Kate's case, her maieutic end directs her to acquire ends that are settled, enduring, and independent. The maieutic end in this case, says Schmidtz, doesn't play a normatively grounding role toward the newly acquired ends. Rather, it is eliminated once it is fulfilled, replaced by the newly acquired final ends.

The point here is worth making absolutely clear. In normal instrumental reason, I acquire A for the sake of B, and the normative significance of A depends on the normative significance of B. If B loses its normative significance, then so will A. Let's say that, in this case, A is *normatively attached* to B. If I acquire money only for the sake of peace of mind, and I discover that having money doesn't get me peace of mind, then I should abandon any interest in acquiring money. But in the peculiar case of settling on life goals, when I acquire a A, a final end, for the sake B, a maieutic end, A does not depend for its normative significance on B. In this peculiar case, A is acquired for the sake of B, but A is *normatively detached* from B. Kate acquires the final end of helping people in order to have a life goal, but the goal of helping people then floats normatively free, once chosen. It must do so, or it is not really a life goal. Kate's case is one of normative detachment between the maieutic end and its chosen final end.

Striving play is quite different. The maieutic ends involved in striving play don't fade; rather, it is the various new ends we acquire that will come and go.

And my choices about which game ends to take up are regulated, in the long run, by my enduring interests. Suppose I have the following end: to have exciting and entertaining after-dinner games with my spouse. To fulfill it, I will need to develop some further ends, like acquiring an interest in winning by collecting green tokens, or an interest in capturing the flag. But I won't best fulfill this end by acquiring those various in-game ends as fully detached final ends. Rather, the original end continues to guide the long-term maintenance, arrangement, and disposal of my in-game ends.

We can tell that in-game ends remain normatively attached to the overarching end, because I do eventually evaluate the worth of the in-game ends in terms of their ability to achieve that overarching end. I mean something utterly mundane here. Suppose I am playing a game for the sake of an experience of absorption. To do so, I must forget about my interest in absorption. But afterward, I reflect back on and evaluate the game experience in terms of its ability to help me achieve absorption. I can step back and ask whether a game is any good or not. I can do so between games ("Should I play that game again? It was more grueling than fun"). I can even do so mid-game ("Are we really having any fun right now? Want to just call it and play something else?"). And I may play with the details of the experience. I may, say, shift the goals of my game— as a trail runner might change their mileage and time goals mid-run in order to zero in on the right state of meditative absorption. I may alter a game, adding house rules to it, all in the name of that original end of having an interesting struggle. In-game ends are not free-standing. But they must appear to us as free-standing during the game in order for us to be absorbed in the game.

To summarize: Kate's process generates detached final ends. It involves birthing genuinely independent ends, and changing her long-term structure of final ends. My process of play does not; it creates attached temporary ends, which take on the momentary appearance of detachment. Kate's story is one of motivational self-transformation. Striving play, on the other hand, is a story of temporary self-manipulation. I maintain my original ends, but I submerge myself in a temporary agency, with a different set of ends, in order to actually get at my enduring, but self-effacing, ends.

Games and the Clarity of Practicality

But thinking about submersion here reveals something interesting about the relationship between games and life. Games can offer an unusual degree of practical clarity within their confines. Most of our reasoning in life is, we might say, "all things considered." We must weigh various considerations against one another: moral considerations, short-term practical consider- ations, long-term environmental considerations, and the demands of our various conflicting values, all piled on top of the needs and interests of family, friends, and community. The result is an unholy mess we must somehow navigate. Many games work by vastly narrowing the scope of practical rea- soning and action, reducing the number of relevant considerations and abil- ities to something manageable. Paintings are made for the human eye, and games are made to fit human practical abilities.

One might then worry that there is something existentially troubling about the artificially crisp nature of these game ends, and about our single-minded pursuit of them. In our full life, we are, if we are adequate human beings, guided by a complex of values, which are often varied and broad-ranging. We must balance considerations. We must sound out subtle values and try to translate them into concrete actions. We are, furthermore, constantly rubbing up against other people and the vast confusing welter of their many values. How different that is from our existences in games, where the goals are usually clear, well- defined, measurable, and few; and where we are usually pitted against others with identical, though opposed, goals. Game goals are usually thin and pre- cise. They are very much unlike the fuller forms of valuing, which are subtle, flexible and ambiguous in their application. In fact, one might note that the assumptions of classical economics—that we are all identically rational, iden- tically self-interested agents engaged in pure self-interested competition—are problematically false in real life, but precisely right in most games.

This would be a problem if we were to suppose that the purpose of games was simply to model or represent parts of life. In that case, the clarity and quantifiability of game values would be something of a lie. In a related thought, Miguel Sicart argues in "The Banality of Simulated Evil" that the ethical harm of video games is not in the representation of evil acts. Such acts aren't wrong, because they're fictional. Instead, it is in the quantification of good and evil acts, as in *Knights of the Old Republic*—a computer game, set in the Star Wars universe, where you are presented with moral choices and then immediately presented with a score for how Light or Dark your character has become. This, suggests Sicart, cuts off moral reflection and promotes the be- lief that morality is simplistic (Sicart 2009).

We might expand Sicart's criticism and claim that all scoring sys- tems promote a banality of value—they present the purposes of life as oversimplified. But that is precisely the point of games! One of the greatest pleasures games offer is a certain existential balm—a momentary shelter from the existential complexities of ordinary life. In a game, for once in my life, I know exactly what it is that I'm supposed to be doing. This helps promote the single-mindedness that is so crucial to many of the desirable aesthetic experiences involved in striving. Furthermore, the very clarity and simplicity of these alternative goals may help players to quickly find their way into the various alternative in-game agencies. It is easier to find your way into a different motivational mode when its outlines have been made tangible. I suspect, furthermore, that the clarity and simplicity of game ends makes it more feasible for the game designer to manipulate and arrange those ends.

What's more, the clarity of purpose can help support the existence of certain aesthetic qualities that emerge in normal life only with difficulty, or help us encounter them more unambiguously. Consider the possibility that some experiences of beauty are grounded in functionality. As Glenn Parsons and Allen Carlson point out, there are experiences of beauty that are best explained as being grounded in an artifact's fitting its purpose. Their examples include elegantly designed machines, architecture, and living organisms. But, they, the primary difficulty for a theory of functional beauty is that the proper function of an artifact is often quite hard to determine. But a judgment about the proper function of an artifact is required for any non-relative judgments of functional beauty. Parsons and Carlson offer a complex solution, one in which we turn to an organism's evolutionary history, or an artifact's market and production history to determine its proper function (Parsons and Carlson 2008, 62–110). For example, we can determine the function of a doll by looking at how and why dolls were originally made, how their audience received them, and what market forces shaped the making of dolls—all of which will help us to infer what the proper function of dolls is. But notice that this requires a significantly complicated cognitive evaluation, and, in actual practice, the results will often be quite epistemically blurry. If I need to know a great deal about the evolutionary history of human arms and human movement to know whether a particular movement fulfills the proper function of human arms and bodies, then, without an adequate schooling in such things, my judgments will be hesitant and insecure.

But that blurriness disappears in games. In most games, the proper functions of objects and actions are entirely clear. Thus, the fact that the action fits its purpose is also entirely clear. Teleologically hazy objects and actions are reconstituted within the context of the game as teleologically obvious. The point of a golf stroke is to drive the ball toward the hole. It is easier to judge functional beauty in a game precisely because the relevant functional purposes are extremely well-defined. If this is right, then the very clarity of in-game goals, and our submersion in an alternate agency wholly focused on those goals, ought to ground clearer and more epistemically confident perceptions of functional beauty in games than in ordinary life. And I think this is precisely what we find. It is much easier to point out a perfectly elegant chess move than a perfectly elegant political solution. Harmonies between agent and world are easier to achieve when the agent is thinner, simpler, and clearer, and when the world has been temporarily cleared of various ambiguities and complexities. Games are a teleologically crisper context for action and evaluation. Thus, teleologically informed aesthetic judgments made in games will be correspondingly crisper and clearer.

But are such unlifelike crystallizations inherently problematic? If we were to presume that games were artistically valuable primarily in terms of their ability to accurately represent the world, then such crystallizations might raise suspicion—especially when the values given in games weren't intended as, say, clarifications or pictures of life, but simply as manipulations for providing some aesthetically satisfying experience. But I hope to have shown that games can be valuable in many other ways. And there are many arts that are valuable in virtue of their unlifelike simplicity. I think here of, say, Bach's *Art of the Fugue* and Rothko's paintings, all of which seem to abandon much of the call for accuracy in favor of promoting other sorts of aesthetic experiences. I suspect, in fact, that the pressure to articulate the value of games in terms of the value of their representational powers has arisen precisely because we have tended to discount the aesthetic value of striving experiences, and to overlook the value of games as agential manipulations, designed to foster those aesthetic experiences of striving.

Which is not to say that those unlifelike crystallizations are entirely without danger. I think they may sometimes encourage us to take unrealistic expectations about the value clarity of the world—a topic to which I will return in Chapter 9. But that is a danger that arises from exporting unrealistic expectations of clarity out of the game, and not from the experience of value clarity in the game itself.

The Paradox of Failure

Striving play involves a complex process of agential layering, where the players create and deploy a temporary agency, nested inside their primary agency, with its own particular ends and modes of practicality. And it's important to think of this as a layered agency, rather than a changed agency, since the temporary agency is still under the justificational thumb of the overall agency. This view I take to have various explanatory benefits. There are many odd features of game playing that I think it explains better than some other accounts. So let's take the theory of agential layers out for a spin.

Let's start with what Jesper Juul calls "the paradox of failure"—that, although we generally avoid failure in life, the practice of game playing introduces extra failures into our lives (Juul 2013, 1–9). The paradox, says Juul, bears some resemblance to what's been called "the paradox of tragedy" or "the paradox of painful art." Though we generally avoid painful emotions in life, we actually seek out art that will introduce painful emotions into our lives. But, says Juul, games are different from painful art, and none of the standard theories meant to explain painful art will work. In painful art, we watch somebody else fail—at most, we might have some empathetic resonance. But in games, it is we ourselves who fail (33–45).

How might we explain our willingness to court failure in games? Juul's explanation is a story of sacrifice and self-deception. Juul suggests that the pains of failure in games are outweighed by the pleasures on offer from games.[3] The greater the difficulty, and the more painful the failures, the more fantastic the triumph we feel when we do pull it off. "To play a game is to make an emotional gamble; we invest the time and self-esteem in the hope that it will pay off," says Juul. But what happens when it doesn't, and we don't get the promised reward because we failed without eventual vindication? What we can do, says Juul, is *deflate* that failure, and claim that it was "just a game"; we can say that it didn't matter anyway, because "games are artificial constructs with no bearing on the regular world." This leads to something of a contradiction, suggests Juul. When we succeed in games, we treat them as normal contexts in which success matters. But when we fail at games, we treat them as deflated contexts, telling ourselves that success and failure in games doesn't really matter anyway (Juul 2013, 13–21). In other words, says

---

[3] This kind of account is what Aaron Smuts describes as a compensation theory of painful art (Smuts 2007, 2009).

Juul, we pivot between treating the value of success and failure as local and confined to the unimportant context of the game, and treating the value as global and generally reflective of our capacities and intelligences (66). This, thinks Juul, is something of a mental trick we play on ourselves, where we pretend, retrospectively, that something didn't really matter after all. Thus, we maintain a "plausible deniability of failure" in games (122). So, following Juul's delightful phraseology, I will call his response the *plausible deniability* solution to the paradox of failure. The situation of plausible deniability may seem somewhat paradoxical, says Juul, but that paradox is an irresolvable one at the heart of game playing.

> The uncertain meaning of game failure is a feature, not a bug: it allows us to take games seriously but also grants us a freedom from consequences. We could have hoped that one of the traditional explanations of the paradox of painful art would be a perfect fit for games, but the truth is rather that games are defined by the uncertain meaning of failure. We therefore have a way to save face, whenever we fail. (44)

Thus, something of a contradiction lies at the heart of game playing, says Juul. We both value and disclaim valuing game achievements. And we shouldn't be so anxious to get out of that contradiction. If we resolved game playing into a wholly normal context, then the failures would hurt too much. If we resolved game playing into a wholly deflated context, then the successes wouldn't matter, and we wouldn't have that lovely sense of triumphing over painful failure. So we must suspend ourselves between these two states, pivoting as needed—caring about the achievement when we pull it off, and pretending to ourselves that it doesn't matter when we fail (123–124).[4]

Juul's account of plausible deniability gets at something very important about the phenomenon of game playing. But the theory, in its details, has some significant problems. First, if Juul is right, we would never engage in the activity if we didn't think that we could win. And as I've argued, this simply doesn't seem true for all game playing. There are many cases where we enter into a game without so much as a hope of winning. More importantly, Juul's

---

[4] Please note that this is something of a reconstruction. Juul's text, while full of interesting claims, never actually puts all these pieces together quite as explicitly as I've done here. He also brings up a number of points that don't quite fit with the theory—perhaps because the book is, as he says explicitly, something more of a personal essay and exploration of failure in games than an argument. However, the argument I've presented I take to be the best reconstruction I can deliver of the primary threads and suggestions in the text. I was helped in my reconstruction by Moser (2017, 138–141).

account ascribes to every player an essential irrationality—a kind of self-protective delusional state—in order to survive the ego pain of game playing. This description is surely right of some players. There was, for instance, a very blustery fellow whom I used to play basketball with on the streets of Los Angeles, who spent a lot of time talking to me about his vast superiority whenever he was winning, but at those rare moments when I would win, he'd laugh it off as "just a game, man."

But this story doesn't seem true of all game players. There are plenty of players who both play with great seriousness and intensity, but don't seem to be terribly put off by losing—not so much that they would require an act of self-deception to protect their ego. Take, for example, my Go mentor Joe—a delightfully odd gentleman who made his living as a chess tutor to wealthy children, but would show up every Wednesday and Thursday night at the Unurban Cafe to anchor the Los Angeles Go Club and give free Go lessons to anybody who wanted them. Joe was a model of game play behavior. He played to the limit, fighting tooth and nail, but seemed to be equally pleased to win or lose, as long as the game was interesting. In fact, at several key moments, when I started being able to give him a decently interesting match (at a significant handicap, of course), I'd make a dumb mistake, and he'd sadly point out that he'd won, sigh at the lost possibility of a lovely game, and then insist that we reset to that moment and play out the game as it might have happened if I hadn't made that dumb mistake, because, you know, it was just starting to get interesting.

If Juul is right, then Joe must have been an exceptionally good liar, successfully pulling off a complex misrepresentation of his motivational state. But I suggest that we don't need to go as far as Juul does in ascribing self-delusion to every single game player. Instead, all we need are the mechanisms I've already offered: submersion and layering. In order to enjoy the *experience* of struggling against obstacles, I set up a temporary agency in which I submerge myself. This temporary agent cares about winning and losing and will feel the pain of failure. But does that temporary agency's failure count as a global failure for me, as saying something about my interest and capacities? It does not. I took up a temporary agency that has an interest in winning for the sake of the experiences associated with struggling under such an interest. But that temporary agency is not me. It is merely a construct that I submerge myself within. In Juul's account, I really want to win, but I have a covering excuse in case I fail. My account offers an alternate solution to the paradox of failure—one in which I never truly valued winning in any sort of genuine and

enduring way. In games, I adopt a temporary agency which cares about winning. Because that constructed agency cares about winning, I can experience
the various thrills of the game: the absorption, the intensity, the drama, and
the like. But it is only a temporary agency, one that I set up and inhabit for the
sake of a particular experience—and, ideally, one I can discard at the end of
the game.

A few caveats: first, I am not claiming that every player does this. For one
thing, not all players are striving players. Only insofar as one is engaging in
striving play does one have disposable ends. Second, even if one wishes to
be a striving player, one is not guaranteed to actually succeed in disposing of
one's ends. A sore loser, for instance, can be understood as anybody who fails
to dispose of their gaming ends when it would be appropriate to do so.

To sum up: the enduring agency of an aesthetic striving player is interested in the experiences of striving. In order to have these experiences, the
aesthetic striving player adopts a temporary agency with its own disposable
end. The pure striving player cares about winning as part of a temporary
construct, introduced for the sake of an absorbed experience. Importantly,
the ends of the temporary agency are not the ends of the enduring agent.
The failures of my in-game agency do not reflect on my full agency. This also
means that, unlike with Juul's account, for the striving player, success in the
game also won't matter to them outside the game. For the striving player, the
value of the game is in terms of experience and not the achievement or the
failure. For an aesthetic striving player, winning doesn't matter if the experience was dull, uninteresting, or aesthetically insipid.

Suppose I am throwing a dinner party; the guests are all rather socially
awkward, and they all seem to be suffering in their sad attempts at conversation. I pull out a party game, in order to give everybody a good time.
Unfortunately, since I've played it so many times before, I turn out to be
vastly better at it, and I beat everybody else horribly, and nobody has any fun.
By Juul's lights, I should take this as a win and be proud. But really, I've failed
in my purpose, and the fact that I won the game should be something of an
embarrassment.

Conclusions

In the previous chapter, I argued that it was possible to take on the motivationally inverted state of striving play. Now, we have a fuller picture of what

that motivational state looks like for us, and the kinds of motivational inversion we're capable of. We have the capacity to submerge ourselves in a temporary agency. We conduct that submersion via a complex motivational structure, whereby we set up a temporary inner layer that will dominate our practical activity, and our awareness of that activity. But that inner layer is held within an enduring outer layer, that must be held at phenomenal arm's length, but which also must have the capacity to step in and cancel our absorption in the inner layer.

And we have remarkable fluidity with the content and character of that inner layer. We may not care enduringly about winning, but we can submerge ourselves in a temporary agent that does care. And our experience with games tells us that we can take in, via games, very different agencies. We can submerge ourselves in a wide variety of agencies, as detailed by different games. We can take on temporary agencies oriented toward beating others, or cooperating with them, or surviving as long as possible in a virtual environment. Our capacity to take on agencies, combined with the fact that games work in the medium of agency, makes it possible for us to communicate and transmit agencies. Our fluidity is how we can step outside our enduring selves, and not just see the world from a different perspective—as we might from reading a novel—but to act for ourselves, from a different agential perspective.

4

Games and Autonomy

At this point, games may begin to look a little creepy. They might start sounding a bit too agentially intrusive. To play a game is, on my account, to take on a new agency—an agency designed by somebody else. This might seem like a strange sort of subservience. When we play a game, we let it dictate the form of our agency for a while. We let others tell us what to focus on, what abilities to use—even what to care about. We may take up that new agency voluntarily, but it is still an alien agency designed by another. In game playing, we reshape our very selves at the behest of another. Perhaps the insight that games work in the medium of agency reveals the problem at their heart: that playing games will inevitably erode our autonomy.

This is a suspicion is common in both the popular discussion of games, and the academic scholarship. There is, according to this worry, something quite unsavory about the subservience to authority involved in playing structured games. It would be better to be free to be as creative as we like, and to pursue whatever goals we like. Thus, goes the suspicion, we should want games that do not tell us what goals we should have or what rules we must obey. We should prefer toys to structured, rule-driven, goal-oriented games. We should prefer Legos to Chess. We should favor creative sandbox games, such as *Minecraft*, which provide virtual environments for exploration and free play, but leave it up to players to decide their own goals for themselves.

This worry has been given a clear formulation by Miguel Sicart. Structured games, says Sicart, are a poor cousin to true play. Play, says Sicart, is essentially free and appropriative; it takes practical objects out of their usual context and transforms their use. Play is essentially disruptive; it disrupts the normal state of affairs. "Play appropriates events, structures, and institutions to mock them and trivialize them" (Sicart 2014, 3). And games are created for play—or, as Sicart puts it, "Games are just a formal manifestation of play" (85). But play is, by its nature, essentially unstructured; it is carnivalesque and appropriative. Structured games resist this sort of reappropriation and so block true play. Taking structured games seriously—submitting oneself

Games. C. Thi Nguyen, Oxford University Press (2020). © Oxford University Press.
DOI: 10.1093/oso/9780190052089.001.0001

entirely to the structures and rules of a game, and earnestly trying to win—actually runs counter to the chaotic and anti-authoritarian nature of play.

Game designers are sometimes lauded for harnessing, controlling, and steering play for their intended purposes. But this runs counter to play's essential spirit as appropriative, creative, and anarchic, says Sicart. The idea that the game designer is something like an artist implies authorship, granting the game designer a special authority over how players ought to encounter the game. Instead, says Sicart, makers of games should provide nothing more than context, a focus for inspiring play (Sicart 2014, 86–91).

> Designing for play means creating a setting rather than a system, a stage rather than a world, a model rather than a puzzle. Whatever is created has to be open, flexible, and malleable to allow players to appropriate, express, act and interact, make and become part of the form itself. (90)

Thus, structured games fail at their purpose, says Sicart. Games aim at fostering play, but structured games undermine that play through their very structure.

Interestingly, we can find almost exactly the same worries in some recent conversations in the avant-garde art world. Consider, for example, the movements of social art and relational aesthetics, which focus on creating participatory, social artworks. Often in these works, the audience's own actions and interactions are considered an integral part of the artwork. Such an artwork might involve, say, creating a fully functioning restaurant in a museum as an artwork. One might think that any such movement would naturally be interested in employing the techniques of games. Nicolas Bourraiud's landmark manifesto on relational aesthetics opens, in fact, with these words: "Artistic activity is a game, whose forms, patterns, and function evolve according to periods and social contexts." (Bourriaud 2002, 11).

But the artistic avant-garde has largely avoided using rules, goals, and any other game-like structures, in their works. An allergy to prescriptive practices seem to run throughout the world of social art. Art historian Miwon Kwon, for example, criticizes the early social artwork *Culture in Action* by saying that the artists presented "prescriptive and overdetermined situations" by mandating particular kinds of social relationships, rather than letting participants be free to establish social relationships as they wished" (Kwon 1997, 140, quoted in Finkelpearl 2012). The presumption lying under this criticism must be that rules have no place in social art, because they undermine freedom. And underneath that presumption must be another: that in order to support the autonomy of the audience, we ought to let them be as free as possible when they experience the artwork. Sicart's and Kwon's criticisms both seem to depend on a particular view about the nature of freedom: that the freer and less restricted the audience when they experience the work, the better for their freedom and autonomy in general. If this position is true, then so much the worse for Suitsian games.

I argue, instead, for the opposite conclusion: that the restrictions and specifications of the agential medium offer a special path to enriching our long-term freedom and autonomy. The prescriptions of games are necessary for games to *communicate* modes of agency. Adopting an alternate mode of agency, at a game's behest, is a way of learning about new ways of being an agent. By surrendering, in the short-term, full creative control over the details of the agency which one will inhabit, one can learn about new forms of agency from the inside. This can support the long-term growth of autonomy. Playing games isn't an intrusion of autonomy from the outside, any more than reading is an intrusion of thoughts from the outside. Playing games is a voluntary form of participation in a sculpted agency. It is a way for us to receive and experience modes of agency that have been prepared by another.

Games can thus provide us with something very special: they can expose us to alternate agencies. And a wider range of agential experiences, I argue, can support and enhance our autonomy in a number of ways. In the sphere of speech and politics, we think that exposure to a wide variety of ideas can enhance our autonomy. Similarly, I argue, exposure to a wide variety of games can enhance our autonomy. Games constitute a library of agencies, in which we may discover and familiarize ourselves with new modes of agency. Free play won't help build that library; what will build that library is the communicative process of making and playing structured games, which specify particular modes of agencies through their prescriptions, rules, and goals.

This chapter focuses on the instrumental uses of game playing—on how they help us develop. I do not intend this to displace the account of games' aesthetic value. It seems entirely plausible that games have both sorts of value. I think my most beloved novels offer intrinsically valuable aesthetic experiences, but also can increase my emotional and moral sensitivity. Games offer us access to a plurality of values. I do think, however, that both the special aesthetic and special developmental value of games arise from the same place—that fact that games work in the medium of agency.

Freedom and Restriction

The rejection of structured games seems to arise from a common, but overly simplistic view of autonomy: that the fewer the rules and restrictions, the greater the autonomy. Call this the *rules-free* view of autonomy. This is an entirely negative view of autonomy, in which we support the autonomy of others by leaving them alone.

This simple view of autonomy, however, has been significantly questioned by philosophers and political theorists.[1] For one, voluntarily taking on rules and restrictions can be part and parcel of our autonomy. This is, after all, what a consensual government is supposed to be. What's more, we can place restrictions on ourselves as a technique of self-control. Such self-restriction is utterly familiar. As Jon Elster argues, any reasonable theory of autonomy must make room for the fact that agents sometimes need to constrain themselves and bind their will. If, for example, I wish to quit smoking cigarettes, I might pay the liquor store owner near my house to refuse to sell me any. Such restrictions aren't a blockade to my autonomy—they are, in fact, expressions of my autonomy. They are my long-term will imposing its choices on my recalcitrant short-term will (Elster 1977).

But there's even more to say. Presume, for the moment, the simple view that we can support an agent's freedom by offering them more options. Restrictions can, then, increase your freedom when they help give you a greater range of options. Here's a simple example. Imagine that I am standing alone in an empty field. My range of movement is relatively unrestricted. Imagine that we add some walls, a door, and a roof. Now there's a house in the middle of the field. In a very simple sense, my movement has been restricted. There are walls now; certain paths of movement are now impeded. But those simple restrictions themselves also help constitute a set of richer, more substantively different options. Now I can be inside or outside, sheltered or exposed. Restrictions can constitute new options, and these new options can be more richly meaningful than whatever options were lost.

Games, surely, can also aid autonomy by adding more and richer options to my menu of possible actions. This was Suits's insight: that games are activities constituted, in part, by constraints. On a smaller scale, restrictions can actually help constitute entirely new actions. The action of "making a basket" in basketball is partially constituted by the dribbling restriction and

---

[1] For a summary of one set of such naive views and my response, see Nguyen (2010).

the requirement for opponents. "Making a basket" is an action that cannot exist outside the rules of basketball. On a larger scale, those restrictions constitute the very activities of game playing. If one refuses to take up new rules for reasons of autonomy, one will end up simply reducing the option space of available actions. One will not be able to play basketball, Chess, *Team Fortress*, Bag on Your Head, *Twister*, or any other Suitsian game. Restrictions, then, can increase one's autonomy by constituting new options.

But these observations are only a prelude. All we've said so far, really, is that game restrictions can increase autonomy by offering more games to play. This might seem a rather trivial insight. It simply restates Suits's observation that constraints help to constitute the very activity of playing the game. I would like to argue for something much more significant: that the structure of games can enhance one's overall autonomy in a systematic and far-reaching way. Games can play a role in the development of the entire shape of our autonomy.

New Alternatives for Agency

Here, in brief, is the argument. In game playing, we take on temporary agencies. These agencies have been shaped by others, and are passed to us via the game. In other words, games are a medium for storing and communicating forms of agency. A collection of games can, then, constitute a library of agencies. Games can store, offer access to, and offer immersive experiences of different agencies, as well as different social arrangements of agencies. So you can expose yourselves to many different modes of agency, by exploring the library of agencies. One game might be focused on high-speed reflexes, another on calculative look ahead, or on diplomacy and bargaining, or on manipulating alliances and shared incentives. Wide exposure to games can enhance the autonomy of agents by making them aware of alternative modes of agency. By communicating agencies, we can enlarge and enrich each other's autonomy. We can help to broaden each other's knowledge of agencies, help to develop our capacities to switch between modes of agency, and our ability to find the right mode of agency. Games, as a medium for communicating agencies, can help us to develop our autonomy as a collaborative project. We can think of new forms of agency, write them down in games, and share them with one another. We can refine modes of agency and store them for future generations. Filling in the details of that argument will take up the remainder of this chapter.

First, what do I mean by a "mode of agency"? An agential mode is a focused way of being an agent. To enter an agential mode is to focus on a particular set of goals and on a particular set of abilities as the method for achieving those goals. Approaching a house with the goal of making it more energy-efficient, by focusing on my abilities as a carpenter and a mechanic—that's one agential mode. Approaching a house with the goal of making it more energy-efficient, by focusing on my economic abilities to purchase the services of others—that's another agential mode. Approaching a house with the goal of making it beautiful, by focusing on my abilities and sensitivities as a painter—that's another.

Cognitively limited beings like us usually approach the world one agential mode at a time. When I want to make my home better, I do so by taking on a sequence of agential modes, which take me independently through the various qualities of the house I might wish to consider—its structural integrity, its daily usability, its beauty—and engaging with each of these qualities while focused on different sets of abilities. And I constantly switch agential modes as I deal with the wildly varying practical demands of my life. When I am at a committee meeting wrangling for resources for my department, I focus on my goals of supporting my department, and on doing so with my political abilities. When I am working with my students, I focus on the goals of education, and on using my communicative abilities. And we often use different agential modes in sequence, as part of the same project. When I work on a piece of writing, I switch between a research mode, a creative mode, a rigorous mode, a communicative mode, and then finally a nit-picky proofreading mode. Often, doing the right thing involves finding an appropriate agential mode. When talking with a student during office hours, I might realize that our conversation isn't just about the details of a paper, but that they are actually profoundly distressed and emotionally overwhelmed. I need to switch from philosophy-teacher mode—focused on teaching rigorous arguments and writing clarity using the tools of argument analysis—to a more therapeutic mode, where I aim at finding and easing their emotional distress using various empathetic abilities.[2]

Obviously, agential modes look a lot like the temporary agencies of games. Games are the formalization of agential modes. They are crystallized and framed agential modes. Each game fixes an agential mode in significant

---

[2] Compare my discussion of agential modes with Elijah Millgram's discussion of segmented agency. In Millgram, all of us are capable of taking of taking on a different agential niche—taking on new values and focusing on a different set of abilities—as we transition between, say, jobs. However, Millgram's niches are long-lasting and slow to change, and he seems to think we can only occupy one (Millgram 2015, 234–268). The agential modes I've described are far more fluid and fleeting.

detail, by specifying precise goals and specifying exactly which abilities to achieve those goals. In ordinary practical life, things are a little more free-form. I often must select the appropriate agential mode for myself. Notice that if one is skeptical of the existence of agential modes, every argument I've given for the possibility of striving play—for our capacity to take on temporary agencies as specified by games—also shows that we can take on agential modes. Game playing, because it is so formalized, makes it easier to see that we have this capacity to fluidly shift within our agency. Once we see it happen so sharply in games, it is easier to see the softer forms of agency shifting that we perform elsewhere in our lives.

So, game playing makes new agential modes accessible to the player. In game playing, one takes on an alternate agency. This can offer exposure to a novel mode of agency. And games don't just simply describe the outlines of such an agency; they plunge the player into it, exposing the player to that form of agency from the inside.

The idea that an artwork might offer such developmental utility should be familiar. Martha Nussbaum has argued for the moral importance of narrative in terms of such experiential immersion. Narrative is essentially moral, says Nussbaum, though not in the sense of offering some annoyingly pithy "moral to the story." Narrative can embody cognitively rich emotional experiences of the world. Crucially, Nussbaum thinks emotions can be cognitive. Anger can be a way of comprehending an injustice; sadness a way of comprehending the value of something lost. But our emotions can be well or poorly tuned. Badly tuned anger lashes out at inappropriate targets, but well-tuned anger can motivate us to act against real injustice. And a rich range of experiences can better tune our emotions. But we are, of course, quite limited in the range of direct experiences we can have. We are finite beings, with limited lives. This is where narratives come in. Narratives—both fictional and nonfictional—can offer emotionally rich experiences from far beyond the borders of our own narrow lives. I myself could never know directly what it's like to work as a woman in corporate America in the 1950s, but I can get a glimmer of that experience through a narrative—and get some of the emotional attunement, too. And narratives don't offer that knowledge in the dry abstract. Narratives experientially immerse me in an alternate life. They bring me to actually feel those emotions, which makes them more available to me in the rest of my life (Nussbaum 1992, 3–53, 125–147, 261–285).

I am suggesting that games can offer an analogous form of experiential immersion. Games can give us access to rich experiences of different modes of agency, and of different arrangements of agency within varying social structures. Games can experientially immerse a player in an alternative agency, making that mode of agency more available to the player elsewhere in life. Games can help to build a broader menu of possible ways of being an agent.

Consider *Spyfall*, a charming recent design from the world of party games. In *Spyfall*, the players are each dealt a single card from a special deck of cards. Say there are eight of you. Seven of you will receive location cards, putting you on a team together, and the other player will receive the "SPY" card, making them the dastardly spy. The seven cards will designate the same location. Perhaps the team players will discover that they are all in the Opera House together. The spy player, however, has no idea what the designated location is. The team's goal is to work together to figure out who the spy is. The spy's goal is to ferret out the team's location while avoiding discovery. But, of course, no team player quite knows who else to trust yet.

What follows is a delicate and hysterical dance of verbal probing, bullshitting, and obfuscation.[3] The team players must ask and answer one another's questions, quietly signaling to the others on the team that they know the proper location, while trying to trip up the spy into answering incorrectly. But the team players can't be too explicit in their questions and answers, or the spy will catch on. If one is at the Opera House, one should certainly not ask, "How are you enjoying this aria?" Good team players must subtly inform their teammates that they themselves are in the know, but must do so in a sufficiently obscure way so as to leave the spy in the dark. This, of course, opens the door for the spy to bullshit their way through, by aping such attempts at strategic obscurity, probing for hints all the while.

The game is, as it turns out, exceedingly funny. But between the gaffes and hysterical laughing fits, the game offers a very delicate and focused epistemic dance, using a very particular set of skills. The team players focus on a very specific kind of informational transfer. They need to hint at their insider knowledge, without giving it away. The spy needs to crack that code while bullshitting their way through conversation with knowledgeable-sounding,

---

[3] I mean "bullshit" here in the technical sense—the attempt to persuade without regard for the truth (Frankfurt 2009).

but informationally noncommittal content. And the team, of course, must become hyperattentive for exactly that kind of bullshit. The experience of *Spyfall* is remarkable for the spareness of its mechanisms and the single-mindedness of its practical focus. Such narrowness, in the normal world, would be problematic—a mark of psychological obsessiveness and insensitivity to the many varied demands of human life. But games permit us to become absorbed in a single facet of practical life.

I have, elsewhere in my aesthetic life, a deep affection for the paintings of Mark Rothko. Sometimes, I think they are paintings of inner moods. Sometimes, I think they are, as a fellow museum-goer once suggested to me, just one long succession of sea and sky horizons—a spiritual extension of J. M. W. Turner's obsession with the textures of horizons. But sometimes, I think they are simple explorations of color itself; they use the mechanisms and institutional practices of painting to focus the viewer's attention, for a moment, entirely on the experience of subtle variations in, and subtle contrasts between, particular colors. *Spyfall* is something like that, but in agency rather than color. It is a single-minded exploration of a very tiny and particular corner of human reasoning and skill. It has sometimes been thought that artworks put a frame around a little bit of the world, and direct the viewer to pay special attention to it. If *Spyfall* is a work, then it is perhaps best described as putting a frame around the practice of bullshit and bullshit detection. And the experience of *Spyfall* doesn't primarily originate in the design of, say, some virtual environment. It originates in a precise paring down of the practical agent—in the creation of an activity in which all the practical agents are united single-mindedly in a focused practice of informational extraction.

Games can encode an incredible variety of practical modes. Broad exposure to a variety of games, and the modes inscribed in them, can help me to expand my inventory of agential modes. I can become more familiar with the mode of agency encoded in Chess, obsessed with looking ahead to possible opponent responses; or the mode in *Spyfall*, looking for hints of obfuscation and double-speak; and so on, for every different mode of agency on offer from the wide world of games. Once I play *Spyfall* enough and internalize the agential mode which is utterly obsessed with listening for obfuscation and pretence, I can don that agential mode during university committee meetings, in order to be more sensitive to those sorts of deceptions.

When we play games, we are exploring the library of agencies. That exploration can expose us to more options about how we might inhabit our own agency. That wider range of options helps us be more autonomous; it makes us freer about how we might go about being rational.[4]

All this is possible because games permit us to record agencies and pass them around. Since we can communicate forms of agency, we can help each other in the project of developing our agency and autonomy. We can help each other to experience modes of agency, alone, we might never have found on our own. The point of communication, after all, is to gain access to states of mind that an individual might not have thought of independently.

Autonomy, Self-Governance, and Games

I've claimed that when we are more familiar with different agential modes, we will have a wider range of options for how we will conduct ourselves in practical situations. Games can help build our inventory of *ways of being practical*. And such an inventory, when well and appropriately managed, can support our freedom and autonomy.

These claims might sound a little fanciful. How could a game actually and concretely help develop our autonomy? To say any more, we'll have to take up the details of some specific theories of autonomy and freedom. Unfortunately, that terrain is tangled and full of controversies, and it is certainly not my intention to plump for a particular theory of autonomy or freedom here. I will, instead, make some general claims about what games do for us, and suggest how those claims might fit in with some specific accounts of autonomy and freedom. I've selected a handful of representative accounts, to help see how the case might go. Hopefully, readers can catch the tune, and apply it to their own favored account.

Let me first offer a simple, bare-bones argument. Suppose you thought that freedom involved having more options.[5] How would agential modes give you more options? In the simplest terms, having a wider variety of agential modes ready and at hand gives you options about which agential modes to occupy. If I am only familiar with the mode of empathy, then I can't switch modes. If

---

[4] See also Elijah Millgram's discussion of Mill on how exposure to alternatives keeps thoughts alive rather than letting them ossify as dead dogma (Millgram 2004, 167–173; Mill [1859] 1999).

[5] For a defense of such a simple view, see Waller (1993).

I am familiar both with an empathetic helpful mode and a Machiavellian manipulative mode, I now have the possibility of switching between them. That, by itself, gives me more internal degrees of freedom. But a wider inventory also gives me more freedom in my decisions. This is because it gives me more options to plan about how I will cope with the world.

In a recent discussion, Chandra Sripada suggests that an agent's freedom is dependent on the size of their option set. Importantly, Sripada notes, those options are constructed. People, says Sripada, have more freedom than animals, precisely because they have a wider range of constructible options. We can construct complex plans, and this widens our options set. Intellectual beings don't only get to choose between going right or left; they get to choose between going right to get a sandwich, or going right to have a pleasant view, or going left to get some fried chicken, or going left to take a shortcut (Sripada 2016a). When we have more agential modes, we have more options for planning. Suppose I am being sent to a key university meeting, where I will have to wrangle for department funding. If I have a wide variety of agential modes, I have more options: I can plan to try to wrangle for funding using my diplomatic mode, my aggressive mode, or my bargaining mode.

But perhaps these notions of freedom seem to thin to you. Perhaps we need to have more than just a wide range of options. Perhaps we want the capacity to self-govern, and to do so well. For these concerns, we should look to theories of autonomy. But much, again, depends on the details of the theory. According to some theories, to be autonomous, we need to able to properly translate our genuine self's desires into actions. Call these *coherentist* theories. The idea here is that there is some division between our genuine self's desire—like to advance knowledge—and interfering local desires—like to start drinking whiskey at noon. We are autonomous when our genuine self rules (Frankfurt 1971; Watson 1975; Bratman 1979; Buss 2012; Sripada 2016b). Alternately, we might conceive of autonomy as *responsiveness to reasons*. Autonomous agents are the ones who adjust desires, motivations, and actions in response to the real reasons that bear on them (Wolf 1993; Fischer and Ravizza 1998).[6] Games can help us become more autonomous under either sort of account.

An example may help. Let's focus, for the moment, on the coherentist notion of autonomy: that autonomy is getting coherence between the genuine self's desires and one's action. I had long nurtured a deep desire to seek the

---

[6] I owe this classification scheme and taxonomy to Buss (2013).

truth via analytic philosophy. But in my earlier years, I was temperamentally ill-suited to analytic philosophy. My attention wandered; I wasn't very interested in looking for potential objections. I wasn't motivated to take the requisite painstaking care in developing my arguments. Thus, my actions did not cohere with my genuine self's interests. I was weak of will.

Then, I started playing a lot of Chess. Chess offered not only entertainment, but an agential mode. Chess gave me access to a way of focusing my practical rationality by making me, for short periods of time, extraordinarily interested in winning through careful calculation and predicting precise countersequences. Playing Chess made the short-term interests that were conducive to analytic philosophy more psychologically available to me. I could then deploy them at the appropriate time, like during graduate seminars. Why does this work? What matters here is that interest come in stages. I have, in general, an interest in finding the philosophical truth. But in order to do that, it helps to have the appropriate agential mode. This can involve any number of mental postures: a certain type of focus, a style of reasoning, some degree of rigid self-control or relaxed fluidity. Perhaps most importantly, taking on an agential mode can transform a merely instrumental interest into a direct interest, for a time.

To be a philosopher, it helps enormously to have a direct interest in getting all your fussy little distinctions right. Certainly, my interest in getting at the philosophical truth generates instrumental reasons for me to get all my distinctions right. But I will be even better at getting at the truth if I also have a direct interest in finding those distinctions—if I take immediate pleasure in finding a good distinction; if I love distinctions for their own sake. I've been given similar advice by my music teacher and by an athletic coach: the best athletes and the best musicians are the people who love to practice for its own sake. Unfortunately, as a young aspiring musician, I didn't have any love for practice at all. I wanted to play great music, but I had little interest in practicing my scales and drilling technique. I went through those dreary exercises only as a means to an end. That kind of purely instrumental justification generates a relatively faint form of motivation. It would have been far better for my development as a musician if, knowing that my purpose was to play great music, I could have temporarily adopted a direct interest in performing repetitive technique drills. I couldn't, so, unsurprisingly, I washed out.

But, interestingly, Chess helped me learn to adopt the sort of detail-oriented, every-possibility-checked love of fastidiousness needed for philosophy. It helped me to adopt the appropriate attentive state and to acquire a direct interest in, and take immediate satisfaction in, working out the fine details. And these two are deeply related. It's much easier to fully enter into and sustain the appropriate state of attention to detail if I have a direct interest in getting those details right. In fact, if my interest in getting all the details right can sometimes supplant my interest in the broader truth, I might actually do better in the long run at actually getting at the broader truth. Schmidtz makes a similar point in his discussion of motivational psychology. A being with only a bare interest in survival, he says, would not actually be very good at surviving. Strictly instrumental means have a weaker grip on our motivational psychology. An agent who eats and has sex only as a means to the end of survival wouldn't actually survive that well. Agents who love eating and sex for their own sakes will actually have a better shot at surviving, because such agents will seek out food and sex with more gusto. Better to be an agent with a rich hierarchy of related ends, and to take a direct interest, not only in survival, but also in the various means for survival (Schmidtz 2001, 251–255).

Suppose I have a genuine interest in doing analytic philosophy right. In order to do that, it would be helpful to adopt a further set of temporary goals, interests, and a narrow focus on the relevant abilities—in getting my distinctions right, in looking ahead to counterresponses. If I can't adopt that agential mode, then I am suffering from a kind of weakness of will. I am failing to *temporarily inhabit an agential mode with an appropriate set of interests, attentions, and focuses* to fulfill my general interests. This also makes further weakness of will likely downstream. If I can't don the agential mode that would make doing analytic philosophy easier, then I'm more likely to fail to perform the actions that will be in line with my genuine self. If I can't take on the agential mode of being rigorous, then I will be far less likely to perform the appropriately careful and rigorous actions when they're appropriate.

Thus, being able to deploy the appropriate agential mode will help me to better translate my genuine self's desires into appropriate actions. The needs of the genuine self may conflict with my mood, personality, and natural tendencies. Agential modes are tools for managing my attention, focus, and interests, and controlling myself, in order to better bring my moment-to-moment practical reasoning and action into line with my genuine self's interests. They are tools for generating appropriate actions. Since the Chess-like agential mode is focused narrowly on a particular set of goals and abilities, other sorts of reasons simply won't come to mind. To put it another way: genuine-self theories say that we are autonomous when we can successfully exert willpower. We impose the interests of the long-term self against the short-term distraction, thus bringing our actions into line with our genuine desires. Agential modes are tools for exerting willpower by acquiring momentary focuses, which exclude whole ranges of reasons.[7] When we deploy them appropriately, agential modes are a form of willpower; they help us focus on the kinds of reasons we need to focus on, and ignore the rest.

What's more, having a variety of agential modes on hand is crucial, since which agential mode is appropriate will vary widely. The agential mode I put on when I am doing analytic philosophy is very particular. It is one that searches for errors, hammers on counterexamples, and cares deeply about clarity and precision. The appropriate agential mode for having a casual chat with my friends is very different—it is one that seeks out opportunities for emotional connections, for ways to support and encourage others. It cares more about intimacy than precision. I need, as it were, to put on a different agential face when I transition from doing philosophy to hanging out with friends. The capacities that render me a decent analytic philosopher would make me, in the social context, something of a jerk.

And it is not simply that I have a plurality of goals. Pursuing even a single goal can require me to put on a series of very different agential modes. I have an interest in finding and communicating philosophical truth. In pursuit of that interest, there are a number of very different tasks I need to perform. Sometimes I need to engage in philosophical research. Sometimes I need to teach introductory philosophy to nonmajor undergraduates. Sometimes I need to navigate the Machiavellian cesspool of university administration in order to keep my philosophy department from being defunded in favor of the business school. Each of these tasks requires a different agential mode. The fussy, slow, delicate, ornery mode of analytic philosophy research turns out to be too cold and ponderous for teaching general education classes. I need a more sympathetic and light-footed communicative agential mode for teaching. And I need a more paranoid, conspiratorial, manipulative agential mode to survive in administrative politics.

---

[7] My thinking here is deeply influenced by Richard Holton's account of willpower as the capacity to exclude certain classes of reasons from rising to mind (Holton 2009, 70–96). Holton's account is, in turn, grounded in Michael Bratman's account of planning as the capacity to, among other things, exclude certain forms of reasoning from arising (Bratman 1999).

But notice: the optimal mode for analytic philosophy is much like Chess; the teaching mode has some significant resemblance to *Sign*; and the political mode is a lot like *Spyfall, Imperial,* and *1830*. So playing a variety of games might give me something crucial. Games expose me to different agential modes. Playing a variety of games gives me a broader menu of agential modes to choose from. They can also familiarize me with how those modes work in a variety of practical contexts, so that I can better recognize when a particular situation might need a particular mode. Thus, games can make me more capable of regulating myself appropriately, by making me more capable of selecting the appropriate mode for the situation.

But now we have another worry. Don't agential modes narrow our awareness of reasons? Don't those thin, game-like attitudes make us miss out on too much of the world? To deepen that worry, let's turn to the responsiveness-to-reasons accounts of autonomy. By such accounts, we are autonomous when we can regulate our drives, motives, and actions in response to the real reasons that bear on what we are to think, feel, and do. Suppose that such an account is right. Wouldn't there, then, be a conflict between narrowed agential modes and the demands of autonomy? As Susan Wolf puts it, autonomy is responsiveness, not only to legitimate reasons, but to a sufficiently broad set of them. If I am a university administrator, and I am responsive only to economic reasons but ignore reasons of, say, social responsibility, then I am not autonomous. Doesn't the use of agential modes, especially game-like agential modes, undermine such broadness? Games promote attentional frames focused around very narrowed modes of agency. They focus me on a narrow set of reasons: looking ahead for opponents, or opportunities to screw people or opportunities to interlock our abilities. Thus the extragame agential modes inspired by game play would, accordingly, be similarly narrow. A narrowed mode of agency is appropriate in a game because, in games, there genuinely is a very narrow set of legitimate reasons. But perhaps exporting that narrowness to the outside world would threaten autonomy.

Indeed, being stuck in a single such mode would certainly be destructive to autonomy. I will explore this possibility at length in Chapter 9. But, I suggest, those narrowed frames can be useful they are properly managed, and if we can move between them. Narrowed frames can be useful, if we are not stuck in one, but if we are capable of deploying the right one from our broad inventory when the circumstances call for it. By appropriately employing a series of narrowed attentional frames, one can, in the long run, increase one's exposure to relevant reasons. Each frame digs narrowly, but deeply. So an appropriate succession of narrowed attentional frames can, in the long run, dig more.

In fact, for limited beings like us, such a controlled sequence of different focusings would be the only way to approach the fullness of relevant reasons. Perhaps a cognitively infinite being could always locate the relevant reasons out of the pressing multitudes, and so wouldn't need to use narrowed agential modes. But we cognitively finite beings have to manage within our limitations. Agential modes, through manipulations of attention and interest, focus us on a particular set of reasons. By temporarily shutting us off to the larger stream of reasons, they enable us to devote our limited cognitive capacities to a narrower range of considerations, and thus see more of the relevant reasons in that range. What we need here is not a single correct focused agential mode, but the capacity to cycle through a variety of them. Agential modes, then, are a tool for the cognitively limited beings to handle a fluctuating series of demands from a world too complex for us to grasp all at once. We cognitively limited beings need to become something like Swiss Army knives of agencies.

But it is not enough merely to have access to a wide inventory of agential modes. To be more autonomous, I have to be able to move between the various agential modes. I also need to be able to select the right one for the situation. I need, not only a large inventory of agential modes, but the *fluidity* that allows me to move between them, and the *accuracy* to select the appropriate agential mode. We not only need a broad inventory of agential modes; we need the capacity for appropriate inventory management. But, of course, the ability to take up and put down agential modes is a kind of agential fluidity quite similar in structure to striving play. In striving play, I submerge myself in temporary agencies. So it will perhaps be less surprising to think that the extragame capacity for agential fluidity is developed by practicing agential fluidity in games. The formal acquisition of designated goals, narrowly specified abilities, and disposable ends in games helps me to develop my extragame fluidity with interests and agential modes. Game playing is a way to practice agential fluidity. Game playing builds familiarity with different agential modes—to help us build our inventory and know which one to pick—and the fluidity to shift easily into our chosen mode.

To summarize: I've argued that we are more autonomous when we can choose the appropriate agential mode for the task at hand. We will be more likely to do so if we are experientially aware of a wider variety of agential modes—we'll have more agencies in our inventory. Since games can expose us to a wider degree of agential modes, they can make an appropriate choice more likely. And each agential mode will also be easier for us to inhabit once we are experientially familiar with it. And we will be more likely to be able to fluidly switch between agential modes and to select the right one if we have practiced such changing through a wide variety of agencies in games. Just as various forms of writing and speech communicate ideas for us to consider, games communicate modes of agency for us to try on. All these forms of communication enhance our autonomy in different, but mutually supportive, ways.

This may seem plausible in the abstract, but might it just be a wild flight of philosophical fancy? But think, again, about the enormous variety of games we've seen, and the extraordinary range of agencies that they contain. *Spyfall* offers me an agential experience of being interested in cooperation, but one where I am unsure of who to cooperate with. It offers me the experience of an agency oriented entirely toward disentangling obscured social relationships. The cooperative board game *Pandemic* offers me an agential experience of trying to arrange myself into better cooperation with others. In *Pandemic*, all the players share a single goal, but have different abilities, and much of the game experience is devoted to figuring out how to deploy one's own particular abilities to best aid the group as the game's challenges evolve. The game offers me the experience of subsuming my specialized practical abilities to a collective enterprise. *Monopoly* offers me the experience of submersion in an agency that is entirely self-oriented, where I am narcissistically bent toward the destruction of others for my own good. *Risk* offers me an experience of an agency that is self-oriented, but which must temporarily form alliances with others. *Imperial* offers me an agency oriented toward manipulating the incentives of others. Old point-and-click computer games, like *Space Quest*, offer me the agency of hunting for the right clues and objects, of searching for tiny missed details and looking for ways to repurpose objects and tools to solve new problems. *Sign* offers me the agency of trying to generate and refine a language under conditions of extreme communicative limitation. Each of these designed agencies is familiarizing us with an agential mode that is more appropriate to some tasks than others. Rock climbing, for example, transformed my sense of possibility for how I might maneuver through a space, how anything in the world might be turned into a point to lever myself around. And it's not just for my own actions; experiences of a wide variety of agencies might help me understand of how substantially different agents might go about their business. Anecdotal evidence: I have become much more capable of understanding and predicting sociopathic business behavior, and of understanding how vast profit-oriented corporations reason, after having spent much time playing the stock-trading and market manipulation game *1830*. Thus, familiarity with destructive agencies—like the narcissistic agency of *Monopoly*—can be useful to a good-hearted agent for understanding the bad actors that they'll have to contend with.

These may not seem like very deep emotional experiences. One might worry that games cannot offer us anything like the meaningfulness and emotional experiences of the great works of literature, painting, and music. But we should be open to the possibility that games might have something to offer us that's very different from other forms of art. The incredible variety of agential experiences I've just described is its own kind of richness. When I read Dostoevsky, Bronte, Kafka, Baldwin, and Basho, I come away with my emotions transfigured. These sorts of work can help me to acquire a richer set of emotional responses to draw from. When I spend time in a museum staring at a work by Van Gogh, O'Keefe, Hiroshige, and Goldin, I come away with a richer sense of ways to look at the world. And strategic games can transfigure my experience of parties, meetings, of navigating social relationships, and the sense of how I might work to bind people together or tear them apart.[8]

I am not arguing that games are the only path to alternate modes of agency. Different careers or hobbies could do it, too. To echo Nussbaum's view: narratives aren't the only way to get access to rich life experiences and so develop one's emotional capacities. One can refine one's emotional awarenesses simply by living life. But narratives offer compressed alternate chunks of other lives—experiences that we either cannot, or did not, happen to have. They can also offer us experiences that have been refined and shaped for particular effect. Games, I suggest, can function analogously, by offering shaped, precise, compressed, crystallized experiences of alternate agencies. And we can have these experiences more quickly and easily through games than through taking up a major life project—though the experiences of games are likely to be less rich.

One might worry that I am being unrealistically optimistic about the psychological effects of game playing. And certainly, my suggestions, however

---

[8] My comments here are specific to the sort of specific examples of novelists, artists, and games I mention locally; I am not intending to make categorical claims about different media, nor make any claims about their limited effect. Surely, some paintings also enrich my emotional experience of the social world; surely some games can transfigure my visual and emotional experiences.

plausible, need empirical investigation. But I do not mean to promise some fantastical level of effectiveness—say, that you can play Chess once and suddenly acquire the right agential mode. Nobody is suggesting, for example, that you can read one great work of literature and be morally transformed. The plausible claim is, rather, that a lifetime of consuming a wide variety of emotionally rich narratives can gradually support one's emotional development. Similarly, I am suggesting that engagement with a broad variety of striving games, over a long span of time, can help one's agential development.

I am also not claiming that playing games guarantee an enhancement of autonomy. Appropriate self-governance is a complicated and delicate affair; it would be absurd to think that there was some simple formula for developing our autonomy. I can't simply play games and be done with it. Game playing has to be directed in the right way; the right lessons have to be learned from it. The experiences have to be integrated in the right way. What I have shown, however, is that game playing can play a significant role in the project of growing and developing one's own autonomy. It is a resource for autonomy development, though not a guarantee— just as reading literature in the proper way can be a resource for developing our various virtues, wisdoms, and sensitivities, even though it doesn't guarantee successful development. You can misuse games, just as you can misuse Jane Austen.

Furthermore, if games are active in our autonomy, we should suspect that could not only help, but also hinder the development of our autonomy. Let's take one extreme case: imagine that I play only a single game, and that the agential mode of that game is not usefully exportable to anything else in the world. Furthermore, imagine that I play this game so frequently that it keeps me from a great number of other rich experiences of agency. Suppose, for example, that playing this game has kept me from having a wide variety of ordinary life experiences, such as different jobs, different social situations, and the like. This sort of relationship to games could plausibly corrode the player's autonomy. Game playing, as a life practice, tends to develop our autonomy when it augments our exposure to different agential modes. Game playing can be corrosive to autonomy when it reduces our exposure to a wide variety of agential modes.

But this extreme case is not actually that fantastic. It is, I suspect, exactly what happens when an addictive game starts to take over one's life. I want to tread carefully here, because what it means to for a game to be addictive is a difficult matter. And I do not have clear views about whether there can be game addiction in the formal, psychiatric sense. But in the common and colloquial sense, an addictive game is one that seemingly compels repeated play, often displacing other life activities. Many addictive games offer extremely simple agencies and repetitive exercises of these agencies. Natasha Dow Schull has documented the design techniques used by the machine gambling industry for video slot machines, and the like. In many of those cases, designers encourage repeated play, not by making play interesting, but by building what Schull calls a "ludic loop" into the structure of the game. A continuous stream of gentle challenges and in-game rewards, offered at the right pacing and tempo, seems to produce something an addictive response. Schull documents many long-time machine gamblers talking about the cherished mental state to which they are addicted—what she calls "the machine zone," in which awareness of the world, time, and the self falls away into nothing (Schüll 2012). Such an agency seems clearly less rich than the agential experiences of even a fairly humdrum sort of practical activity. Insofar as wide exposure to rich agencies supports autonomy, an addictive game would, by displacing those richer exposures, corrode autonomy. And crucially, Schull thinks that the techniques of machine gambling design are no longer confined to the casino; they are currently used to make addictive computer games, like *Candy Crush* (National Public Radio 2014). Obviously, an addiction is, by itself, a direct reduction in autonomy. But my suggestion here is that game addiction in particular might lead to a further reduction in autonomy, by blocking my access to other rich experiences, and thus decreasing the availability of alternate agential modes.

If I'm right, then lack of exposure to a sufficiently broad variety of games, or constant exposure to a very limited range of games, might interfere with the development of our agency and autonomy. We might also think that certain games would encourage modes of agency that, if adopted outside of the game, would be bad, non-useful, or crippling. And if games do have the power to help and hurt our autonomy, we might also expect games to be employed badly by malicious actors as a means of impeding our autonomy. Again, the analogy with literature is useful here. If literature has the power to shape and develop our moral capacities, we should expect bad actors— malicious states and malevolent institutions, especially—to use those powers for evil, by control the spread of literature, and create and distribute literature for their own ends. Obviously, fascistic and oppressive states do use literature as an instrument of state control. We should, then, also expect oppressive regimes and the like to use games to further their oppressive ends. (I will explore some related possibilities in Chapter 9.)

Autonomy and Rigidity

My claim may have a certain ring of perversity to it. First, I've argued that one may enhance one's autonomy in the long term by taking on alien agencies, as specified in a game. The very sociality of this process might strike some as strange. Some of that strangeness may arise from some the view that we all must develop our autonomy on our own. Such individualism has held sway over theories of autonomy in the past, but I think that it isn't actually tenable.[9] Any genuinely plausible view of autonomy and freedom must make room for the fact that we learn from others and that we learn from others using a wide variety of techniques (Nguyen 2010). And learning from others involves temporarily submitting ourselves to them, in a controlled and consensual way. When I take an art class, I put my attention in another's hands for a while. I look where they tell me to look, attend to the features they tell me to (Nguyen 2017d, 2019c). We learn and develop by adopting different states of mind that others help us to find our ways into.

But even we accept all that, we run into another seeming paradox. I've claimed that games can help us achieve fluidity through temporary rigidity, and achieve autonomy through temporary submission to an outside design. How could this possibly be? The answer is that rigidity in the short term is sometimes crucial for flexibility in the long term. This is because, among other things, new states of mind and new emotional postures are subtle, delicate things, and not easy to access. It's easy to learn a simple fact about the world. It's much harder to learn to see the world with a mixture of pity, affection, and laughter—though one might begin to get a feel for it by reading Dostoevsky's *Brothers Karamazov* and *The Idiot* and sinking into his descriptions of Alyosha and Prince Myshkin's strange, affectionate, and sad inner responses to the world. Consider, too, meditation practice. Learning to move into a sense of open, relaxed mindfulness often involves following a careful set of structured exercises that have accumulated through the centuries of meditative practice. When I learned to meditate using Christmas Humphrey's excellent manual, I followed a rigid set of exercises—staring at

---

[9] In general, the sweep of much recent philosophy has been to question this fantasy of radical individuality and autonomy. On the epistemic front, philosophers have pushed away from radical Cartesian intellectual autonomism, toward a view of a network of epistemic interdependencies (Burge 1993, 2007; Hardwig 1985, 1991; Millgram 2015; Jones 1999). My own views on the matter can be found in Nguyen (2010, 2011, 2017, 2018b, 2018a, 2018c). On the practical and political scale, consider also recent work in the nature of joint commitment, group agency, and collective intelligence (Gilbert 2013; List and Pettit 2011; Bird 2014; Bratman 2014).

candles, counting my breath. I followed the directions, despite not under-standing exactly what they were for at first, and they brought me to a new mental state I had not ever experienced before (Humphreys 1999). A similar notion of strictness often shows up in traditional Zen manuals. My favorite exercise, from one early manual for monastic living is the "Hello" exer-cise: Zen monks, upon encountering anybody else, must immediately and unhesitatingly shout a hearty greeting.

The point is to move past deliberation and reflection toward an auto-matic embrace of the world. However, the actual mental state of meditation is so delicate that it cannot be taught directly, but only indicated through some oddly strict-sounding procedures. One cannot acquire the Zen spirit by reading a theoretical description of it, or through an argument, or by reading a Zen manual. One must follow that direction, and actually prac-tice the prescribed actions. (Incidentally, I adopted the "Hello" practice for a good few months in a few limited contexts—my academic department and on hikes—and I can attest that, for me at least, even the limited deployment of that rule transformed my experience of the social world). Those involved in athletic practice often find that strictness about motion in the short term creates greater freedom of movement in the long-term. In rock climbing training, you can often find that a particular technique isn't part of one's nat-ural technical repertoire. The right response is to *drill*—to force yourself to repeat a single technique over and over again, until it becomes an instinctive part of your repertoire of movement. When I started climbing, I did what most novice rock climbers do: I relied too much on cranking with my upper body and didn't use any hip rotation. The movement pattern of hip rotation is very counterintuitive, but it works astonishingly well, especially in steep, overhanging terrain. But even if you know about how hip rotation works in theory, it is hard to find that pattern of movement within yourself in the frantic intensity of the moment. The following exercise is an excellent cura-tive: do a lot of easy climbs, but without ever bending your elbows. The ex-ercise forces you to discover a thousand different subtle ways to inflect your hips and rotate your trunk to maneuver through space. And, after enough practice, you internalize the movement patterns, they become part of your natural and intuitive vocabulary of movement. The temporary restrictions create short sessions of intense practical focus, which result in a long-term increase in your freedom of movement.

Consider the practice of yoga. Yoga builds fluidity and freedom of move-ment, and gives access to particular delicate states of mind. But to get there, you must follow extremely detailed directions about how to move your body: where to turn, where to look, how to direct your attention. That strictness is a way for us to learn to do what we find unnatural. Strictness is a technique for surmounting one's natural impulses and learned routines. Most people tend to move in habitual patterns and hold habitual postures. Strict, precise, demanding instruction help to break you out of the trap of your own nature.

Let's translate all this back into the language of autonomy. Those who resist games often do so from the naive view that the fewer restrictions we have, the greater our autonomy. The naive view presumes that people have a natural tendency toward autonomy. But that presumption seems inapt with respect to our psychological reality. Left to our own devices, we are often creatures of habit. To get out of our habits, we often need artificial strictures, to help us find our way into different patterns of doing and thinking. Others can provide us with such artificial strictures; they can help us to get out of our own patterns of thought and action.

Here, too much freedom, in the strictly negative sense, may simply lead to a repetition of one's own ruts and habits. We need a richer conception of freedom, in which an agent can impose restrictions on themselves in the short-term as part of the long-term project of developing more freedom and autonomy. In this light, the absolute, unyielding resistance to ever submitting oneself to another's rules turns out to be, not some proud victory for autonomy, but a symptom of profound distrust. Sometimes, we don't yet know what mental states and practical patterns we need, and the only way to get a hold on them is to trust other people to mold a little bit of ourselves—for a little while.

We can now start to see why, in some cases, it might be easier to acquire a mode of agency from a game than from real life. Recall, it was playing Chess that helped me find my way into the appropriate mode of agency for doing analytic philosophy. You might have thought that I would have soaked up the right agential mode just by being in graduate school. But games offer easier entry points into novel modes of agency precisely because they are thinner, narrower, and more precisely specified. It is easier to find your way into novel way of being when somebody tells you exactly what to do. This is true with yoga and other kinds of physical training. If there is a mode of movement or a postural stance that is unfamiliar to me, the easiest way for me to find my way there is to submit myself to very precise directions that tell me exactly where to place my feet, exactly how to turn my hips.

Similarly, I suggest that a new agential mode is easier to find under very specific direction. And what will directions toward new agential mode look like? They will tell us what to focus on, what to pay attention to, what kinds of abilities to concentrate on. And games do exactly that. In yoga practice, you take up exact physical postures at another's direction. Strict instruction from the outside can help you to discover new possibilities of posture and movement. The exact nature of those postures might also help you find your way to some particular and delicate mental states. In games, one accepts direction from the outside about *the kind of agent to be.*

Games are agency yoga. Each game specifies, through a precise set of directions, an agential posture. And these postures might be quite are unfamiliar. Before I played *Spyfall*, I rarely attended so closely to the social cues that accompanied obfuscation. Before I played *Sign*, I had never focused completely on the attempt to stabilize the meaning of a new basic term. Before I played *Imperial* and *1830*, I had never focused so intently on how to manipulate others' actions by manipulating their incentives. Each of these is a new agential outlook, which can be transmitted through the medium of agency.

Another personal anecdote: learning and studying Go over the course of a decade has transformed parts of my practical agency. For those unfamiliar with the game, Go is to much of East Asia as Chess is to Western Europe. It is the dominant deep abstract strategy game. Go was invented in China approximately a millennium and a half ago; it is still played, studied, and theorized with great vigor to this day. Go has a much wider scope of action than Chess. My first Go teacher told me: Chess is like one fight; Go is like ten fights all going on at once. As a result, the Go player is constantly evaluating the relative value of each fight they're involved in. The good player knows when to abandon a particular fight to make a higher-value move elsewhere. The bad Go player becomes obsessed with a single fight and can't let it go. To play Go well, one needs to be emotionally detached from each particular fight. A Go player needs to constantly evaluate the strategic value of each particular fight against the whole landscape. This way of thinking has leaked out to the rest of my agential life. Go has made the mental move of stepping back and reflecting on the comparative value of my current pursuit more available to me. The strict, controlled environment of the game made it easier for me to get a hold on and practice that evaluative maneuver.

In some sense, what I'm saying here is something like that old chestnut: that games teach you "life lessons." There is, in fact, an entire genre of such semi-autobiographical, motivational texts, especially in sports.[10] Basketball helps you learn to think like a team and act unselfishly; rock climbing helps you learn to control your fear and focus; Chess teaches you how to think ahead and anticipate your opponent's moves. These thoughts are tropes, though surely, they have some truth to them. And, obviously games teach particular skills and practice particular practical abilities. My claim is positioned at the next level of abstraction. Each of these "life lessons" arises from a particular agential mode, built from the rules and goals of the particular game. Playing a variety of games and absorbing the different available agential stances grants the player something more than just one, very specific life lesson. It exposes the player to a variety of agential orientations and styles and so enhances their options for self-determination, and thus their autonomy.

All of this is simply a more formal way of rendering a well-worn observation—that playing games is a good part of a childhood education and an important part of our development. What I've argued for is a specific thesis inside this broad umbrella: that playing games can expose one to a broader set of agential modes, and so make one more able to fluidly and appropriately select different agential modes. Most importantly, I've argued that this particular benefit arises specifically from structured games, rather than from free play. I don't mean to argue against the importance of free play. Surely, free and creative play is an essential part of a human life. But I've argued that structured games make their own distinctive contribution.

We have a response now to that suspicion about structured games, and to Sicart's argument that free play was always better than structured games. Structured games are ways to inscribe and communicate agency. They are vessels for transmitting agential modes. Thus they are a particularly useful tool for the collaborative social enterprise of enhancing our autonomy, together. They are a way to harness the inventiveness of great numbers of people, and to make the development of our agencies into a collaborative and social project. Games let us codify, transmit, and store highly crystallized modes of agency. They are a library of agencies.

---

[10] This genre is vast and full of tired clichés. But a particular lovely one is the novelist Haruki Murakami's memoir about how running helped him learn to write (Murakami 2009).

PART II
AGENCY AND ART

5

The Aesthetics of Agency

Here's the picture so far. Suitsian games are structures of practical reasoning and practical action. Game designers aren't just creating constraints; they are designing forms of action and agency. A game designer creates a practical environment and the agential skeletons that will inhabit that environment, designating abilities and motivations ("Run, but don't hit. Dribble while moving. Care about getting the ball in the basket.") Game designers sculpt an agency and an environment to shape a particular kind of practical activity. Players adopt the proffered agency, filling it out in various ways. The exact nature of their gaming activity is up to them—but its outlines are shaped, in profound ways, by the game designer. Game designers work in the medium of agency.

So far, I've focused on the players and their capacity for agential fluidity. In the next three chapters, I turn to consider my claims about art and aesthetics. I claimed that one of the uses of the medium of agency is to shape aesthetic experiences of agency—of deciding, solving, and doing. But can there really be aesthetic experiences of agency? Could there really be an art of agency?

In this chapter, I look more closely at the sorts of aesthetic experiences that games can provide. Though games can offer some of the more familiar sorts of aesthetic experiences by telling stories, presenting striking images, and even making arguments, they can also do something else for us: they can provide designed experiences of our own agency. And the agential medium is particularly good at shaping the character of our practical engagement. Chess focuses us on thinking ahead down a chain of logical possibilities; *Tetris* focuses us on high-speed spatial reasoning. And those designed experiences of agency can be aesthetic. I don't mean here to imply that aesthetic experiences are essential to art, nor to claim that games' sole purpose is to provide aesthetic experiences. But games are particularly well suited to providing aesthetic experiences of agency.

Such aesthetic experiences are not unique to games. They often arise in ordinary practical life. I search for the right answer to a particularly thorny logic problem and the solution hits me like a bolt out of the blue—elegant, beautiful, perfect. A car swerves into my lane and I react smoothly, dodging

Games. C. Thi Nguyen, Oxford University Press (2020). © Oxford University Press.
DOI: 10.1093/oso/9780190052089.001.0001

perfectly. Afterward, I am struck by the gracefulness of my own instinctive response. Games can refine those pleasures, concentrate them, and present us with novel aspects of them. For example: doing math, philosophy, and the like, can give rise to aesthetic experiences of calculation, puzzle solving, and glorious leaps of the mind. Chess takes this sort of activity and crystallizes it. Chess offers us a shaped activity particularly fecund in aesthetically rich experiences of the intellect.

Rock climbing is another clear example. We experience the grace of our own effective movements sometimes in life; rock climbing concentrates these experiences. In rock-climbing gyms, a designer sets a particular climb by selecting and arranging holds on an artificial wall. In the subdiscipline of bouldering, such climbs are often set to induce climbers into some particular subtle, refined motion—for the sake of their experience of their own beauty and grace in motion. I touched on these issues briefly in Chapter 1; in this chapter, I will expand upon those opening thoughts.

Other Game Aesthetics

The contemporary discussion of the aesthetic and artistic value of games has rarely touched on the aesthetic of agency. It has, instead, often been concerned with showing that games can provide some of the more familiar aesthetic and artistic values: absorption in characters and narrative, political commentary, and the presentation of ideas. For example, Leo Konzack claims that games can only reach real cultural importance when they convey philosophical ideas (Konzack 2009). John Sharp praises those games that move beyond merely inducing instrumental efforts in their players and, instead, represent and comment on the world (Sharp 2015, 77–97). Mary Flanagan argues that games can be worthwhile as conceptual art, comparing them to avant-garde performance art. She praises what she calls "serious games," which deliver social and political criticisms. These serious games, she suggests, deserve praise because they engage in political subversion and social criticism. They can be called art because, by engaging in such political and social critique, they resemble many recent works of politically relevant conceptual art and performance art (Flanagan 2013).

Brenda Romero's work has become something of a poster child for the argument that games can be a serious and worthwhile form of art. Her game *Train*, for instance, is an art installation piece built around a board game.

Audience members are invited to play what appears to be a normal European-style train game, in which they are tasked with efficiently moving some yellow pieces across the board via railways. As the players continue to play the game, the game offers increasingly suggestive contextual information, until the players realize that they are, in fact, shipping prisoners to concentration camps during the Holocaust. The game, in both critical interpretation and Romero's own words, is built to create in its players an uncomfortable sense of complicity. *Train* often serves as a prime exemplar of respectable game design for various theorists (Baker 2013; Sharp 2015, 63–68).

Such attention to the representational and critical capacities for games is common. For example, Gonzolo Frasca argues that games can express ideas about causal systems in a more fluid and complex manner than other media because games are interactive simulations, rather than static tellings of particular stories. Imagine, for example, an artist trying to portray how labor unions might fail or succeed. A novel could represent one narrative of such a struggle, and show a single outcome. A game, on the other hand, could simulate such a struggle interactively and show the wide variety of possible outcomes. Thus, a game could represent a causal network (Frasca 2003). Similarly, Ian Bogost argues for the value of games by showing that they can function as a kind of rhetoric. Games are particularly good at representing and commenting on causal systems, such as economies and political structures, because games can simulate such systems. By highlighting particular features of those causal systems—for example, the way that capitalist systems tend to sacrifice environmental considerations—games can offer critiques of social systems (Bogost 2010, 28–64). Others have offered an artistic redemption for games by treating them as a kind of fiction. Grant Tavinor, for example, argues that video games are art precisely because they are a special kind of fiction: they are an interactive fiction, where the interactive features serve as props for the imagination.[1]

I have no quarrel with any of these accounts, so long as we treat them as each describing only one way, among many, that games can be artistically valuable. Games can surely function as political commentaries and social critiques; games can surely be fictions. But the aesthetic aspects of

---

[1] Tavinor's account builds on Walton's account of fictions as props for the make-believe (Walton 1990; Tavinor 2009). That account has been further developed by Aaron Meskin and Jon Robson (Robson and Meskin 2016). I have argued elsewhere that striving play and Waltonian play are not the same category, nor is either reducible to as a subform of the other (Nguyen 2019b).

practicality and agency are largely absent from these discussions.[2] The games that Flanagan, Sharp, Frasca, and Bogost praise sometimes involve struggling against obstacles, but they are not praised not in virtue of the quality of the struggles they engender. Rather, these games are esteemed for their representational qualities—how they model and comment on the real world. When agency shows up in these sorts of discussions, it is usually considered a subordinate technique for the purpose of representation. For example, in Tavinor's account, difficult obstacles are important for the artistic value of games when they help the game's fiction. Tavinor shows how difficulty in a game might serve to augment the immersion in the make-believe world. The player's frustration in manipulating the controls of the game can help them better identify with, and imagine themselves into, the frustrations of the character they control (Tavinor 2009, 130–149). One way to put it is that all these accounts approach games by asking for their *meaning*, in the strict sense of the term. What do they represent? What stories do they tell, what fictional worlds do they build, what parts of our world do they comment on, what philosophical notions do the convey? But I think we can find, in games, an aesthetic value unrelated to meaning. It is in the aesthetic qualities of doing—in the aesthetics of agency.

We can find the aesthetics of agency in virtually any game. It is not confined to narrative, cinematic videogames, or politically serious game design. It is a kind of aesthetic experience common to sports, video games, board games, role-playing games, card games, and more. The general neglect for the aesthetics of agency arises, I suspect, from a certain anxiety about the value of goal-oriented play.[3] As long as the goals of a game seem so arbitrary, pursuing them so vehemently seems childish. Thus, in many of the recent attempts to raise the cultural status of games, writers have sought to find other aspects to praise than mere instrumental, goal-oriented play. The seriousness and importance of fiction and social critique are well-established. If we can show that games can and do function as a form of fiction, cinema, or modern art, then the status of games as art—and thus their cultural worth—can be secured.

---

[2] Those familiar with the narratology vs. ludology debate will recognize my position as somewhat aligned with the ludologists. The differences between my account and those of other ludologists will emerge in the details, especially in Chapter 6.

[3] Some writers outside analytic philosophy have begun to focus on various aspects of the aesthetics of obstacle-oriented play, including Daniel Vella's continental approach to what he calls "the ludic muse," and Jesper Juul's brief discussion of "the aesthetics of mind" and "the aesthetics of challenges" (Vella 2016; Juul 2005, 92–94, 110–116).

But we've already seen how we should respond to such a worry. Suppose we accept that the goals of a game, by themselves, are worthless. What explains our intense pursuit of those goals? If we confine our answer to the goals themselves and to what follows from them, we may struggle to find an answer. But this misunderstands the justificatory structure of striving play. Somebody can pursue a goal for the sake of the struggle for that goal. And, I am suggesting, one way to explain the value of a struggle is in aesthetic terms. We can justify our pursuit of an arbitrary-seeming goal in terms of the aesthetic value of that struggle.

The aesthetics of agency offers a way to explain the distinctive aesthetic value of games. Without such an account, we will be inclined to cash out the aesthetic value of games in terms of some other, more established form of aesthetic value. But this assimilation threatens to obscure the unique potential of games as an art form. This has happened before in other emerging art forms. Take, for example, the beginnings of art photography. In the early days of photography, the very clarity, crispness, and detail afforded by the technology seemed, to many, uncomfortable. Photography was starkly unlike the nearest available recognizable art form, painting. Early photographers who aimed self-consciously at making photography an art form often engaged in various manipulations to undo that clarity—like blurring and soft-focus. Their goal was to make photographs more closely resemble traditional painting. It took the rejection of the traditional painting paradigm for photography to begin to explore some of the artistic potential special to the medium (Bunnell 1992). I am certainly not claiming here that an art form must confine itself to those effects unique to its medium. I am only claiming that we can obscure a new medium's artistic potential when we bid for its art status by trying too desperately to assimilate it within a more traditional art form.

Finally, I am not suggesting that our aesthetics of agency displace other aesthetic approaches to games, especially those which are devoted to particular types of games. We have recently seen some extremely interesting and sophisticated treatments of the aesthetics of video games that do take agency into account. Graeme Kirkpatrick, for example, offers a useful account of the aesthetics of video games in terms of the formal timing and rhythmic structures involved in the dance of the hands over the controller (Kirkpatrick 2011, 87–158). There have also been some extremely useful investigations into the meanings of the video games, especially of story-based video games, which focus on the meaningfulness of the special interactive structure of games (Arjonta 2015). These are all worthwhile approaches, and none of them are incompatible with the attempt to build an aesthetics of agency. It will be useful to search for an aesthetics in common to all games, as well as an aesthetics specific to video games—just as it is useful to study both the aesthetics of film in general, and also look at the aesthetics of horror movies (Carroll 2003). It is useful to study the aesthetics of music on its own, and then to think about how the aesthetics of music and story interact in opera and film. And I think that the attempt to think about the aesthetics of agency, on its own, will also help us to understand how it can interact with the aesthetics of stories and meaningfulness.

Toward an Aesthetics of Agency

But can there really be aesthetic qualities in our goal-directed activity? Can we have aesthetic experiences of our own struggles? Let's start by throwing ourselves into actual gaming practice. As David Davies suggests, aesthetic theory should be largely beholden to actual aesthetic practice and language (Davies 2004, 16–24). And ordinary talk about games is full of aesthetic language. Games talk is full references to familiar aesthetic qualities: harmony, elegance, grace, and the like.

Some of the most obvious cases occur in the aesthetic talk over athletic beauty. The appreciation of sports is replete with undeniably aesthetic language. Athletes are graceful, beautiful, poetry in motion. The poet Marianne Moore—a true connoisseur of unexpected beauties—writes of her love of animals and athletes:

> They are subjects of art and exemplars of it, are they not?. . . I don't know how to account for a person who could be indifferent to miracles of dexterity, a certain feat of Don Zimmer—a Dodger at the time—making a backhand catch, of a ball coming hard from behind on the left, fast enough to take his hand off. (Moore 1961, xvi)

When John Dewey looks to find the basis of artistic practice in everyday life experiences, among the very first examples he reaches for is, again, baseball.

> In order to *understand* the esthetic in its ultimate and approved forms, one must begin with it in the raw; in the events and scenes that hold the attentive

eye and ear of man, arousing his interest and affording him enjoyment as he looks and listens: the sights that hold the crowd . . . The sources of art in human experience will be learned by him who sees how the tense grace of the ball-player infects the onlooking crowd. (Dewey [1934] 2005, 3)

Obviously, aesthetic qualities abound in the athletic sphere. Philosophers of sport have argued at length about the more specialized question of whether sports deserve to be called art (Best 1985), but there is no controversy over whether an athlete's movement can be beautiful. (The debates in the aesthetics of sport concern relatively fine matters, such as whether or not an athletic movement's gracefulness is conceptually dependent on the movement's effectiveness [Best 1974; Cordner 1984].)

But the philosophers of sport have mostly focused on the aesthetic experiences of spectators. We're after something quite different here: the aesthetics of deciding and acting, as experienced by the players themselves. We're looking, not for an aesthetics of skilled performance, but for an aesthetics of agency. Still, the aesthetic experiences of spectators surely show something about the aesthetic experience of the players. If a spectator can see the grace, elegance, or beauty of an action, then surely the player can, too. Chess moves are often described as elegant or lovely (Osborne 1964). Surely the inventor of a strikingly elegant Chess move can recognize and appreciate its elegance. And, as Barbara Montero argues, dancers can perceive the aesthetic qualities of their own movements through proprioception (Montero 2006).

The Harmony of Self and World

But the player of a game is not simply the spectator with the best seat in the house. The player has a special relationship to the activity of play. They have a direct experience of their own action and agency. There are special aesthetic qualities that are available primarily to the player themselves—aesthetic qualities that arise in the act of analyzing, deciding, seeing, responding, and doing.

Each player has access to agency from a first-person perspective. Players are the ones who analyze the situation and discover that particularly effective move. They have access not only to the aesthetics of the Chess move itself, but also to the aesthetics of the process of generating that move. They can have a special experience of their action as *practically harmonious*. (I do not mean to claim here that harmony is some necessary part of the aesthetic. It is merely one familiar aesthetic quality, among many, and a good place to start.)

There are many sorts of practical harmony. First, there can be a harmony between act and challenge. In a beautiful Chess move, there is a harmony between the move and the situation it addresses. Here is a trap; there is an elegant resolution. Call this the *harmony of solution*. The harmony of solution is strictly a harmony between the solution and the obstacle; it makes no explicit reference to the actor or their capacities. The harmony of the solution is available to both spectator and player.

But there is another form of harmony, which includes the player's agency. Let's call this the *harmony of action*. When you time a jump just so in *Super Mario Brothers*; or when you figure out, during a rock climb, that you need to slide your hips over just enough to balance on that tiny nubbin of rock, you're experiencing more than the harmony of solution. You're experiencing your agency and action as fitting the demands of the environment. You experience, not only the fit between the obstacle and the solution, but the fit between the obstacle and yourself as the originator of those solutions.[4] The harmony of action expands on the harmony of solution. The harmony of action concerns, not only how the solution fits the problem, but how my decision-making and action-generation were just right to generate that fitting solution. And though the harmony of action is, in principle accessible to both player and spectator, the player has better and deeper access to it. After all, they came up with the move themselves; they chose a course of action. They know what it feels like to analyze the situation, to find the solution, to react with precision and grace, and to have inspiration strike.

There are also social versions of these harmonies. You can have a sense of your actions and abilities as fitting with those of other players, and of those collective actions as fitting the challenges of the game. Traditional team sports offer these harmonies aplenty. Think of the moment when you are playing basketball, when you're penned in with the ball, and you and a teammate simultaneously spot the opportunity for a pass—and you bounce the pass between two opponents and your teammate slips into just the right place to catch it. Modern multiplayer computer games offer it, too. The social harmonies of solution and action are particularly evident in role-based team games like *DoTA* and *Team Fortress 2*, where each player's character has

---

[4] Some of this may strike readers as similar to the positive-psychology literature on flow. See Juul (2005, 112–116) for a treatment of flow-state in games, as well as a useful criticism of the view that flow-state is the paradigmatic desirable state for all game play.

a particular specialty (sniper, medic, tank), and good play involves coordinating the roles in just the right way.

But the harmony of action is not the end of the story; there is yet another kind of harmony available in games. Take *Super Hexagon*, a cult favorite in the realm of modern ultrahard, twitch-based arcade games. *Super Hexagon* involves using only two basic controls—rotate clockwise and rotate counterclockwise—to navigate a tiny arrow through a swirling, onrushing maze. Your ship is in the center of the screen; new sections of the maze appear at the outer edges of the screen and rush in toward you. In the early levels, the game offers a simple reflex challenge. You must react to oncoming walls, avoiding them and steering between the gaps. Then the maze gets faster and more complicated. You must now split your brain. You must monitor the nearest walls, to execute the precision reflex movements, and simultaneously monitor the more distant outer walls, to plan your long-term flight path. Then, as the game progresses, the walls get faster still, and the only way to survive is to realize that the maze progresses according to certain repeating patterns, and to suss out those patterns with that remaining tiny bit of your brain. The game keeps speeding up until you come to the very limit of your capacities. But as long as you can survive at that limit, then you can experience an especially delicious sense of the connection and harmony between your abilities and the world. Your abilities must work perfectly—a microsecond's slip, and you die. This is an experience, not just of a particular action's fitting the requirements at hand. It is an experience of your whole self fitting the task. It is the experience of your abilities, worked at their maximum, just barely making it.

This experience is not merely of one particular action fitting the solution. It is an experience of harmony between one's *overall capacities* and the demands of the practical environment. It is the sense that one's total capacities fit precisely with the demands of the world. Let's call this the *harmony of capacity*. By contrast, the harmony of action makes no reference to how difficult that action is, compared to the actor's total capacities. The harmony of capacity, on the other hand, is particular to the experience of doing difficult things—of engaging your abilities fully. The harmony of capacity arises from a fit between one's maximum skill level and the demands of the task. It is only available when you are pushed to your limit.

When I'm warming up for rock climbing, I climb easy climbs. As I warm up, I try to maximize my grace and elegance. I choose and decide just the right movements for the task. That is the harmony of solution and the harmony of action, without the harmony of capacity. After all, I'm only warming up and nowhere close to my limit. But when I'm working near my limit—when I'm just barely managing to succeed—I experience now also experiencing the harmony of capacity. In fact, the harmonies of solution and act are most present in the warm-up. I am at my most elegant when I am fully in control and operating well within my abilities. When I am maxed out, on the other hand, my movements will be far uglier to the outside observer. My movements are clutching and desperate, and I lack the perfect harmony of solution that I had managed when I was in total control. But it is in these desperate moments, at the outermost edge of my capacities, that I experience the harmony of capacity most fully.

Some small whisper of the harmony of capacity may be accessible to spectators; they may have some dim sense of when athletes are near their limits. But players relationship to their maximum capacity is often not on display. We spectators often only find out afterward that a player was near that limit, when they tell us so, or when a commentator announces that an athlete has broken a personal record. Sometimes we have some external cues—the body in strain, the face in anguish—but not always. (I challenge any reader to watch a videotape of one of Michael Phelps's record-breaking swims, and then one of Michael Phelps's daily, run-of-the-mill workouts, and judge, without a timer, which is which.) The relationship between a player's actions and their maximum practical capacities is particularly difficult for spectators to access with largely mental games, such as Chess.

The sense that one's abilities are working perfectly in tune and performing actions right at the limit of one's capacities is, I think, a particularly special and profound experience of harmony between self and world. That specialness helps to explains why we might seek games that are difficult for us. We want the harmony of capacity because it is offers us a feeling of fitting the world, practically speaking. An experience of beauty here, of harmonious fit, is something of a balm to the perpetual sense of friction between ourselves and the world. The satisfactions of this fit help to explain why pure striving players might be interested in difficulty, even if they uninterested in the value of difficult achievements themselves. Striving players here aren't doing it in order to have done something difficult; they are doing something difficult for the experience of harmony between their utmost capacities and the practical world.

This explanation is significantly different from many of the other explanations on tap. For example, Juul offers a compensatory theory of why we play difficult games and risk failure. Says Juul, we take pleasure in the sense of achievement after we're done; the pleasures make up for the risk (Juul 2013). R. Scott Kretchmar offers an explanation of difficulty in terms of the dramatic arc. When one has failed many times, the eventual victory is ever so much more dramatic (Kretchmar 2012). But the explanation I've offered is quite different. It is not a retrospective pleasure in the achievement, but a sense of harmony in the process of being engaged with, and fitting to, the task. Only in a difficult game can we experience the harmony of capacity. And that fit can explain the enjoyment of difficulty even if there is no dramatic arc. Climbers value what's called a *flash*—successfully climbing a problem on the first try. One of the greatest satisfactions in climbing is flashing a particularly hard problem. One's body must respond perfectly on the first try; one's mind must work quickly enough to figure out the right sequence on a first encounter. The explanation in terms of the drama of failure and defeat has little to say about beating a challenge or a game first try, but the explanation in terms of the experience of practical harmony explains those pleasures quite well.

And the harmony of capacity is far rarer than the harmony of action. The harmony of action occurs frequently in my everyday life. Sometimes, I even take the time to notice it as it goes by. I have experienced the harmony of action in perfectly organizing my clothes in my luggage, in chopping wood and placing the axe just so. (I read some Zen instruction manuals as instructing the reader to try to appreciate the harmony of every single one of their actions.) But the experience of that most delicious of harmonies—the harmony of capacity—is particularly rare in the wild. I've had it very occasionally: finally solving a difficult philosophy problem that had been tormenting me for years; swerving and weaving perfectly through a tiny gap in traffic to dodge an out-of-control drunk driver. Harmonies of capacity occur so rarely in ordinary life because so much of the world, and the tasks it forces on us, do not fit us well. There are things that we must do that are boring, because our abilities are too great for them, but we must do them (folding laundry). Then there are the things we must do that, though they are difficult, are also unpleasant (proofreading a book for the seventh time). There are things we must do that might start out as interesting challenges, but the world forces them on us in such mind-numbing volume that they lose all interest (grading). And then there are all the tasks we wish to do that are far beyond our capacities: curing cancer, fixing the politics of climate change, easing intercultural conflict. But in games, the obstacles can be engineered to fit us. Some of this is the work of the game designer; some of it is the players finding the right game, or the appropriate opponents, or even just fiddling with the difficulty level. But in our life with games, we design, fiddle, and pick until the struggle is tailored just right.

The Negative Aesthetics of Games

The examples I've just given are all of various forms of consonance between self and world. Most of the literature on the aesthetics of sports also focuses on positive aesthetic features—beauty and grace, and the like. But what of dissonance—disharmony, unfitness, and other such experiences? Elsewhere in our life with art, we find negative aesthetics aplenty. We value so many aesthetic experiences that are horrifying, disgusting, disquieting, jarring, or dissonant. Tragedies, horror movies, modernist symphonies, and avant-garde jazz: all modulate various forms of unpleasantness as part of some greater aesthetic achievement. Is there an analogue in games? In our experiences of practical activity, can there be an aesthetics of awkwardness, inelegance, and failure?

I think so. Examples here will do more work here than arguments, I suspect. There is a recent minigenre of video game which involves interposing arcane and difficult control mechanics between the player and the game. For example, *QWOP* is a sprinting simulator in which a player controls a physics-modeled rag doll in a running race. The controls are awkwardly and counterintuitively mapped to a computer keyboard. The Q and W keys control the runner's left and right thighs, and the O and P keys control the runner's left and right calves. The goal is to make the rag doll run; but given the unhelpful interface and the deconstructed relationship to the body parts of the rag doll, most efforts to run are comically unsuccessful. The rag doll flops, stutters, flails, and falls. When one finally manages to make the thing run, it is, for a while at least, a constant fight against one's intuitions and instincts. (It is a fairly significant victory to make the rag doll run for over two seconds.)

Consider, too, the video game *Octodad: Dadliest Catch*, a cult favorite in which the player takes control of the eponymous octopus. Here's a review:

> The . . . let's say, awkwardness of Octodad's situation is represented well by *Dadliest Catch*'s bizarre controls, which map one of his leg tentacles to each trigger and one of his arm tentacles to the thumbsticks (when they

aren't controlling leg direction, that is). Octodad's head and mantle are sort of amiably dragged along for the ride. Much of the joy and hilarity of *Octodad* is derived from just how ineffective a control scheme this is. Watching Octodad attempt to pour milk for his daughter as he simultaneously flips a living room table, pulls a painting from a wall and accidentally chucks the carton at his son is endlessly entertaining. If through sheer will and inspiring determination you manage to become competent at steering the game's hero, you can ramp up the madness by activating co-op mode. With each player controlling individual limbs, you'll be lucky if you can manage any ambulation for Octodad that doesn't resemble a grand mal seizure. (McElroy 2014)

Armor Games has designed a number of free web-browser games in a similar spirit. Their games often revolve around a carefully designed awkwardness of control mechanics. My favorite is the game *Minotaur in a China Shop*, in which you play a large and clumsy minotaur, who is trying to fulfill his lifelong dream of owning a china shop. The game involves maneuvering your minotaur through his overcrowded china shop to fetch objects ordered by the customer. But the control scheme is frustratingly erratic by design. Your minotaur lumbers, corners terribly, and moves with considerable inertia. And, for extra comedic value, as your minotaur inevitably breaks more of his own stock, he becomes angrier and angrier, and moves ever more unpredictability, as he falls into a vicious downward spiral of clumsiness and rage.

These cases suggest that dissonance and unpleasantness in games can be just as valuable and interesting as dissonance and unpleasantness elsewhere in the aesthetic world. They offer the flip side of the experience of effectiveness. They are the gaming equivalent of horror movies. They are eloquent and crystallized portraits of ineffectualness. They are horrors of practical incapacity. Interestingly, when one reaches for explanations of the value of these sorts of experiences, the language of expressiveness comes most readily to hand. *Minotaur in a China Shop* is expressive, among other things, of the experience of having one's heart's desires and one's actual abilities fail to fit; it is an expression of practical disharmony. But we don't get that expressive content by contemplating the game design, as was the case with Frasca's *September 12*. Rather, it is an expressiveness that arises from being engaged in the difficult act, from the experience of trying to pursue a specified goal under some specific, and very irritating, limitations.

There are other ways to account for the place of negative experiences in the aesthetics of games. Some negative experiences may help us to have aesthetic experiences, because they accentuate and intensify the final positive experience. In rock climbing, early awkwardness might give way to learned gracefulness. In an arcade game, early failure may give way to gradual progress and eventual mastery. Juul's and Kretchmar's accounts suggest such a compensatory account. But the examples I've surveyed showed there is also a more immediate value to negative experiences in games. The negative experience is a constitutive part of what we aesthetically value, rather than merely a technique for accentuating a positive experience of eventual achievement. Juul's and Kretchmar's accounts require that we eventually succeed to make sense of the value of the difficulty and failure. But you don't need to win at *Octodad: Dadliest Catch* to have a worthwhile experience. Sometimes, the experiences of awkwardness, difficulty, and failure can be aesthetically valuable in themselves.[5]

Experience and Disinterest

But are these sorts of experiences really aesthetic? So far, I've talked in relatively broad strokes of harmony and drama and other aesthetic qualities that we might find in game play. But can these really be called aesthetic qualities? Are what I've called the harmonies of solution, act, and capacity really of the same ilk as, say, the harmonies we find in music, painting, or nature? One might think that there cannot be aesthetic qualities in the instrumental activity of game play. I now turn to consider whether these qualities can be genuinely aesthetic ones, in the face of certain worries from particular theories of the aesthetic.

In many ways, the way we critically evaluate games is strikingly similar to the way we evaluate the more traditional aesthetic objects. Take, for example, the requirement for direct experience. It is often thought that one of the markers of aesthetic judgments is that they ought to be made from an immediate experience of an aesthetic object (or some adequate surrogate). Aesthetic judgments, it is thought, are judgments of taste. We cannot render an aesthetic judgment of a thing without having actually experienced it for

---

[5] My discussion here has been influenced by Matt Strohl's discussion of negative aesthetics and painful emotion in horror films and other art (Strohl 2012, 2019).

ourselves. This is in direct contrast to how we use testimony in ordinary empirical contexts. I am free to trust my mechanic about the state of my engine block, and base all manner of beliefs on my trust of that testimony. But things are different in the realm of the aesthetic. I should make aesthetic judgments about Van Gogh's *Irises* based only on my actual direct experiences of *Irises*. I ought not pronounce on the beauty of *Irises* merely on the basis of expert testimony to that effect (Budd 2003; Livingston 2003; Hopkins 2011; Wollheim 1980; Nguyen 2017d; Nguyen 2019c). Many have thought this demand for first-person experience to be an essential marker of the aesthetic.[6] Notice that our attitudes toward judgments about the quality of games also conforms to this experiential requirement. In order to judge a game, we need to have played the game for ourselves. Similarly, we expect game reviewers to have played the game for themselves and had the experiences for themselves, in order to make their pronouncements about the quality of the game. Game reviews work like movie reviews and fiction reviews, and not like *Consumer Reports* surveys of dishwasher reliability. In this regard, at least, judgments about games are significantly like other aesthetic judgments.

But from other angles, there seems to be a significant tension between the nature of aesthetic experience and the nature of striving play. Aesthetic experience, it is often thought, requires a very particular state of mind. This requirement has been cashed out in any number of ways. To have aesthetic experiences, it has been suggested, we must be disinterested in practical outcomes, or we must be contemplative, or we must maintain a particular unfocused quality of attention. But all these various requirements seem to conflict with sort of the focused, practically oriented, instrumental attitude we find in the kinds of games we've been focused on. How, then, can we reach an appropriately aesthetic frame of mind, when we are wholly absorbed in instrumental calculations of game-play?

Let's start with the most familiar version of the conflict. One might worry that aesthetic striving play is impossible because the motivational state of aesthetic experience is incompatible with the instrumental attitudes involved in games. The worry is easiest to put in the Kantian language of disinterestedness. Suppose that aesthetic experience is essentially disinterested—that

---

[6] For example, Dominic Lopes suggests that the experiential requirement is the best candidate for marking off the realm of the aesthetic from the non-aesthetic (Lopes 2014, 163–184). Elizabeth Schellekens relies on the experiential requirement in her argument for the aesthetic value of ideas in conceptual art to explain why it might be reasonable to think that an entirely non-perceptible work might be reasonably considered aesthetic (Schellekens 2007).

it is pursued, not for any practical purpose, but for its own sake. But the activity of playing a Suitsian game is essentially interested. It is pursuing an end, absorbed in the practicality of means-end reasoning.[7] How can I have any disinterested experiences, when I have devoted myself entirely to winning the game? This worry has haunted the philosophy of sport. It leads Stephen Mumford, for example, to argue that aesthetic experiences are available, not to the player or the spectating partisan, but only to the spectating purist. Partisans, who want one particular side to win, cannot experience the beauty of sports. The only person who can see beauty in a sport is the observer who cares not which team wins, but is only in it for purely non-partisan experiences of athletic beauty (Mumford 2012, 2013, 1–18).[8]

Is there a way out of this apparent conflict? First, let's get clear on which aesthetic judgments we're talking about. Aesthetic judgments about games might be made from several different stances. I might be playing a game, utterly absorbed in its particular challenges. I might be watching other people play, or studying classic Chess matches from a book. I might also be admiring the elegance of the game design itself. My favorite board game designer, Reiner Knizia, is revered in game-design circles for the astonishing elegance of his work. Some of the loveliest Knizia designs consist of a handful of rules that give rise to complex and subtle play. One of my favorites of is the board game *Modern Art*, in which all the players play modern art dealers, auctioning paintings from hot new artists to one another. At the end of each round, they sell the paintings they've bought from one another to the general public. The game (cynically) fixes the resale value of a given artist's work based solely on how many times that artist's work has been traded during the game. A small handful of rules creates a wildly fluctuating, complex market simulation, in which players must forecast and manipulate their fellow player's actions, and in which they can set off booms and busts in investment. There are so many ways to approach the game, and different groups of players create wildly different market dynamics—but almost everybody loves the experience. When I say that *Modern Art* is an elegant design, I am not speaking

---

[7] The worry can also be put in the language of aesthetic empiricism—the view that aesthetic experiences must be intrinsically valuable to count as properly aesthetic (Goldman 2006; Stang 2012), but nothing significant for my discussion hangs on this difference. For an excellent survey, discussion, and criticism of theories of this sort, see Lopes (2018, 53–87).

[8] Mumford's earlier writings on the topic took a hard line: that no aesthetic experiences are available to the partisan. He has softened the view, in the cited works, to include the possibility that partisan spectators may have a greater experience of drama. However, he still thinks that there is a trade-off between emotional drama and a purely disinterested aesthetic experience, because the two kinds of experience are still essentially in conflict

of any particular playing experience of mine, but rather of its capacity to support wonderful gaming experiences for a wide variety of players, all from such a simple rule-set.

There are, then, three distinct stances we can take up toward games, from which we might have aesthetic experiences. There is the *play stance*, in which one is directly involved in the practical activity of playing a game. There is the *spectator stance*, in which one surveys a part or whole of a game session, while not actively engaged in the practical activity of the game. Finally, there is the *design stance*, in which one attends, not to a particular session of a game, but to the design of the game itself and how that design supports different instances of play. Notice that the play stance and the spectator stance both focus on particular playings of a game, while the design stance focuses on the stable artifacts which underlie many different playings—the rules, the graphics, the pieces.

The spectator stance and the design stance can obviously support aesthetic experiences. Neither requires any form of instrumental goal-oriented thinking on the part of the audience. Only the play stance seems in tension with the disinterest requirement for aesthetic experience. But our analysis of striving play and disposable ends gives us a ready solution. Zoomed in, the moment-to-moment phenomenology of aesthetic striving play seems clearly interested. I am choosing my actions for the sake of winning the game. But the aesthetic striving player only adopts ends temporarily, for the sake of the aesthetic experiences which arise from the pursuit. Zoomed out, the aesthetic striving player is playing games just for the sake of the aesthetic experience of play.

Aesthetic striving play is, then, curiously both interested and disinterested. In the midst of the game itself, we are interested. Our minds and wills are bent to the task of winning. We have submerged ourselves in a temporary agency, wholly devoted to that disposable end. But our overall purpose for playing can still be disinterested. We can set up that temporary agency and submerge ourselves within it for wholly aesthetic reasons. In pure striving play, I—the enduring agent—care not if my striving succeeds. I am only in it for the experience of striving itself. It is only the temporary agent who is interested. The interestedness of striving play is thus crucially bracketed. Aesthetic striving play is *disinterested interestedness*. It is a disinterested attitude taken toward the interested states of an activity. To put it another way, striving play is *impractical practicality*. It is practical reasoning and practical action engaged in, not for the outcome, but for the sake of the engagement in the practical activity itself.[9] This solution can also apply to the interested spectator, who takes up a bracketed interest in their team winning, for the sake of a valuable experience of partisan spectatorship.

Disinterested Attentional States

Let's turn to a different account of aesthetic experience, which will yield a slightly different sort of difficulty for aesthetic striving. Perhaps what marks off the aesthetic realm is a particular quality of attention. In Jerome Stolnitz's well-known account, what marks off the aesthetic realm is a special attitude in the perceiver: the aesthetic attitude. Normally, says Stolnitz, our attitudes toward objects are practical and interested. Crucially, the practicality or impracticality of our attitude changes how we will perceive something. When we are interested in something for practical reasons, says Stolnitz, we focus only on those features that are relevant to our interest. If I am interested in a kitchen knife for the purpose of cooking, I will attend to its sharpness, its balance, and its durability. I will not attend to the aspects of its shape that are irrelevant to those functions, nor to its color, nor to the pleasant ringing sound it makes when tapped. Practical interest filters and focuses my perception. But when I am interested in something just for the sake of experiencing it, that filter goes away, and I attend to the whole thing (Stolnitz 1960; Kemp 1999). For Stolnitz, the impractical attitude engenders a particular kind of open, unfiltered state of attention.[10]

Suppose this kind of view is approximately right, and that the aesthetic attitude is marked by an impractical and unfiltered attention. During striving play, I attend practically to a very specific range of factors. I attend to what matters for winning. I do not focus on the look or the odor of my Chess pieces. Those details all drop away as I focus narrowly on the strategic potential of my pieces. Empirical research has shown that as players become more deeply involved with a game, their perceptual focus narrows. As Simon Dor argues, novice players usually engage with a wide range of visual and auditory

---

[9] Daniel Vella, working from a background in continental aesthetics and critical theory, comes to a strikingly similar solution in (Vella 2016, 80–81)

[10] Stolnitz's account has fallen into relative unpopularity of late, due to some apparently compelling criticisms (Dickie 1964). Bence Nanay has recently revived and improved the theory, overcoming Dickie's criticisms in a convincing way (Nanay 2016, 1–35). I take Nanay's account to be superior to Stolnitz's, but the details won't matter for my discussion, so I will speak in terms of Stolnitz's simpler and more familiar framework.

details: they soak in the pretty graphics and dramatic music, and engage with them as they might a fiction. But experienced players filter out such details, focusing narrowly on only those elements relevant to the win. This is why games like Chess and *Starcraft* often use simple, repetitive visual patterns to represent core game elements. This makes it easier for experienced players to ignore the visual details, and focus only on the strategically relevant features of their various units (Dor 2014). Isn't this filtered, focused form of attention the opposite of the aesthetic attitude?

The response comes, once again, by noting our capacity for agential layering. The inner layer—the temporary game agency—may be entirely absorbed in practical modes of attention, and thus be incapable of aesthetic attention. But the outer layer—the player's overall agency—can take the aesthetic attitude. Aesthetic striving should, then, work like this: the inner layer pays a wholly focused attention to some practical problem. The outer layer reflects on the inner layer's activity, but attends to it in a nonpractical and unfiltered way. The aesthetic experience in games, then, won't be found in the narrowed experiences that arise in the practical activity itself. The aesthetic experience is a reflective experience, had by the outer layer, which takes as its object the inner layer's practical activity, including the inner layer's experience of being absorbed practicality. The aesthetic experience of striving is, among other things, a contemplation of *what it is like* to engage in that narrowed, practical mindset.

When I am fully engaged in a difficult rock climb, I am wholly focused on overcoming the challenges. I don't pay much attention to the lovely shade of green on the rock, or how the granite smells. I am largely focused on what matters to the practical task—where the holds are, how slippery the feet are, how the rock is textured. This is a fully focused and filtered practical form of attention. But I can also pay a second-order unfiltered aesthetic attention to those first-order unfiltered experiences. In this second-order reflection, I distribute my attention to all the aspects of my first-order activity: the feel of the calculations, the intensity of pressure, the explosiveness of the solution.

Consider the differences between me, rock climbing for aesthetic reasons, and Shauna Coxsey, former world champion, training for the next Bouldering World Cup. When I climb, my first-order practical attention is devoted to the rock and to my own movement. The same is true for Coxsey. Both of us also reflect on our practical activity. In particular, we can both meta-attend to features of our own first-order practical attention. But when I reflect on that first-order practical attention, I can do so aesthetically. I give second-order aesthetic attention to the totality of my first-order experience of climbing: what it felt like to be so desperate, so out of balance, and to pull off that delicate move anyway. I can aesthetically attend to the very experience of having my attention narrowed. This is, in fact, one of the best parts of climbing—that lovely feeling of having the world disappear, all my worries about my obligations and my finances vanishing. My whole consciousness is lost in complete devotion to this one problem, this body position, this solution. My first-order perception of the rock is practical and focused, and therefore not aesthetic, but my second-order perception of my first-order perception is unfocused and, therefore, aesthetic. But any wholly devoted competitor would, in their second-order attention, only narrowly focus only on those first-order climbing experiences most relevant for improvement. Shauna Coxsey, while training, would likely meta-attend to those features of her first-order practical experience that were practically useful to her. Coxsey would both have a practical, focused first-order perception of the rock, and a practical, focused second-order perception of her first-order perception.

Previously, I suggested that aesthetic striving players have complexly layered motivations. Here, I also suggest that aesthetic striving players have complexly layered attentional states. But if we hold any sort of aesthetic attitude theory, this should be unsurprising. According to such a theory, the characteristic form of aesthetic attention arises from our motivations for attending. We see the hammer narrowly when we are motivated practically; we see the hammer broadly when we are motivated aesthetically. So as long as there are layers of agency with different motivations, we should also expect layers of agency with different forms of attention. And that layering makes it possible to take up the aesthetic attitude toward the experience of our own practical activity.

6

Framed Agency

I've argued that there is an aesthetics of agency. We can have aesthetic experiences of our own agency and action—of analyzing, deciding, and doing. But this is only a start to understanding the art form of games. For one, the aesthetics of agency can be found in the wild. I have had aesthetic experiences of my own agency when I have come up with an elegant solution to a scheduling dilemma or gracefully plucked my laptop out of the reach of my toddler's filthy hands. But these experiences can also be constructed. In games, the game designer shapes our activities, and often does so in order to enable, encourage, and even construct aesthetic experiences of agency. Up to this point, I have been largely focused on the game player—on their experiences and motivational states. But in order to understand games, we also have to think about them as constructed, designed artifacts. We need to understand how designers can work to encourage and support the aesthetics of agency. We need to investigate games as an art form.

But what kind of art form are games, exactly? There are two familiar approaches to answering this question. One approach, as we've seen, is to assimilate games to more familiar forms of art, like fictions. Another approach is to deny that games are any kind of art at all. Sicart urges us to take such an approach. It's problematic to think about games using concepts like "art" and "artist," says Sicart, because games are such profoundly different things from artworks. When we get too caught up in the particulars of the rules, or when we worry too much about honoring games as a kind of art—when we care too much about discovering the artist's meaning—then we'll miss what's really important: that games are there to inspire us to play, and that play is essentially free and creative (Sicart 2014).

I think the right answer is somewhere between these two extremes. Games are unique in many aspects, but they are also like traditional artworks in some very significant ways. Games share with traditional artworks a *prescriptive frame*. That means that, in order to experience the artwork, you have to follow certain prescriptions about how you will confront it. You must attend to the work in a prescribed way in order to experience the work.

Games. C. Thi Nguyen, Oxford University Press (2020). © Oxford University Press.
DOI: 10.1093/oso/9780190052089.001.0001

Artworks have a peculiar form of existence; an artwork is something slightly above and beyond its mere material. To really understand what a work of art is, we will have to think about the social norms that surround and regulate our experience of art. I mean something very elemental here. To experience a painting, you have to look at it from the front. Looking at it only from the back, or only smelling it, doesn't count. The rule that we have to look at a painting from the front reveals something deep about what a painting *is*—which is something more than just the material stuff of paint on canvas. The fact that such rules are public, and held in common in a social practice, makes a certain kind of communal experience possible. Games are also works of this sort, with one foot in the material and one foot in a social practice. To experience a game, you have to follow the rules and aim at the given goals. This is why it is important to acknowledge the similarity between games and other, more traditional forms of art. Traditional artworks and games both use prescriptions to direct our attention along common channels, and to structure our experiences in a shared way.

This chapter marks a return to themes and issues, first raised in Chapter 4, concerning the relationship between freedom and communication. In this chapter, we'll address some key concerns by using, and extending, some useful insights from the philosophy of art. Why would we ever play structured games when we could instead play freely and creatively, with nobody telling us what goals to pursue or how to pursue them? Why should we ever submit ourselves to goals and constraints invented by another? My answer is that certain kinds of prescriptive structure help to stabilize our experiences, and make them, to a limited extent, sharable. That stability makes it possible for the designer to sculpt a particular kind of activity and pass it to the player—and so to help shape the player's aesthetic experience of their own agency.

Games, I will argue, have a very different function from free play. Free play offers creativity, raw freedom, and an unrestricted playground for the imagination. In games, we submit ourselves to publicized prescriptions, in order to pass stabilized experiences between people. Games are a technology of communication. And efficient communication depends on using some norms and prescriptions of some sort. We need some common rules to have a language—to stabilize the meanings of words, for example. And games are a language, of sorts, for communicating modes of agency and forms of activity. Games are a frame hung around specific and sculpted forms of our own activity.

But Is It *Art*?

I will spend much of this chapter talking about the notion of a "work," and arguing that games are works. I will not, however, be directly addressing the question of whether games are art by this or that formal definition of "art." As it turns out, most of the plausible definitions of art won't actually help us to answer the really interesting questions. Take, for example, the institutional theory of art, which states, approximately, that the "art" is whatever the sociohistorical institution of the art world says it is (Dickie 1974). This does seem to get at something of the sociolinguistic truth of how we use the term *art*. But using this account won't really got to the heart of the questions that matter. When most people ask, with some urgency, whether video games are art, they are not asking a whether a particular social institution has, in fact, accepted games. Similarly, suppose we subscribe to a cluster theory of art—that is, that certain things are called art because they share a sufficient number of the typical properties of other things that have been called art. It would be easy to demonstrate using such a theory, that some games are art. Others have already provided such arguments, at least for video games (Tavinor 2009, 172–196; Smuts 2005). If it helps, here are my own views on the matter: I take the term *art* to be best explained by a cluster theory. Thus there are no good necessary and sufficient conditions for being "art," but only a loose set of family resemblances. One traditionally significant member of that cluster is the class of artworks that are made for the sake of aesthetic experiences. And games are often made for the sake of such experiences, and resemble traditional forms of art in other significant ways as well, so they plausibly belong in that cluster.

But again, this doesn't quite seem to satisfy the real itch for many questioners. The reason, I think, is because the question "Are games art?" isn't really about whether games share enough properties with other, more established arts. The underlying question is one of value. It is a question about whether games could ever be worth spending time with, in the way that reading Marcel Proust and listening to Charlie Parker can be worthwhile. It is a question about whether games can help us lead rich and fulfilling lives, or whether they are just a way to idle away the hours.

So I propose that we elide the question of the proper definition of art, and largely skirt around the struggles about whether games do or do not fit that definition. I'll show some ways in which games are significantly like traditional forms of art and some ways in which they are significantly novel, and leave it at that. I will use the term *art* because it is the readiest at hand. Games, in my picture, are artifacts that have been intentionally constructed for the sake of, among other things, engendering aesthetic experiences in their audiences. "Art" seems to be best term that we have to talk about such things. But nothing much of terrible significance hangs on the term, above and beyond the specific claims I'm going to make about the prescriptive structure and aesthetic value of games. What matters to me is the particular story of how games serve as vehicles to communicate agencies, and how designers can use that medium to sculpt aesthetic experiences of agency. If the reader is strongly committed to some definition of art that excludes games for some particular reason, then they may feel free to substitute, for all incidences of the term *art*, the phrase, "works which are art-like in many significant regards."

Works and Prescriptions

On the other hand, it is crucial to my account that games are works. I intend "work" here to include any sort of intentionally authored, stable object, made for some specified form of appreciation and consumption. This category includes artworks, but also many non-art objects, such as newspapers and history books. I implicitly relied on the view that games are works when I argued, in Chapter 4, that games are stable vehicles for communicating modes of agency. I will now defend that assumption.[1]

The standard view in contemporary analytic aesthetics is that a work is partially constituted by prescriptions about what its users must do in order to encounter that work. For example, says Davies, the practice of painting, at least in its traditional European form, prescribes that users look at, but not taste, the canvas. It also prescribes that they look at the front of it and not the back. Imagine that an alien species has a practice whereby they make things that look very much like our paintings, but that those objects are embedded in a practice where audience members look at them from the side and admire the shape and power of the outward protrusions of the paint. Even if one of their artifacts happened to be materially identical to, say, Van Gogh's *Irises*, it would be an entirely different work (Davies 2004, 50–79). This kind of view is

---

[1] The remainder of this chapter is adapted, with some improvements, from Nguyen (2019a). That earlier article does include more detailed engagement with the game studies literature and the intentional fallacy.

sometimes called a *prescriptive ontology*, which means the prescriptions help constitute the very artwork itself. The novel *Moby Dick* isn't just the words on the page; it is the words as experienced under the prescription to read them in order. If I read all the words of *Moby Dick* in a random order, I wouldn't have read *Moby Dick*. This shows that the work isn't just a physical object. The work is some physical material, as encountered according to a certain set of prescriptions. The prescriptions help to delineate what the work *is*.

Note these prescriptions have only contingent authority. Nothing says that you have to read the words of *Moby Dick* in order, all things considered. You are utterly free to read those words in any order you please, for all sorts of reasons. Rather, prescriptive ontologies only say that *if* you want read *Moby Dick*, then you must read all these words in order. Whether or not you want to read *Moby Dick* is up to you. The prescriptive ontology merely tells you what *Moby Dick* is, by telling you what you have to do in order to experience it. Consider, for example, the rules specifying what it is to dance the waltz. Nobody is telling you that you must follow these rules, because nobody is telling you that you must dance the waltz. They are only telling you that, in order to dance the waltz, you have to move your feet this way and that. These prescriptions have no more normative force than the rules of a game, which tell you that you must follow them if you wish to play this particular game. You are free to play by different rules, but then you will simply be playing a different game. In other words, both artworks and games are social practices with constitutive rules. One might then complain that prescriptive ontologies make artworks and games out to be utterly artificial, socially contingent affairs. But that is exactly the insight on offer. Artworks and games are our creations, and their basic nature emerges from our decisions and practices.

Yuriko Saito puts it rather elegantly. Traditional art objects, she says, are aesthetically *framed*. Just as a painting has a physical frame, which marks off a particular space as the proper object of attention, all works have a *prescriptive frame*. The prescriptive frame consists of norms which tell the observer what to pay attention to and what to ignore in order to encounter the work. Saito traces the existence of the aesthetic frame to our presupposition that art objects are intentionally authored. The artist intended to create a particular artistic object. The practice of art appreciation aims at retrieving the particular artistic object that the artist intended to create. That practice assures us that we're appreciating and talking about the same thing. A perfumer has spent an enormous amount of effort getting the smell of a perfume right, and has selected their ingredients in an effort to manipulate the smell—while ignoring their taste. The perfumer has relied on the existence of a social practice with certain contours: on the understanding of the audience that they are to smell, and not taste the perfume. The material substrate of perfume is a liquid; but the *perfume* is that liquid approached in a certain way—by smelling it. If I pour that liquid over my steak and consume it, I have not experienced the *perfume*. To retrieve the artist's intended object from the material, we must follow the prescriptions.

The author sets what's in the frame. When I declare something to be a novel, I am telling readers, when they are thinking about the novel, to ignore the physical arrangement of the words on the page. The line breaks aren't part of what matters; they aren't part of the thing I've crafted for your attention. If we reprint Alice Munro's short-story collection *Open Secrets* and change where the line breaks as it curls down the page, we have not changed the work at all, or its meaning. On the other hand, if I declare that my work is a "poetry collection," then I am prescribing that my readers attend to the line breaks as part of the work—as part of what matters.

Contrast this with what Saito calls "everyday aesthetics"—the aesthetics of ordinary life, and not the aesthetics of officially sanctioned art objects. For such things as beaches, our daily housework, the crowd at a baseball game, and the ambiance of a classroom, there is an "absence of an equivalent conventional agreement on medium or evidence of the artist's intention" (Saito 2010, 18–23). Non-art objects are frameless. We, the appreciators, frame the object for ourselves. We are free to decide what the object of our attention will be. Art objects, on the other hand, are framed; there are rules for encountering them.

Saito suggests that games are part of everyday aesthetics because we can attend to whatever we wish. In a baseball game, she says, we can decide to appreciate the crowd, the ambiance, and the weather, just as much as we can decide to appreciate the game itself. Perhaps this is true of baseball games—though I suspect that Saito is talking about the cultural event of a baseball game, rather than the game itself. But when we turn to other gaming practices, especially those that are more obviously authored, such as video games and board games, our social practice reveals that there are most certainly prescriptions for adequate encounters. These games are framed works. In such games, as with other framed works, we create prescriptions to stabilize certain aspects of our experience, so that we may communicate and share experiences—or, at least, so that we may bring each other into a substantially similar space of experience.

We can detect the existence of these frames—and their associated prescriptions—by thinking about how we might fail to meet them. Imagine, for example, writing a review of *Grand Theft Auto* based on how the programming code looks, or reviewing a board game having only imagined a story from the box art. Or, imagine that a player declares to their friends that the video game *Elder Scrolls: Oblivion* is a terrible game, after only having played around with the character generator, and then running their character in a circle in the opening location for twenty hours. What we want to say is: "You can't review that game based just on how the box looks; you haven't even played the game yet!" This reveals something about what we take the work to be. Of course, what the work is turns out to be relative to a social practice. But, again, that is exactly what this sort of ontological analysis reveals: what a particular artwork is, is a particular object of attention, specified through an entanglement of certain material with prescriptions for encountering that material, where those prescriptions are usually specified through some common social practice.

Are there really such prescriptions for encountering a game? Some have resisted the thought. Olli Taipo Leino, for example, argues that we ought not accept any norms restricting how we might play a game, or on our interpreting it. Leino argues that game scholars usually presume the *ludic imperative*": that in order to study a game, one has to play it in the spirit intended by the designer, adopting the goals of the game and trying to win by the rules of the game. But, says Leino, this normativity is problematic, for it is a form of intentional fallacy. It forces the audience to follow the author's intent. Players of games should be free to interact with a game as they please, just as readers are free to interpret a text in any way they wish (Leino 2012). But I do not think Leino's argument is right. Accepting the mere requirement that we must follow the rules of a game, in order to encounter it, does not commit the intentional fallacy. As Sherri Irvin points out, the intentional fallacy is no barrier to accepting a prescriptive ontology. Prescriptive ontology accounts do not claim that the author gets to set a work's meaning, its interpretation, or the terms by which it will be judged successful or unsuccessful. A prescriptive ontology says only that an author gets to set what the work *is*, by setting what counts as a minimally adequate encounter with the work.

Importantly, William Wimsatt and Monroe Beardsley's original argument against the intentional fallacy turned on the inaccessibility of the author's private intentions (Wimsatt and Beardsley 1946). Suppose we grant that the author's intentions about a work's meanings are too subtle to be publicly accessible. But the prescriptions that set out a work's ontology involve very simple rules, which are easily publicizable. In most cases, says Irvin, artists make declare these prescriptions by setting their works within familiar and publicly available social practices. Suppose I write a book. I would make one prescriptive declaration by selling it in bookstores ("You have to read the words in order") and another, very different declaration by exhibiting it behind glass in a museum ("You have to walk around and look at this thing"). Authors can also, says Irvin, declare novel sets of prescriptions simply by explicitly stating them, as many contemporary conceptual and performance artists do (Irvin 2005).

Note that these prescriptive frames leave plenty of room for other modes of encounters with a game's material substrate. Nothing forbids me from cutting up my copy of *Moby Dick* and putting the words into a new order. It only says that, in reading the re-ordered version of *Moby Dick*, I have read a different work. Similarly, consider the practice of speedrunning. Speedrunning is a relatively new gaming practice, where players change the goal of a game. When you speedrun *Super Mario Brothers*, the point is no longer to get the most points possible. It is, instead, to get to the end of the game in as little time as possible. Some styles of speedrunning involve taking advantage of glitches in the game and unintentional consequences of various programmed phenomena. Speedrunners relate to a game in an entirely different way than standard players do (Scully-Blaker 2014). When I say that *Super Mario World* is a framed work, and that one has to play the game by the specified goal to really experience it, I am not saying that speedrunning is bad or that you shouldn't do it. I'm only saying that speedrunning is an alternate mode of encounter with the physical materials of the game, and not an encounter with *Super Mario World*. You shouldn't judge or review *Super Mario World* just by speedrunning it. The speedrunning version is played with the same materials as *Super Mario World*, but it is a different game—just like Chess variants are different games from Chess, but played with the same pieces.

What we've learned is that there is a crucial distinction, in an artwork, between the *material basis* of the work and *the work itself*. Leino's view—that scholars of games ought not be bounded by any prescriptions—is right of the material basis. Art historians can study any aspect of a painting in doing historical work. They may inspect its back, smell its paint, x-ray its contents. But they are not interacting with the work itself, only its material basis. And the forensic analyst who has only examined the back of Van Gogh's *Irises* with a microscope, and has never seen the front of the canvas with their own eyes, has never encountered the work that is *Irises*—just as somebody who has only studied some blood cells extracted from my back has not met *me*.

Works and Stability

Why is it important that games are framed works? Why do we engage in the practice of setting prescriptions, and why do we think that it's important to follow them? We now have the beginnings of an answer. Such prescriptions help ground the structure and specificity of a work. They help guide the attention of many people along similar lines. They stabilize the experience, making it more shareable between people. They steady the lines of transmission between designer and the player, and between one appreciator and another. Prescriptions help us achieve communicative stability.

The delicate awareness of inner life in *The Remembrance of Things Past* depends on the particular ordering of the words. In order for there to be effective aesthetic communication, I must read the book in a particular order and hold to certain norms of what words mean. Similarly, the rules and goals of striving games are the means by which a game designer achieves experiential specificity. For example, the restriction on speaking in partnership Bridge helps to create the particular experience of deduction, information management and communication under adverse conditions. The restriction on looking at the other person's cards in Poker helps to create the particular experience of trying to deduce the other person's cards from their behavior. The goal of going right in *Super Mario Brothers* helps to create the activity of precision platforming.

In rock climbing, a climber must climb within specific restrictions. In free climbing—what most rock climbers practice—you cannot ascend by pulling or standing on your gear. The rope, the clips—these are all only there to catch you if you fall. They should not be used for ascent. This rule strikes many novices as restrictive. Why aren't they allowed to pull on the gear? But this rule is responsible for much of the incredible variety of rock climbing. If you could ascend by pulling on your gear, most climbs would involve a very similar range of movements. The rule that forbids pulling on the gear forces you to adapt yourself to the vast varieties of rock. It frames the activity of puzzling out new sequences, in response to each rock face's particular and unique features, rather than the activity of pulling down over and over again on the same pieces of gear.

The importance of restrictions in climbing is especially clear in artificial rock climbing gyms, where many routes overlap each other. Usually, each route is marked off with a particular color, in tape or in the hold itself. To count as having climbed a route, a climber may use only the designated holds. Novices will sometimes complain about all these rules and proceed to use all the holds on the wall. They are certainly engaging in free play. But if they never climb according to those rules, then they will never experience that particular experience of difficult motion that has been sculpted by the route setter. They are failing to experience the work, just as surely as somebody who reads all the words of *Moby Dick* in a random order doesn't experience the novel. The fact that a route setter can rely on a climber to follow the rules enables that route setter to sculpt particular movements and particular epiphanies of motion through an arrangement of physical holds.

Communication involves shared norms. The more I reject shared norms, the more freely I can play, but the less I can receive communication. And the more I wish to communicate, the more I must bind myself, for the moment, to a set of shared norms.[2]

A prescriptive frame focuses the viewer's attention. In painting, the prescriptive frame is partially delineated by the actual physical frame, but much of the aesthetic frame is simply a part of a conventional social practice. I ignore everything visually that is outside the physical frame, but I also ignore the smell and taste of the paint and the sounds of the passers-by. This prescribed focus brings me into contact with a particular delineated object of attention.

The rules of a game also function as a frame, focusing the attention of the reader on a delineated object of attention. They focus us on a delineated activity. *Spyfall*, for example, is a frame hung around the activity of bullshit creation and bullshit detection. *Sign* is a framed experience of inventing the means of communication. *Super Hexagon* is a frame hung around semi-defocused reflex challenges. The social practice of framing, as executed through traditional artworks, is a structured technique for calling somebody's attention to a particular set of features. And since these frames are usually embedded within common social practices, they enable us to share experiences, or at least to come close.

---

[2] My discussion here is influenced by Gary Iseminger's analysis of aesthetic communication (Iseminger 2004, 31–61).

With games, a game designer can use the medium of agency to get the player to perform a particular activity and attend to it. Just as a painter is framing a particular visual experience, isolating it and drawing attention to it, the game designer is framing a particular kind of practical activity by instructing the player to approach a particular practical environment from a particular motivational angle. Games are frames hung around aspects of the player's own activity. In short: games are framed agency.

Here it will be useful to make an attempt at a sketch of what the actual prescriptions for aesthetic striving games are. *Spyfall*, *Sign*, and *Super Hexagon* all are part of closely related social practices, that all follow the same fundamental prescriptions for engagement. Let me suggest, as a first pass, that the social practices that surround the appreciation and criticism of such games involve the following prescription:

General Prescription for Aesthetic Striving Games: The appreciator will play the game, following the indicated rules and aiming at the indicated goal, and then appreciate the resulting activity.

This might seem like a rather loose directive for directing the attention of the player. But notice that, because of the special nature of games, that general prescription typically leads to very predictable and specific channels of attention. The specified goal strongly conditions the nature of the player's practical attention in the inner layer. The rock climber must attend to tiny ripples in the rock, to their own balance, to the exact trajectory and intensity of their motion. The *Spyfall* player must attend to informational and social cues, to signs of deceit, to informational slip-ups.

But what of aesthetic attention? In my simple formulation of the General Prescription, there is only the simple prescription that players attend to their own activities. There are no further directions about where players should direct their attention, nor do most games explicitly instruct players where to attend via rules. But the nature of the practical activity can *call* players' attention to where the action is the thickest, and the exercises of agency most interesting and memorable.

Consider, by way of an analogy, Jane Austen's novels. The general prescriptive frame for novels tells us what counts as a minimally adequate encounter with the novel. The reader is supposed to read the words in order and imagine the world described. Nothing in that prescriptive frame tells readers to direct their attention to the social commentary or to the psychology of the characters. But the fact that so much of the content of those novels concerns matters of society and psychology naturally draws readers' attention to those topics. The prescriptive frame directs the attention enough to enable the basic transmission of some content, and then the nature of that content itself suggests or draws readers' attention in certain directions. The prescriptive frame of novels is only a brute way of directing readers' attention in a particular direction; once the attention has been brought to bear on the common object, then the artists can bring to bear all the techniques of their art to draw the attention in various ways.

The same is true with games. The General Prescription only tells each of the players to follow the rules, to try to hit the goal, and then to attend to their own activity. But the nature of the activity, as generated by the game's design, calls the players' attention in certain directions. Climbers will pay aesthetic attention, in reflection, to the details of their own movements and how those movements got them past challenges. They will likely pay much less to the taste in their mouth or the smell of their sweat. Chess players' aesthetic attention will be drawn to the aesthetic qualities of their tactical solutions and calculations—and relatively less to how they are sitting, or the color of the Chess pieces. When reflecting on one's own activity *as activity*, one's attention is naturally drawn to where that activity is the thickest—to the regions where one's agency was most active. The self-reflecting agent's gaze should naturally be drawn to the *agential center of gravity*.

And this is the toolset for the game designer to direct the player's aesthetic attention and to foreground certain aesthetic qualities. The game designer designates rules and goals, and designs the practical environment. That package—the game—is entered into a social practice, where it falls under the General Prescription that I've described. The player, following that prescription, is lead to follow the rules and chase the designated goal. The combination of abilities and obstacles pushes the player to concentrate on a particular part of their agency: on their capacity for tactical reasoning, or their reflexes, or their social-manipulation capacities. In aesthetic reflection, the General Prescription simply tells the player to attend to their own activity. But the densities of agency that have occurred—that have been *designed* to occur— draw the player's aesthetic gaze toward certain aspects of their activity, in predictable ways. And this is one of the ways that game designers can shape the character of the player's aesthetic experiences of agency, even if designers must relinquish complete control over every detail of that experience's precise content.

Three Kinds of Game Prescriptions

Perhaps it will help us to digest all this theory if we apply it to some actual games. So let's consider the particular nature of the prescriptions we encounter in games, and spend a little time looking at their variety. All aesthetic striving games, I suggest, have the same prescriptive foundation. But there are, I think, some significantly different types of gaming practices within that broader category, each with a slightly different prescriptive frame.

I suggest that there are at least three distinct types of games, with slightly different prescriptions. Let's call them *party games, heavy strategy games*, and *community evolution games*. All share the General Prescription. But each adds subtly different further prescriptions as to how many times one must play, and in what spirit, to count as having adequately encountered the game.

First, consider two party games: the supposedly funny tabletop game *Cards Against Humanity*, and the video game *B.U.T.T.O.N.* In *Cards Against Humanity*, players answer questions or finish incomplete phrases by selecting from their hand of cards, each with some intentionally absurd, ridiculous, or supposedly offensive phrase. For example: to the prompt "If you detect it early, you can stop ____," different players might respond with such cards as "A sneezing fetish," "Old people smell," "Vigorous jazz hands," or "Totally fuckable aliens."[3] *B.U.T.T.O.N.* (a.k.a. *Brutally Unfair Tactics Totally OK Now*) is a multiplayer Xbox 360 game in which players are surprised with any variety of mini-games. For example: the game will first order all players to put their controllers down and take five paces back. After a brief countdown, the game will abruptly provide a randomly selected mini-game: such as telling the players that when the X button on their controller is pressed by anybody or anything, they will lose. Sprinting, wrestling, and occasional fisticuffs typically follow.

Party gaming, I propose, is a practice in which the long-term development of skill is unimportant or actively discouraged. (Imagine if you found out

---

[3] These are actual examples from the game. *Cards Against Humanity* is, in my view, a truly abysmal game. Far better uses of the same basic mechanic can be found in *Dixit, Why Did the Chicken . . . ?* and *Funemployment*.

that I had scoured the online forums for charades tips and strategies, studied YouTube videos to watch effective charades players, and carefully practiced those techniques to be sure that I won at the next charades event.) In fact, in both games, the system for deciding the victor is obviously and patently arbitrary. In Cards Against Humanity, one player each round is the judge and selects which of the other player's responses strikes them as funniest. As for *B.U.T.T.O.N.*, here's the co-designer, describing the inspiration he took from an earlier party game, *WarioWare: Smooth Moves.*

> *Smooth Moves* features a collection of zany "micro-games" that only last a couple of seconds. In each micro-game, one player uses their wiimote to adopt a silly pose, such as "The Elephant" or "The Samurai." From that pose, the player attempts to complete a simple little task, such as tracing a shape or slicing a virtual piece of wood. None of these micro-games would work very well individually. Rather, they work together in series, synergistically. Because *Smooth Moves* fires off these micro-games at such a manic pace, it is difficult to get too emotionally invested in any one challenge. The focus is shifted away from the game-delineated reward system of winning and losing, towards the human beings performing and willfully making fools of themselves. (Wilson 2011)

Notice the lack of any discussion of elements of skill development, decision trees, or possibility spaces. There is no reason to think the practice of party gaming involves a prescription for repeat encounters, or for skill development. The design, in fact, foregrounds arbitrariness, skill-lessness, and intentional chaos.

Incidentally, while it may be tempting to merge the category of party games with the category of stupid games, they're actually quite distinct. Party games are those games for which skill-less encounters are prescribed; stupid games are those games which you must try to win to play properly, but where the best part is failure. Though many party games are also stupid games, many are not. The game *Cards Against Humanity* is built for low-skill play. The goal of the game is to assemble, from the provided cards, a really funny joke. You get points when the referee thinks the joke is funny. And, for most players, the game is satisfying when they have successfully assembled a really funny joke. Thus, success, and not failure, is the cherished state. So *Cards Against Humanity* is a party game, but not a stupid game.

On the flip side, there's the ridiculous and ironic game of finger jousting, which involves clasping hands, extending a forefinger, and, while staying clasped, attempting to be the first to touch the opponent's body with one's forefinger.[4] It is a stupid game—the times I've most enjoyed it involved moments when I was sent head over heels and stabbed by my opponent while I passed above her shoulder. But the game actually becomes funnier and better as the players acquire some skill at the various ridiculous awkward-wrestling stratagems, and groups of players who regularly play with each other seem to get more out of it. In fact, an awareness of the decision space and an attempt to anticipate which clever maneuver one's opponent is about to pull off, heightens the hilarity. Actually acquiring skill just makes the failures more elaborate, and thus more hilarious—but it is still failure which is cherished. So finger-jousting is a stupid game, but not a party game.

Compare party games to *heavy strategy games*. First, consider the board game, *1830: Railways & Robber Barons*, created by Francis Tresham. (Tresham also designed the board game *Civilization*, precursor to the *Civilization* computer games, thus introducing the idea of technology trees into board gaming and video gaming (Woods 2012, 40). *1830* is an extraordinarily complex game; it is almost two separate games merged into one. Half of the game is about stock manipulation. Players buy and trade stock in train companies and thereby manipulate the prices of the stock market. The other half of the game is about managing those companies: laying track, designing efficient routes, improving one's train technology. Much of the complexity of the game evolves from the relationship between these two halves, as the stock valuations of the companies change and shift with the companies' operations. A player can build a train company with a hidden flaw, trick others into investing into it, and then loot the company and dump its broken remains on another shareholder. And predicting which companies will flourish depends on predicting which other players intend to manage their companies well, or which intend to loot and dump their companies for profit.

1830 is full of features that make no sense on a first playing. First, some features don't make sense until players are skilled enough to make intelligent

---

[4] More details can be found at the fairly comedic www.fingerjoust.com, which purports to be the home of the World Finger Jousting Federation. Almost everything I say here also applies to the stupid game of hat jousting, in which two people attempt to be the first to knock off their opponent's hat.

use them, which can take many playings. For example: when a particular company's stock price declines sufficiently, its stock becomes junk stock and can be traded in greater volume. This rule only makes sense once players understand the mechanics of stock-market manipulation enough to intentionally bring about and take advantage of a junk rating. Second, there are early decisions in the game that, on a first playing, simply cannot be made intelligently. For example, when players start a company, they must set its *par value*—its price per stock. Players set par values on many of their companies in the very first round of the game, but the implications of that decision will not be apparent until players fully understand how the various subsystems of the game interact—which cannot happen until after at least one, and probably many more, playings.

Next, consider the computer game *Dream Quest,* part of a family of games called *rogue-likes*. The key features of rogue-likes are that each playing involves a new procedurally generated environment to explore; and that character death is permanent. Thus a given playing is your only chance to defeat a particular dungeon layout. *Dream Quest* adds to this a deck-building element: you fight monsters using a deck, and you build that deck piece by piece, picking up new cards one at a time as you explore the dungeon. *Dream Quest* is fiendishly difficult, requiring hundreds of plays to even get past the first level.[5] When starting a particular play-through of *Dream Quest,* the game immediately presents the player with choices whose consequences cannot be properly evaluated until after the player has gained considerable experience with the game. Many of the early card powers have synergies and possibilities that can only be understood after the player has seen how they will interact with later-stage card powers. In many cases, some early cards that seem strong turn out to be problematic because are incompatible with many other cards and force you to build your deck in one particular way. Other early cards, which might have seemed weak at first, turn out to be compatible with a greater variety of deck builds, and so allow for more flexible deck development. These are core features of the game, but they are invisible or incomprehensible on early playings. In heavy strategy games, core

---

[5] At least as it was originally released. Eventually, designer Peter Whalen relented to various requests and installed both an easier mode as the default, and an even easier "kitten" mode. The originally difficulty level has been relegated to a special difficulty setting called "velociraptor" mode. A small set of players of the original version view this update as something of a betrayal of the original version's gorgeously harsh purity. This set of players includes myself.

features of the work *only become visible and coherent after repeat playings, and after the acquisition of significant skill.*

The social practice of heavy strategy gaming is very different from that of party gaming. Players of heavy strategy games may study the games, devise new strategies, discuss strategies with others, and master the games through many playings. Games like *1830* and *Dream Quest* have design features which make sense only within that context. Irvin suggests that, in most cases, we can determine the relevant prescriptions by looking to the social practice, and we can determine the right social practice simply by looking at a work's context of display: whether the artist displays it in a museum, concert hall, or bookstore. But I think this can't be the whole story. Consider: novels and short story collections involve slightly different social practices, with different prescriptions. Novels are supposed to be read entirely in order. Short-story collections need to be read in order inside each short story, but the collection need not be read in order. But sometimes, I encounter novels, short-story collections, poetry, and essay collections all jumbled together on a bookshelf. I can figure out which social practice each one belongs to, however, and figure out something about what the prescriptions must be, by looking at clear and fundamental features of the work, and looking for the best explanation of those features. This book follows the same character over its entire course; events in one section cause events in a later section. The best explanation of these facts is that it is a novel and was written to be read in order.

There are publicly accessible features in *1830* and *Dream Quest* which make absolutely no sense in low-volume, unskilled play. The best explanation for their being there is that they are part of a practice that prescribes multiple playings. Some features of the work—relationships between the mechanisms—only come into view after multiple encounters, and after the acquisition of significant skill. These features, though unobvious to the new player, are, in fact, central. And we can tell they are central because they are the best explanation for evident design elements of the game. Thus, for a work of heavy strategy, *a player must play multiple times to adequately encounter the work.* This claim turns out to have a bit of a normative sting. Consider the many popular online reviewers of heavy strategy games, who typically review several new games a week and, as a consequence, only play each game a handful of times each. Our analysis suggests that these reviewers have never actually adequately encountered any of the games they review.

One might reasonably object that this demand for skill is a feature common to many other artistic practices. Charlotte Bronte's novel *Jane Eyre* and Hieronymous Bosch's painting *The Garden of Earthly Delights* are full of subtle details that reveal themselves on repeat viewings. But recall the distinction between a deep encounter and a minimally adequate encounter. Though multiple readings of *Jane Eyre* may reveal all sorts of nuances and foster a profound and subtle understanding, a single reading suffices for a minimally adequate encounter. Not so, for Chess, Go, Bridge, *1830*, and *Dream Quest*. The difference is that central features of *Jane Eyre* are visible on any competent single reading, but central features of Chess are not visible on a single playing. Consider: if we asked somebody who had read *Jane Eyre* for the first time and somebody who had read it for the thousandth time what the basic narrative features were, they would largely agree. The basic features are Jane Eyre, her poverty and helplessness, her relationship with Rochester, and Rochester's mad spouse. But if one were to ask the same questions of an experienced Go player—if one were to ask what the central features of their attention were—one would receive entirely different answers than from a novice. An experienced Go player constantly attends to features like *influence*—that is, the way a piece or structure on one side of the board radiates potential power in complex ways toward other areas of the board. In order to even begin thinking about influence, a Go player needs to have internalized enough of the basic mechanics of the game to be able to read certain basic sequences effortlessly (Kageyama 2007, 55–64, 87–109). It is, in fact, hard to even understand the concept of influence in your first few hundred games. I was warned by my first Go teacher to not even look at any of the texts on influence until I'd advanced through the first ten levels of the Go ranking system. But with skill, a player's basic experience of the game is transformed. Dor calls this effect *strategic perception*. Experienced players of both Chess and *Starcraft: Brood Wars* have different perceptual experiences of the game. A hardened Chess player, for example, looks at a rook and sees, not a particularly figured piece, but lines of movement and potential. In fact, says Dor, visual design decisions can help foster strategic perception—the shape of Chess pieces is consistent across most non-novelty sets, and *Starcraft* repeats visually identical tiles, which aids this transformation of perception (Dor 2014). For many games, key elements of the game only come into view through training and experience. Many such games are built for the player for whom strategic perception has become second nature.

When those skill-dependent elements are central to the work, then the work can only be adequately experienced by a skilled player.

Finally, let's consider what I'll call *community evolution* games. Key examples in this genre include *Magic: The Gathering, Android: Netrunner,* and *Hearthstone.* This is a relatively new practice in gaming. I will discuss *Android: Netrunner*, since it is the one I know best, but all the comments I make here are applicable to the whole class. *Android: Netrunner* is a customizable card game designed by Richard Garfield and Lukas Litzsinger. Before play, each player designs their own personal deck from a large pool of possible cards. Decks are usually designed around some particular strategy, so that the various card powers will interact in some exciting way. Some decks are fast and aggressive; others build to great power, but slowly. Some use brute force; others depend on deceit and misdirection. The possibility of different deck-types gives rise to an emergent, complicated form of second-guessing, like rock-paper-scissors with a doctoral degree. Serious players become deeply involved in what's called "the meta," or "metagaming"—what Marcus Carter and his colleagues describe as "a complex interplay between the game community and the game itself" (Carter, Gibbs, and Harrop 2012, 2–3). Serious play of these games involves a constant flow of information and strategic analysis through the community of players, usually via Internet sites and forums. Certain types of decks become known as particularly effective or powerful, and thus become popular. Players must design their decks to cope with the various deck-types they might encounter. And so the strategic space evolves as players respond to the deck-types currently in play, and then respond to those responses, and so on (Johansson 2009, 5–7). What's more, the pool of available cards constantly changes. Fantasy Flight Games releases a new set of cards every month; after two years, older card sets rotate out of official play. This creates a constantly changing, unstable meta. Most serious *Netrunner* players will tell you that the constant flux of the meta is the point; that the most interesting part of the game is when the new cards are released and all the players scramble to figure out how they change play (Smith 2015; Majewski 2014). And, in fact, the designers of *Netrunner* are constantly monitoring the meta, and creating new cards in response to the current state of the meta, to tweak it, to break emerging strategies that seem to dominant, and to keep things interesting (Browne 2017). For example, when the meta recently started to get stale, devolving into a small number of deck designs, designers introduced a new mechanic specifically to encourage a greater diversity of decks (Ventre 2016). There has been some debate about whether the metagame is part of the game or external to the game (Carter, Gibbs, and Harrop 2012, 2, 4). Our analysis offers an answer: insofar as major features of the game design are publicly declared as attempts to alter the metagame for the purposes of better play, and they are best explained in terms of their effect on the community's strategic discourse, then the metagame is surely part of the *work*.

Magic, Netrunner, Hearthstone, and their customizable kin are, it turns out, quite ontologically unique. What might their prescriptions be? Given the actuality of the practice and evident design features of the game, the prescriptions demand not only multiple playings, but they prescribe *participation in the larger community of players* for an adequate encounter with the work. Many central features of *Netrunner* can only be explained in virtue of their interaction with the community of players and the evolving meta. Most obviously, the constantly changing card pool—especially the way older cards drop out—only makes sense as an attempt to keep the meta interesting. And since this central feature of the game only makes sense in relationship to the meta, then being in contact with the meta—reading the forums, thinking about the currently popular decks, responding to them—is requisite for an adequate encounter with the work. Two players who purchase the game and play it at home may have a very nice experience, but they have not had an adequate encounter with the full game—just as I have not had a minimally adequate encounter with Proust's *Remembrance of Things Past*, even though I thoroughly enjoyed the first eighth of it that I have actually read. Central features of the game are incomprehensible, invisible, or dormant without the player's active participation in a gaming community.

Games are works, because they have prescriptive ontologies and because they are authored. They are like traditional artworks, in that they are often authored for the sake of bringing about aesthetic qualities, and something about the nature of those qualities is attributable to the intentional efforts of their creators. They are unlike traditional artworks, in that there is a gap between the stable artifact that the artist creates, and the object of appreciation. It is to this gap that I turn to next.

7

The Distance in the Game

Like traditional works, games have prescriptive frames. But games are also very distinctive from traditional works. They are works that prescribe the active, practically engaged participation of the audience. I discuss that difference in this chapter.

In games, the player takes a crucial role in constructing the object of the appreciation. In aesthetic striving games, players appreciate their own activity. The object of their appreciation, then, isn't entirely fixed by the artist, but is at least partially created by the players themselves. Game designers are interestingly distant from the aesthetic effects at which they aim. Their works leave a special sort of gap for the agent to occupy. I will call this gap *agential distance*. The goal of game designers is to shape a particular practical activity, but they must shape it through the active, and often creative, agency of the player. The designers of *Spyfall* have created a game that is reliably funny and surprising, and that regularly spews forth moments of insight, cleverness, and creativity from the players. But those moments arise from the highly variable actions, choices, and participations of the various players.

This might start to seem like something of a miracle. The game designer needs to reach through the active participation of the player and create relatively reliable aesthetic effects, even when the players are substantially freely exercising their agency. Game designers, however, turn out to have a special tool to bridge that gap. In games, the designer has significant control of the nature of the participating agent. In other words, game designers use the medium of agency to overcome agential distance.

I have claimed that games are the art of agency. I can now break this slogan down into several different components. First, game designers achieve aesthetic effects of agency. Second, they do so by accommodating the agency of the player, which creates agential distance between designer and effect. Third, the designer overcomes that distance by using the medium of agency: by sculpting the player's agency, as it will occur in the game. To put it all together: games are the art of agency because games use agential manipulation to create aesthetic experiences of agency across an agential distance.

Games. C. Thi Nguyen, Oxford University Press (2020). © Oxford University Press.
DOI: 10.1093/oso/9780190052089.001.0001

The Self-Reflective Arts of Agency

Aesthetic experiences of agency, as I've described them, are essentially re-flective. They are not experiences of the game as a designed object. Rather, the player appreciate the aesthetic qualities of their own activity. This seems utterly distinctive from traditional artworks. Most traditional artworks are *object-centered*. When we make aesthetic judgments in response to them, those judgments are ascriptions of aesthetic properties and qualities to the object itself. It is the novel itself that is clever or thrilling; it is the painting it-self that is graceful or dramatic. Games, I'm suggesting, are *process-centered*. When I make aesthetic judgments in response to a game, I am ascribing aes-thetic properties and qualities to my own processes—to the actions and ac-tivities that I perform in response to the game.

Let me take a moment to sketch a larger picture. I think that there are two broad categories of intentionally created aesthetic artifacts. One type consists of the *object arts*, which are made for the sake of the aesthetic qualities that lie in the artifact itself. The other type consists of the *process arts*, which are made to call forth an activity in an audience, for the sake of the audience's ap-preciation of the aesthetic qualities of their own activity. The object arts are well-theorized. The process arts, on the other hand, are everywhere, but they are undertheorized and undervalued, especially by the art world establish-ment. I think the process arts likely include social dances, including group tango and square dancing; social eating rituals, such as fondues and hot pots; cooking; and perhaps urban planning. Note that these activities are usually not considered part of the fine arts. They are, at best, usually considered lim-inal candidates for art status.[1]

Often, there are aspects of both object art and process art entangled within an artwork or an art form. But, even then, we tend to emphasize their object-art aspects. Take, for example, cooking. Cooking has both object-art and process-art aspects. Cooking is an object art, in that it produces a finished product—a dish—which has aesthetic qualities. But cooking is also a process art. The process of cooking itself is full of aesthetic qualities—the gorgeous smells drifting up from your frying pan and delightful sizzles and pops. Cooking is also full of the aesthetics of agency—of movement, decision, and action. And these interact in complicated ways, for example, the savory

---

[1] There are some theories of aesthetic that think that all appreciation is centered on the activity of the audience—see, for example, Collingwood (1938). I will not address those theories here; my target in this chapter is accounts that might serve to elevate objects arts over process arts.

process of smelling the browning onions, then waiting for them to smell just right before adding the wine. Crucially, cookbooks contain directions that inform both the process of making a dish, and the finished product that is the dish. They involve process-art and object-art qualities. But reviewers usually fixate on the quality of the dish and rarely comment on the fun, gracefulness, or pleasurableness of the cooking process—even though that process is part of the cookbook's content. Reviewers typically neglect the process-art aspects, and dwell on the object-art aspects.

Obviously, games are a kind of process art. I think the process arts are extremely important to think about. They occupy a central part in our daily lives, and deserve far more respect and investigation than they have, as yet, been given. I plan to explore the broader category of the process arts in future work. Here, I will take the first step toward that larger picture by focusing on how games work as a process art.

Games are a very distinctive form of artwork, which will force us to rethink some of our foundational concepts about artworks. They expose that there are two crucially different aspects of an artwork that we usually blur together. First, the artwork is the thing that the artist makes; and second, the artwork it is the thing that we perceive and appreciate. But these concepts are separable, and we should be careful to distinguish between them. First, there is the *stable artifact created by the artist*. Let's call this the *artist's work*. Second, there is the *prescribed object of attention for the audience*. Let's call this the *attentive focus*.[2] In most traditional forms of art, the artist's work and the attentive focus are one and the same, or they overlap very closely. For painting in the tradition of European art, the artist puts paint on canvas; the audience is prescribed to look at that painting from a particular angle and pay attention to its visual features. The audience ascribes aesthetic qualities to stable features of the artist's work—the form, the brushstrokes, the color. In dance, the dancers create a performance, which is the stable artifact that all the different members of the audience can appreciate. The dance performance is both the artist's work and the attentive focus.

---

[2] One might see certain similarities between my notion of an attentive object and Davies's notion of a "focus of attention." But the two are importantly different. Davies does distinguish between the material object associated with an artwork, and the prescribed focus of attention. (He's trying to show that various historical factors and various features of the artist's working method are part of the focus of attention). But the focus of attention is, for Davies, a collection of viewer-independent features. Davies distinguishes between the generative act of the artist and the receptive act of the audience, and restricts the focus of attention to features created through the generative act of the artist. The presumption that the prescribed focus of attention is limited to features generated by the artist would preclude the participatory ontology I'm offering (Davies 2004, 26–27, 50–79).

But it's very different with aesthetic striving games—those games created for the sake of the aesthetic experiences of pursuing the in-game goal. Let's return to the General Prescription for aesthetic striving games: that players are prescribed to play the game, following the rules and pursuing the indicated goal, and then to appreciate their activity of pursuit. The General Prescription means that, in aesthetic striving games, the artist's work and the attentive focus come apart. The artist's work is the game proper: the rules, the pieces, the software, the environment. But the attentive focus is the players' experience of their own activity. An aesthetic striving game is successful, not when the game itself is aesthetically good, but when it inspires and shapes aesthetically valuable striving in the player.

Notice, crucially, the difference between dance performances and aesthetic striving games. At a dance performance, the audience members all look outward—they all appreciate the same thing, which is the publicly perceivable dance performance. In an aesthetic striving game, the players each appreciate something different—their own particular activity of play. My run through *Super Mario Brothers* is different from yours. Of course, one can also attend to the artist's work in a game. Players do, in fact, sometimes attend to aesthetic features in the game itself when they adopt the design stance. But this is, for aesthetic striving games, secondary. For the most common gaming practice, I take the primary prescribed focus to be the player's own activity.

Contrast my account of aesthetic striving games with Lopes's account of the interactive ontology of computer art. Computer art, by Lopes's definition, is an artwork that is interactive, and interactive because it is run on a computer. Lopes defines interactivity thus: "[A] work of art is interactive just in case it prescribes that the actions of its users help generate its display" (Lopes 2010, 36). Since computer art is essentially interactive, the audience of a computer art work can only adequately experience the work by exploring its interactivity. This requires multiple encounters with the artwork, so that the user can try different actions and see how the artwork generates new displays in response. Only then can the user start to get a picture of the way the artwork responds to different kinds of interactions (60). Thus, the ontology of interactive art yields a clear prescription: one must have multiple encounters with the work in order to adequately experience it.

But it is a mistake, says Lopes, to think that the user actually generates the artwork or participates in its creation. We must get clear on what the work is, exactly. For Lopes, the work isn't a particular sequence on the displays. Rather, the work is the stable underlying *algorithm* which controls those displays. The user, it turns out, has no role in creating the work itself. The user merely interacts with the work and generates displays *in order* to grasp the algorithm and thereby appreciate the stable underlying artifact.

Despite the variability of user experiences, Lopesian computer art turns out to be, ontologically speaking, much like more traditional forms of art. In computer art, users are supposed to attend to the artist's work and not to their own activity. Their activity is merely the method by which they come to grasp the algorithm. A user's interaction with a work of computer art is something akin to, say, an appreciator's walking around a statue. It is an activity in which the user must engage, in order to see the whole of the artwork. It is not an activity whereby the user constructs a new object of aesthetic attention.

Lopes claims that if computer games are an art form, they will be a type of computer art. And Lopes's account does seem a good fit for some very particular sorts of computer games. Imagine a narrative computer game in which there aren't any significant challenges in the game, but only a virtual space to be navigated and narrative choices to make. The game, let's say, is a meditation on free will. When players explore all their narrative options, they will discover that, no matter what choices they make, the ending turns out the same. The algorithmic structure and its implied possibility space seem to say that free choice is only an illusion. Suppose, also, that the game is short and that the narrative branches are obvious. The point of the game seems clear: the game player should explore all the narrative options and then reflect on the interactive narrative structure as a whole.[3] This kind of structure seems to indicate that players ought to attend to the underlying algorithm, rather than to their own activity of striving.

But many other games seem to indicate a different form of attention. Consider sports. In order to count as having experienced a sport, players don't need to reflect on the design of the game; they just have to play it. And there are many computer games that seem to have more in common, appreciatively, with sports than with computer art. The appreciative talk that surrounds, say, a multiplayer shooter like *Team Fortress* indicates that the practice of appreciation there is much more like that of sports than it is of computer art. *Team Fortress* players don't have to reflect on the relationship

---

[3] This imagined game is loosely based on aspects of the games *The Stanley Parable* and *Photopia*, simplified for the sake of discussion. For an extended discussion of *The Stanley Parable* as a narrative structure that a player is supposed to reflect on as a whole, see Zhu (2018).

between algorithm, input, and output in order to have encountered the art-work. They only need to play the thing.

Consider, too, the importance of multiple playings. For Lopes, in order to adequately experience a work and explore its possibility space, a user must have multiple encounters with it. But suppose I am playing a puzzle game like *Zen Bound*—a computer game consisting of a series puzzles to be solved one after the other, with no branching story or virtual space to explore. Suppose I take a look at each puzzle, think very hard, and solve it on the first attempt. When I have solved all the puzzles, I take myself to have properly experienced the game. If this were a piece of interactive computer art, I should play the game again and explore different outcomes; I need to experience the "you have failed" screens, and so on. Only with more playings and more explora-tion will I count as having experienced the work. But with a puzzle game, it's quite the opposite. The truest experience of that game is the very first time it is played, when the puzzles are new and unsolved. Once they are solved, re-peat plays are only shadows of the first time.

Other sorts of video games offer no interactively explorable possibility spaces, but only precision reflex challenges. They place the same challenges before us every time. If we fail, the game simply ends. Some rhythm games, for example—such as *Guitar Hero* or *Dance Dance Revolution*—don't signif-icantly respond to inputs by changing their displays.[4] They only rate players on their successful ability to hit the right spots at the right time in response to input. The social practice of playing such games, again, does not seem to require an exploration of the possibility space, because there is virtually no possibility space to explore. They are built, instead, to issue an evaluation of our skilled activity. For these sorts of games, the algorithm and possibility space cannot be the prescribed object of aesthetic attention.

A Taxonomy of Participatory Arts

It will help to situate games among some other, related arts. Aesthetic striving games are a kind of participatory art; the audience needs to actively partici-pate in order to aesthetically appreciate the work in the prescribed way. But

---

[4] The two named examples, and most popular rhythm-based games, do in fact respond in minor ways to input—giving positive feedback during the game for successful play and adjusting the diffi-culty levels. But it is easy to imagine a game that does not and only rates the player at the end. This would still be a playable striving game, with no possible exploration of an interactive possibility space.

they are not the only kind of participatory art. Consider Rirtrik Tiravanija's artworks, which are part of the newly emerging avant-garde art practice called *relational aesthetics*. Relational aesthetics and other forms of social practice art explicitly make the audience part of the artwork. Tiravanija's artworks consisted of a makeshift kitchen, with plastic cutlery, paper plates, and various curries prepared by the artist. The audience, he declared, was part of the materials of the work. The main focus of the work, said Tiravanaja, was not the food, but the audience's very involvement with the food and the place. The food was simply a means for developing a certain sort of convivial relationship between artist and audience (Bishop 2004, 55–56).

Let me propose a taxonomy, which helps us make games' relationship to other participatory arts clear, and also their unique place within that landscape. A work is *participatory art* whenever the user is prescribed to substantially participate in order to experience the work. At the very least, the user has to engage in some kind of activity—they make a choice, or take some action—as part of their appreciation. Aesthetic striving games, Tiravanija's food-making works, and Lopesian computer art are all examples of participatory art. They all require that the audience act, choose, or otherwise interact with the work in order to encounter it. There are, I suspect, a great many forms of participatory art. For example, electronic dance music concerts and social tango *milongas* both seem to be participatory arts. In order to have a minimum adequate encounter, one needs to dance to the music.

There are two types of participatory arts: *generative* and *nongenerative*. In the nongenerative participatory arts, the attentive focus is some object that exists prior to, and independently of, the user's participation. Users participate as part of how they attend to and appreciate that independent object. Lopesian computer art is nongenerative. The attentive focus is the algorithm, which was not generated by a user's participation. The algorithm was generated ahead of time by the artist. Participation, here, is merely a way of *exploring* the attentive object. I suspect that some sorts of rock concerts may also be nongenerative participatory art. You need to dance to appreciate the music, but you're dancing in order to appreciate something outside of you: the music.

In the generative participatory arts, on the other hand, the user actually generates the attentive focus through their participation. An aesthetic striving game is such a generative art. In play, the player creates that which they are prescribed to attend to: their own activity of struggling to reach the goal. Tiravanija's food-making works are also generative arts. Tiravanija wanted the participants to pay attention to each other and the social atmosphere they were collectively generating. For his work, the attentive focus is the very act of socializing, as enacted by his audience.

There are, furthermore, two kinds of generative arts: the manufacturing generative arts and the process generative arts. In the manufacturing arts, the user creates, through their participation, a distinct artifact, which they will then appreciate. In the process arts, the user appreciates their own activity of participation. Compare a game to a smoked salmon bagel platter. The platter comes as a tray of carefully arranged smoked salmon, some fresh bagels, a dish of cream cheese, a pile of artfully arranged red onion slices and capers. The intent, of course, is that the eater will assemble their own bagel precisely to their taste. The lox platter is a generative art, because the intended object of appreciation—the assembled bagel—is created through the actions of the appreciator themselves. But it is a manufacturing generative art rather than a process one, because the eater is supposed to pay attention to the bagel they have made rather than to their process of creating it. The object of appreciation is something the eater has made, but it is external to and independent of the eater (at least, for the moment).

An aesthetic striving game, on the other hand, is a process generative art. Consider the game *Jenga*, in which players carefully rearrange a tower of blocks to make it taller and taller (and progressively shakier). The object of aesthetic attention is not the tower they are building, but their own desperate efforts in building it. The process arts involve essentially self-reflective modes of appreciation.

Finally, some process generative arts focus specifically on activities of practical agency. There, an audience member is prescribed to actively pursue some goal, and then aesthetically attend to the pursuit of it. Aesthetic striving games are focused on the aesthetics of practical agency in a way that Tiravanija's works are not. In Tiravanija's work, one participates by doing as one will—chatting, relaxing, eating, or simply relaxing. Of course, a participant could invent some personal goals, but pursuing such a goal isn't a prerequisite for experiencing the work. But in aesthetic striving games, pursuit of a goal is prescribed for expressing the work.

So aesthetic striving games are an *agential process generative participatory art*—or an *agential art*, for short. To summarize, something is a work of agential art if:

1. An audience is prescribed to participate in order to appreciate the work.
2. That participation takes the form of generating the attentive object.
3. That attentive object includes features of the audience member's process of participation.
4. That prescribed process of participation includes the pursuit of a goal.

Note that I have made no particular use of the term "interactive" in these various definitions of participatory ontologies. While I think that all aesthetic striving games are agential works, I do not think they are all interactive. Following Lopes, a work is interactive when it generates varying displays in response to user input, like responding to a key-press by generating new graphics. But many striving games are not interactive. Here are some examples: logic puzzles; the Where's Waldo series of game books and other hidden picture puzzles; and, arguably, rock climbs and crossword puzzles. These are static objects and do not generate new displays in response to input. Often, the solution, once found, is obvious to the player. Certainly, in logic puzzles and in the Where's Waldo books, there is nothing mechanically sophisticated enough to generate differing displays. But I can engage in aesthetic striving play with such a puzzle; that is, I can aesthetically appreciate my experience of trying to solve it. Note that the physical object doesn't change or provide variable displays in response to input, and the inner experience of solving the puzzle is highly variable between players—it is generated by each player's own deductive efforts. Thus the attentive object can vary, even though the work itself isn't interactive.

Recalcitrance and the Medium of Agency

Let's think more directly about what it means that games work in the medium of agency. Richard Wollheim suggests that we can usefully think about an artistic medium in terms of its characteristic recalcitrance. Artistic media "present difficulties that can be dealt with only in the actual working with them" (Wollheim 1980, 42). The artist cannot overcome this recalcitrance by reasoning about the nature of the medium ahead of time. The artist must work with the medium and see what happens. Painters who work in oils must bury themselves in the slowness of oil; painters who work with watercolors must bury themselves in the fluid and unpredictable movement of water. And each medium has its own special form of recalcitrance.

The characteristic recalcitrance of a medium can be quite abstruse. Consider, for example, Katherine Thomson-Jones's analysis of digital cinema. There is, says Thomson-Jones, a characteristic recalcitrance to the digital medium, different from that of the medium of traditional film processes. With traditional film processes, the difficulties for the artist involve all the physical difficulties of getting the shot itself—getting the camera in the right place, finding the right objects and actors. But this form of recalcitrance seems to disappear in the digital medium. Digital filmmakers can simply create any location or object, manipulating the look of a shot at will. Does this mean that the achievement of the artist in the digital medium is less than it is in traditional film? No, says Thomson-Jones; it simply means that the recalcitrance of the digital medium is quite distinctive from that of traditional film. The recalcitrance of the digital medium is actually the overload of possibility itself. The traditional filmmaker struggles to get a difficult shot. The digital filmmaker struggles, instead, to decide on a particular shot from an overwhelming option space. When computers can easily generate and manipulate images and sounds, what the artist must cope with is limitless possibility itself (Thomson-Jones 2016).[5]

What, then, is the particular recalcitrance of the medium of agency? When we think about games as designed aesthetic artifacts, one feature leaps out. In aesthetic striving games, there is a considerable distance between the artist's work and the attentive focus. The artist creates the rules, goals, and environment, but the aesthetic striving player is primarily prescribed to appreciate, not the artist's work, but the player's own activity. The game designers must achieve their aesthetic effects through the agency of the player. The recalcitrance of the medium of agency is a kind of *distance*.

Notice, though, that other kinds of generative participatory arts involve a version of distance. Generative participatory arts are, again, where the audience participates in creating the attentive focus. So long as the player has genuine choices, and isn't being railroaded into a particular sequence of actions, then there must be some form of distance between artist's work and attentive focus. But agential works offer a very specific sort of distance. There, the artist must cope with the player's practical activity interposing

---

[5] Thomson-Jones brought these passages of Wollheim and the notion of recalcitrance to my attention, and my understanding of these notions draws from her discussion.

itself between the artist's work and the attentive object. Let's call this *agential distance*. Agential distance, I propose, is the characteristic recalcitrance of the medium of agency.

One might be tempted to say, instead, that the characteristic recalcitrance of the medium is the player's freedom—that is, that the designer has to cope with the player's freedom of choice. But I think this way of putting things isn't sufficiently broad to cope with the full variety of aesthetic striving games. Certainly, the recalcitrance of agential distance often involves player freedom. Many games are designed to allow a significant degree of freedom of choice, and even creative expression, on the part of the game player. But that is not the case for all games. For example, single-solution puzzle games and exact-timing reflex-challenge games do not significantly engage with a player's freedom of choice. Still, the practical agency of the agent is interposed significantly between the artist's work and the attentive object—this time in the form of skill, rather than free choice. (Notably, the experience of doing well in certain reflex-challenge games is sometimes the experience of oneself as a reacting mechanism, responding instinctively, rather than as a thoughtful, deliberating agent.)

So how does the maker of games cope with agential distance artistically? One way might be to surrender control altogether. An artist might create a situation, but abjure any control over the resulting player activity and experience. In so doing, the artist wouldn't be confronting the recalcitrance of agential distance, but avoiding it entirely. As we'll see in the next chapter, this seems to be the solution of many artists working in social art and relational aesthetics. But many game designers do, in fact, attempt to exert significant control over the nature of the game-playing experience. Game designers often design games to be difficult, intense, calming, funny, gleeful, wild, or chaotic. And game players often seek out a game specifically because it is reputed to provide such experiences. Each player's exact path—the particular contours of the activity—is often up to them. But, still, many such games seem to be able to reliably inflect players' activities with particular moods, textures, and aesthetic qualities, despite the enormous amount of player-driven variability.

What I mean here is rather mundane. Surely, the creators of *B.U.T.T.O.N.* set out to create an experience of manic hilarity and foolishness. And the fans of that game appreciate it precisely for how it tends to bring about such states. The designer of *1830* seems to have put many elements in place to create an experience of thrilling, brutal, calculative intensity and ferocity—the experience of being at each other's throats, looking for any advantage, desperately trying to manipulate others without their knowledge. All these qualities are cherished by the game's many fans. (A whole community has now arisen around building and enjoying variations on *1830*, with a distinctive and shared aesthetic. A common form of praise in those circles is that a particular game feels like a knife fight in a phone booth, but with spreadsheets.)

So how can game designers achieve any measure of control over the experiential qualities of the game, across the gap of agential distance? One method is to narrow the possible range of solutions from the player. Take, for example, the construction of rock-climbing problems. Certain climbs will be praised for having interesting movement or good flow. Climbers might say that a problem was really graceful, or intricate, or explosively thuggish. What this means is that the climbs require, from most climbers, a particular style of movement. One climb might involve tiny handholds and footholds, usable only when one's center of gravity is jammed right against the wall. This then enforces, for most climbers, a strict style of movement: slow, delicate, precise. And to achieve that movement, most climbers must maintain a certain mental state—careful and deliberate, but calm and free of gripping anxiety or excess tension.

So, here we have one kind of response to the recalcitrance of agential distance: making the solution very specific and singular, which will enforce at least some degree of uniformity of experience. Let's call this the *path of the puzzle*. Here, the game designer aims at allowing only a very narrow set of solutions. Note that the attentive object still won't be precisely the same across all players, even in a puzzle with an utterly singular solution. After all, the process of solving the puzzle will vary between players, and that process is the primary attentive object of an aesthetic striving game. But the narrowed range of possible solutions provides, at least, a common anchor to different players and playings. This path, I take it, was particularly common in an earlier age of computer gaming, one dominated by text adventure games such as *Zork*, point-and-click adventure games such as *Space Quest*, and puzzle-oriented games such as *Myst*. Even though players controlled their movement through a virtual environment, progress through such games is frequently impeded at a various choke points by single-solution puzzles.

But the path of the puzzle only accounts for some games—and is, notably, largely limited to nonoppositional games. The path of the puzzle won't work once players are actively playing against each other.[6] In most oppositional

---

[6] Note the possibility of nonoppositional but competitive games. Players trying to solve the same puzzle faster, or competing to solve the same rock climb in fewer attempts, are not in direct opposition. For more thorough discussion of the difference between competition and opposition, please see Nguyen (2018d).

games, the obstacles are generated on the fly by the players during game play. There are plenty of single-player games, too, that don't take the path of the puzzle, for example, any game where the player has to manage a simulated system or do combat with artificially intelligent enemies. In many such games, the exact nature of the obstacles emerges through interactive feedback loops between the game system and the player's choices. In such games, the basic features of each playing will vary widely. And this unpredictably is not simply incidental. For many of the most valued types of aesthetic striving experiences, it's important that the player make genuine choices—that a player genuinely *invent* a solution, or *choose* one from a rich set of distinctive possibilities, each with different downstream consequences. As game designer Sid Meier put it, players want to make interesting decisions with real consequences (Meier 2012). And in that case, the game designer must cope head-on with the recalcitrance of agential distance. Games designers must constantly keep in mind the option space for the players, what solutions they might come up with, and how early solutions might condition later solutions.

There is no single solution of how game designers can cope with the recalcitrance of agential distance. As Wollheim suggests, the solutions to any medium recalcitrance will be endlessly varied, and cannot be found by any form of abstruse reasonings. Artists find solutions by actually grappling with the medium they work in. Every successful game is its own solution to the recalcitrance of agential distance. But games, as works in the medium of agency, share a particular strategy. That strategy can be brought to light by thinking about other forms of design that must also cope with agential distance.

Kinds of Agential Distance

The game designer is trying to bridge a gap of agential distance in order to achieve some aesthetic effect. At the same time, for many games, it's important that the game player genuinely contribute—that the choices of players matter, and that they have some degree of creativity and make a genuine, consequential contribution. So the challenge looks something like this: the game designer must create the conditions of game play such that a player, in responding to them, responds in certain moderately predictable ways to generate a moderately predictable attentive object.

That agential distance is already vast for heavy strategy games. Not only must the agent take practical action in the game, they must embark on a long-term process of learning and skill development between games. And for many games, different players' skill development can take very different paths. This, of course, will vary depending on the game. A game like *Super Hexagon*, which depends on a very narrow set of pattern-recognition and reflex skills, seems to encourage a very similar skill set in many players. But a game like *1830* promotes a very broad range of skills and approaches. In my playing circle, one player approaches the game by focusing on building an efficient track layout and developing good companies; another player carefully does the math on each possible stock for sale and buys the optimal stock in each moment. I, on the other hand, am a mathematically and geometrically careless player. I play by considering the economic relationships between the other players and manipulating their stock holdings to induce conflicts among them.

Making room for many different practical approaches is often an explicit desideratum for game design.[7] The designers of *Magic: The Gathering* explicitly design for three different player profiles—which they call "Timmy," "Johnny," and "Spike." Game designer Mark Rosewater explains: Timmy wants to experience something; he wants a particular feeling from the game. Johnny wants to express something about himself—perhaps his originality in deck design, or his stubbornness in the face of the community. And Spike plays to prove something—either how innovative he is or how skillful (Rosewater [2002] 2013, 2006). The game designer here is trying to provide a variety of different types of experience, each tailored to a different player, and to somehow ensure that these experiences will reliably arise when these different player types meet each other, using differently designed decks, across newly emergent strategies.

And think of how particularly massive that distance is for community evolution games like *Magic: The Gathering*. Here, the game designer must design across nested layers of emergence. The players' actions emerge from choices and decisions they make during the game, as part of a complex feedback loop between their own choices and those of their opponents. What's more, the strategic space of a particular playing comes in part from the designed decks that each player has brought. And each player's design choices come in response to the strategies that are currently live in the community, where those strategies have emerged through another long-term process of feedback

---

[7] There's a vast amount of literature from the game-design side of the world on designing for different player types. One useful summary of such considerations, at least for European board games, is by Stewart (2011).

and interplay. How could game designers ever negotiate the chaos of such strategic emergence and exert any sort of control over the player's aesthetic experience?

But game designers do, in fact, cope with agential distance. Game-playing experiences have moderately reliable experiential characteristics, which are shared across many players, and which seem to be related to the intentional efforts of the game designer. *Half-Life* is pulse pounding; *Civilization* is absorbing and addictive; *WarioWare* is hysterically funny; *Candy Crush* destroys your sense of time and self. And it is particularly striking that such reliable characteristics can arise from multiplayer games, where the main oppositional feature is another agent. In fact, that reliability is so common that it is easy to overlook the extraordinariness of the game designer's achievement. *Super Mario Kart* is usually gleeful and ever so slightly nasty; *Diplomacy* tends to be thrilling, gut-wrenching, and alienating; *Spyfall* is usually amusingly labyrinthine. Each of these successes is a rather remarkable bridging of the agential distance.

I love the board game *The King Is Dead*, in which each player starts with an identical deck of eight different action cards. Each card represents a single different action a player can take. Over the course of the game, each player only gets to act eight times, each time permanently using up one of their cards. The map is small, the choice space is tiny, and every action waterfalls consequences. What's more, every used card is displayed face up, so you know exactly what options your opponent has left. The decision space is claustrophobic, the possibilities almost within one's mental grasp. The game is a nauseating, masochistic delight. I have a (perhaps sadistic) tendency to whip the game out and inflict it on people without preparation or description. The responses, afterward, are remarkably uniform. "It's like a cage match, but in slow motion, and the cage is too small," said one friend. "It's like we get to take turns sucker-punching each other," said another. "It felt like we were stabbing each other in the gut, until we got to the end, and then we were stabbing each other in the eyes," said another. "I almost puked. Twice," said my spouse, before demanding to play again immediately. (Interestingly, most people do seem to want to play again, but only after a stiff drink.)

But games aren't alone in negotiating agential distance. In many other places in human life, we set up rules and constraints for autonomous agents in order to bring about certain outcome. Here are some examples: landscape design, urban planning, and government. Traffic-flow patterns, for example, emerge from the behavior of vast numbers of people interacting while pursuing goals inside a set of designed rules and constraints—in this case, traffic rules, and the physical layout of roads. Those agents take action in response to their goals and desires running up against those rules and constraints— but also in response to the actions of other agents. Many of these actions provoke further responses, creating significant emergent complexity.[8] The game designer, the urban planner, and the architect face a similar sort of agential distance. They are all trying to shape the sorts of activities that arise from autonomous agents encountering the systems of designed constraints while engaged in the practical pursuit of some goal.

Here's a favorite example from the study of human interactions in architecture. Christopher Alexander's *A Pattern Language* is a set of guidelines for people to construct their own spaces—to design their own towns, office spaces, and homes (Alexander 1977). He offers advice about how to encourage a lively public space, such as a living room or a common room. The key, he says, is the relative spatial relationship of the private spaces, utility spaces, and public spaces. People always go to their private spaces—their offices or bedrooms, for example. They also need to go to utility spaces— the bathroom, kitchen, copy room. This creates a natural and inevitable flow of traffic between private spaces and utility spaces as people go about their daily activities. If you design a space so that the public spaces lie outside the natural flow of traffic, then the space will be dead. But if you put the public spaces between the private spaces and the utility spaces, then natural traffic patterns will create plenty of unplanned encounters, and the public space will come alive. For example, suppose we put a public lounging space between the people's offices, on the one side, and the kitchens and copiers, on the other. Then people will naturally run into each other when they're grabbing a cup of coffee or a snack or making copies.

But, says Alexander, this can also start to feel a little forced. People might resent the fact that they have to cross the public space every time they need to do some little practical task. Sometimes, they might be feeling shy, or they're absorbed in an interesting new idea and want to avoid others. The solution, says Alexander, is to offer an alternate difficult path from the private spaces to the utility spaces—but one that is sufficiently longer or more annoying that people will only use it when they actively wish for privacy. This gives people the option of avoiding the public space, but also encourages crossing through the public space as the default traffic flow. According to Alexander,

---

[8] I mean "emergent" in the casual and colloquial sense, and not the strong sense that is the subject of debate in philosophy of science, where emergent properties, to count as such, must have new causal powers.

the social topology of loops has better circulation than the social topology of lines. A loop can be engineered to subtly steer people toward interaction, yet leave people feeling unforced.

This is a case where a set of environmental features and restrictions creates an emergent social effect. And this is also the work of governance. Public policy, behavioral economics, user-interface design: all these fields study how rules interact with psychologically semipredictable agents to yield, hopefully, the desired range of emergent outcomes.

But it's important not to collapse some very important differences here. Urban design, governments, architecture, and traffic design are crucially different from games in several respects. For one, the agencies involved in the non-game examples are typically more varied. Different agents can be pursuing all sorts of different goals when they interact with buildings, cities, and governments. Still, cities, buildings, and governments share a clear similarity with games. In all such agential designs, the designers use various tools—rules, constraints, and, sometimes, incentives—to shape the activity that will emerge from the agency of users. So games are a part of an extremely well-established category of human artifacts. Games, it turns out, are the artistic kin of governments, architecture, and urban design—at least as much as they are the kin of fiction, rhetoric, and conceptual art.

But notice the significant difference between the degree of intrusiveness available to designers across these disciplines. Under some theories of liberal government, such a government should respect the autonomy of its citizens by leaving them to settle their own ends for themselves. This, John Rawls (2005) says, is the basic problem of political liberalism: how do we cope with a pluralistic society of individuals with widely varying values, conceptions of morality? A government may offer incentives, but offering an incentive to an individual is different from designing the agency of that individual. Incentives don't set citizens' ends; they ought only place instrumental leverage on citizens, as citizens pursue their own individual ends. And even if the designers of urban spaces, buildings, or governments are willing to attempt to alter the agency of their inhabitants, actually effecting those alterations would be quite difficult. People's full agencies are fairly recalcitrant, and it will take some doing for the designer of an urban space to have any significant impact on its users' goals.

But game design is distinctive. Game designers do not need to abide by those Rawlsian restrictions; nor are they limited by the sludgy recalcitrance of our full agencies. Agency, as it occurs in games, is quite malleable. The game designer creates both the practical environment and key skeletal details of the in-game agent. As part of that agential skeleton, the game designer specifies the player's in-game goals. In this way, the game designer plays a role closer to that of more traditional artists, and less like those of engineers and designers of buildings, cities, and governments.[9] A novelist may invent characters, situations, societies. Similarly, game designers have a vast degree of control over the agents that will occupy their created environments—far vaster than the designers of our public infrastructure have. Game designers can simply designate the goals and abilities. They can depend on their players to mold themselves to the specified agencies, though game designers, obviously, do not have complete control over the nature of player's agency. Many features of personality, motivation, and play style are outside their control. But as a matter of degree, game designers' control over the nature of agency is far greater. They can specify the basic motivation; they set the skeleton of the in-game agent.

Game designers can use their extraordinary control over both agency and the practical environment to create surprisingly fine-tuned effects. In other words, designers of governments, urban environments, and roads largely work in the medium of *constraints for agency*, where game designers work powerfully and directly in the medium of *agency itself*. In all of these areas, the designers must allow for the considerable intervention and active participation on the part of their end users. The agential medium is marked by the existence of a gap—a space for the participation of an autonomous agent. Game designers can, with considerable leeway, reach across that gap and shape, directly and forthrightly, the skeleton of the participating agent.

Android: Netrunner is a particularly telling example, because so much of its experiential character come from the very different agencies assigned to the two opposing players. In *Android: Netrunner*, one player takes the role of an enormous corporation; the other player takes the role of a sneaky hacker. The two roles have entirely different sets of abilities and goals. The corporation cannot attack the hacker directly; its goal is to execute a certain number of Agenda cards, which it must guard from the hacker using a variety of defenses and traps. The corporation executes its Agendas by placing them face down on the table, surrounding them with defensive structures, and slowly sending

---

[9] It may be that some illiberal governments also seek to determine and design the agential nature of their citizens through the deliberate exercise of control over education, media sources, etc., in which case, the design resources are even more like those of a game designer, though without games' morally excusing factor of voluntariness and disposability.

resources to those Agendas over the course of many turns. The hacker, on the other hand, wants to steal those Agendas. In the game, only the hacker can initiate an attack. And they can attack anywhere—they can try to raid the Agendas laid down on the table, or they can search through the corporation's draw pile, their discard pile, or their hand. No card is entirely safe from the hacker. But the corporation's defensive abilities are many, including the capacity to drain the hacker's bank account, destroy their equipment, or even brain-damage the hacker (which, in game terms, results in a permanently lowered maximum hand size). The corporation can win by either executing a sufficient number of Agendas or brain-damaging the hacker to death. Much of the hacker's job, then, is to figure out what kinds of defenses the corporation has and plot a way around them. But, crucially, this is a designed deck game, where players assemble their own particular decks from a wide pool of possible cards before the game. A corporation player can come in with a deck that is built to win by executing Agendas or a trap deck built to kill the hacker, or some flexible mixture of the two. And it is also a community-evolution game. The hacker player must have a deck capable of responding to any of those possibilities—and the corporation player must have a deck capable of responding to any of the hacker's possible strategies, all of which are built partially in response to the decks and strategies that are currently popular in the meta.

The experience of *Android: Netrunner* is concerned with the enormous range of possible strategies, of sussing out what the other players' intentions are. The corporation player is given an agency focused on bluffing, deceit, and misdirection. The hacker player is given an agency focused on carefully managing their resources to gather information. And the successes are both glorious and agentially specific. The corporation wins by being deceptive, by bluffing, by forcing the hacker to waste their resources attacking unimportant nothings. The hacker wins by reasoning, by deducing, and sometimes by gambling at just the right moment. Notice how the precise character of these two agencies, and how their interlocking relationship, arises from the particular distribution of agential interests and abilities, as set by the game designer. It is crucial that the corporation can't initiate an attack and can only lay plans and prepare defenses. It is crucial that the corporation plays its cards secretly, but that the hacker's cards are played openly. It is crucial that the corporation can certainly win if it is given enough time to execute its plans, and the hacker must go on the offensive. It is crucial that the corporation can kill the hacker, but not vice versa. For *Android: Netrunner*, it is the game designers' absolute control over the arrangement of the in-game agencies that gives them the ability to provide, with laser-like specificity, a particular experience of play—even through the fully creative agency of the player.

One of the primary tools for the game designer in bridging the recalcitrance of agential distance, then, is the design of the in-game agencies themselves. Game designers can't control all the choices and actions of the player. But they can create the option space from which the player chooses and the goals of the player, and so condition the types of actions and choices the player makes. The player has many decisions to make, freely, in *Android: Netrunner*, but the corporation player must always think in terms of defense and stealth and building defensive structures, because these are the tools the corporation player is provided. In *Spyfall*, there are many creative things a team player can say to root out the spy, and those things are truly the invention of the team players themselves. But the entire experience is given its basic shape by the agential design—by the specified goal of discovering the spy, and the narrowed toolset granted the team player to accomplish that task. Game designers doesn't necessarily fix what happens, but they sculpt the skeleton of the in-game agent, which profoundly shapes how players will act in the game. Creators of cities and governments have to cope with the agential distance, but they cannot avail themselves of the medium of agency. But game designers can. For the game designer, the agential medium both poses the recalcitrance, and offers a particular set of tools by which to attack that recalcitrance. This should be unsurprising; it is true of many other artistic mediums. The basic nature of the medium of watercolor—its speed, fluidity, and transparency—both gives us the basic difficulty and sets the basic approach for coping with that difficulty.

And occasionally, a key part of the experience of the game is a self-conscious experience of direct intrusive manipulation of agency itself. Consider the agential insanity of *B.U.T.T.O.N.* and *WarioWare*. Both these games get their laughs through the wild and blunt manipulations of agency. They are certainly a kind of comedy, but they achieve their comedic effects along a route unique to the medium of agency. Remember that both games consist of a rapid sequence of mini-games, played at high speed. Each mini-game has a very different goal—pressing a certain button, say, or swinging your controller faster. The experience of the game is actually one of wrenched and chaotic agency. You suddenly learn what you are supposed to be interested in; you have to jump in and snatch up that agency in an instant, and then, a moment later, throw it away and pick up a new agency.

These games, despite their lowly status as party games, are actually about the essential nature of striving play. They are experiences of fluid agency itself—so fluid as to be wild, chaotic, and hysterical. Their comic effects come, at least in part, from bringing to the foreground all the agential manipulation and fluidity inherent in game play and, by exposing the very arbitrariness of interest that makes such manipulation possible. These games are, we might suspect, comedies of agential fluidity, and are thus reflective on the nature of gaming practice. They bring our attention to the very process of game playing itself, and expose—with the particular sharpness of comedy— the agential fluidity underneath.

In fact, there seems to be some relationship between comedy and meta-reflection on the nature of a medium. Literature is full of such meta-comedies, such as Laurence Sterne's *The Life and Times of Tristam Shandy* and Italo Calvino's *If on a winter's night a traveler. WarioWare* and *B.U.T.T.O.N.*, I suggest, are their game analogues. They are comedies of medium self-awareness.

Aesthetic Responsibility

Let me briefly touch on one last, very large question raised by my account. In aesthetic striving games, players are prescribed to attend to aesthetic qualities in their own activity. This raises some very interesting, and very complex, questions about the nature of authorship and artistic responsibility. The game designer surely bears responsibility, and deserves the praise, for the artist's work. But what of the attentive object? How much artistic responsibility does the game designer have for the player's efforts?

I don't think there is any uniform answer we can give for all games. In some games, the exact nature of the attentive object may be somewhat or largely attributable to the player. In other games, we may largely credit the game designer. In others, the aesthetic qualities seem to emerge from something like a collaboration between the two. There is an enormous variety of possible arrangements for artistic responsibility—far wider than we might have found in the traditional object arts. To start to come to terms with that variety, let's narrow the question a little, and focus on the *intentional* creation of aesthetic qualities.[10] This surely won't capture the whole of aesthetic responsibility, but it's a decent instrument to start thinking through the issues at hand.

---

[10] This locution adapted from Bacharach and Tollefsen (2010) and Zangwill (2007).

To whom we might attribute the intentional creation of aesthetic qualities in the attentive focus? In some cases, it seems largely the responsibility of the players themselves. Take, for instance, an improvisational dance competition, where the rules are simple: the judges will select a piece of music, and the dancers will all improvise a dance to it. The aesthetic qualities of their activity—their grace, their expressiveness—are surely largely attributable to the dancers themselves. On the other hand, take a logic puzzle. A logic puzzle is a game, and can be played for the sake of the aesthetic experience of epiphany. Suppose that, for a particular logic puzzle, there is pretty much only one way to figure out the solution. We one might plausibly think that the exact contours of that aesthetic experience were largely set by the puzzle's creator, since the nature of the puzzle and its solution are so constrained.

Other cases are much more complex. Let's return to *Portal*. In *Portal*, the game designers have created a physics model, a unique set of physics-based puzzles, and an entirely original affordance with which to solve those puzzles—the wormhole gun. The wormhole gun lets the player shoot out portals, sticking them to most surfaces. Once two portals have been created, the player can enter one and instantly pops out the other. This allows the player to radically alter the topology of the game space—albeit in one very specific manner. Still, it opens up a fairly astounding number of possibilities. In one of the early puzzles, the player must get past a deep trench, one far too wide to jump over. One simple solution is to fire the wormhole gun straight down the trench, pasting one end of a wormhole to the floor of the trench, fifty feet below. Then, you paste the other end of the wormhole to the top of the wall behind you, facing the trench. Then you jump into the trench, gathering plenty of inertia as you fall, and fly into one end of the wormhole and come shooting out the other end—this time flying high over the trench.

The game designers seem to have created the game, in part, for the players' aesthetic experience of their own process of struggling and solving those puzzles. And there is plenty of wiggle room for the player to devise their own solutions. The game is based on three-dimensional movement through a simulated virtual reality, and the solutions depend on the physics-based manipulation of the environment and the avatar. Some of the solutions are only slightly different. A perfect wormhole placement might let the avatar float through the puzzle with ease, where a slightly sloppier wormhole placement might require a bit of split-second platform-jumping skills to get through. But players have also devised radically different portal placements that take them through the same puzzles, even inventing solutions that the designers never expected.

Suppose one of those new solutions is inventive and elegant. Who's aesthetically responsible for that elegance? First, the action is the player's own, so surely the player bears at least some responsibility. But its contours are, in many ways, dependent on the conditions created by the game. In one way, that dependence is quite straightforward. Much of our aesthetic experience in games is of our actions *as game actions*. I mean, for example, that when I elegantly pass a basketball between two opponents to my fellow team member, the elegance of that pass isn't just a matter of my motion, considered in isolation. It's elegant *as a basketball pass*. It is elegant as a solution to a set of difficulties and obstacles that have been constituted, in part, by the game's rules. So, in many cases, the aesthetic qualities are dependent on the particular design of the game. That basketball pass itself couldn't exist without basketball. What's more, in many cases, the exact nature of those aesthetic qualities is deeply entangled with the design of the game. The elegance of the basketball pass has a lot to do with how the rules of basketball create dense thickets of opponents and the constant need to scan for and make use of opportunities. Thus, the elegance of the basketball pass arises, in part, from the design features of the game and from how these features intentionally create obstacles with a certain character, in conjunction with their designation of the abilities to get past those obstacles. But that elegance also arises from the player's athleticism and skill—though much of that skill is grown specifically in the artificial context of the game.

One last step: in many cases, it is imaginable that a game designer creates the obstacles and the agency of a game in order to give rise to a particular aesthetic character in the player's activity. This seems very likely with *Portal*. The designers can't have imbued a particular player's action with the precise aesthetic quality it has. There is too much wiggle room—and the wiggle room is much of the point. The purpose of games like *Portal* is, I take it, to create opportunities for the players to be creative, to generate their own forms of elegance. But the designers may have done much of the work to make elegant solutions possible and likely, by creating background conditions that encourage a certain kind of elegance. And the intentionality here is curiously split. For the game player is intentionally solving the puzzle, but probably is not intentionally imbuing it with aesthetic quality in any way. When I play *Portal*, I'm not aiming at elegance at all. I am utterly absorbed in the practical challenges at hand. The fact that my solution turns out to be elegant is, from an intentional standpoint, merely a byproduct of my absorption in the instrumental struggle. To whom or what do we attribute that elegance? Well, partly to me: it is certainly my skill, and the elegance resides in my solution. But also, I didn't intentionally pursue elegance. It was the game designer who created the game. It is the game designer who chose its rules and designed its agencies, and plausibly did so to encourage the emergence of such elegant solutions.

Aesthetic responsibility, then, is complexly distributed between game designer and player, in a way that is hard to map onto traditional conceptions of artist and audience. In some cases, the responsibility largely resides with the player; in others, with the designer. In many cases, however, the responsibility involves a complex form of collaboration, in which the game designers achieves many of their intended aesthetic effects *through the agency of the player*, and where the end result is aesthetically attributable to both designer and player.[11]

Conclusions

We started our inquiry into the aesthetics of games with various accounts that tried to subsume games under more familiar forms of art—fictions, conceptual art, and the like. But, I've argued, some of the most important kin to game design are actually urban planners, traffic planners, and government designers. All these are attempts to cope and corral the agency of users, to achieve certain effects. Games are an artistic cousin to cities and governments. They are systems of rules and constraints for active agents. But game designers have a trick up their sleeves that the designers of cities and governments do not. They can substantially design the nature of the agents who will act within them. The medium of agency is active, then, in two directions. It creates a distinctive recalcitrance—the recalcitrance of agential distance. And it offers a distinctive sort of solution—the manipulation of agency.

[11] Paul Crowther (2008) offers an account of all game art as co-created. My view splits the difference between Lopes and Crowther; the artist's work is not co-created, but the attentive object often is.

PART III

SOCIAL AND MORAL TRANSFORMATIONS

8

Games as Social Transformation

I've focused so far on games as manipulations of individual agency. But another thought has hovered in the background. In multiplayer games, game designers not only shape the agency of the players; they also shape the social relationships between players. By intentionally manipulating the goals, abilities, and obstacles facing individual agents, game designers can create specific relationships of interdependence, vulnerability, and antagonism between the players. So in many cases of multiplayer games, game designers work not only in the medium of agency, but also in the medium of sociality.

What uses might there be for the medium of sociality? First, it can offer aesthetically valuable experiences. The aesthetic experience of practical harmony can be had , not only between self and environment, but also between self and teammate. But the medium of sociality promises another possibility: one of political action and moral transformation. As has often been pointed out, art can offer us more than just aesthetic experiences. Art can be morally and politically active; it can be personally and morally transformative. Nick Wolterstorff (2015) argues that the museum practice of art—where we make art specifically for disinterested aesthetic consumption—is just one historically localized art practice among many. There are all manner of other socially functional art practices, such as memorials and social protest art. (He suggests, in fact, the museum practice arose as an attempt to offer a new context for religious art, by which religious icons might be conserved rather than destroyed by other conquering religions.)

So let's grant that art can be politically active and socially transformative. And let's also grant that, as some contemporary art theory has suggested, art can stage direct interventions on society and politics. Consider the recent interest in practices of social art. There, artists have explored how they can stage social events, and play with the fabric of our social connections, as a form of art. Art, for such artists, can include designed social interactions, which transform our experience of our social world. Community gatherings, protest marches, and political happenings can all be kinds of art. Art can

Games. C. Thi Nguyen, Oxford University Press (2020). © Oxford University Press.
DOI: 10.1093/oso/9780190052089.001.0001

bring people together, or, as Nicolas Bourriaud has put it, perhaps even create micro-utopias of community.

Multiplayer games also seem like a rich venue for staging such active interventions. Games can create alternate social arrangements and alternate political structures. Games have been plunging us into designed social structures for millennia. They are, we might even say, the original social art. This is part of why I think it's so important to look broadly at the wide variety of games, including multiplayer games, board games, and party games. A focus on single-player computer games makes it easiest to think of games as, say, a special type of fiction. But when we focus on single-player games, we leave out one of the most interesting aspects of games: that they can be designed social structures, and thus can specify social relationships— oppositions, alliances, and dependencies.

Consider the particularly unusual social structure of games like Mafia and Werewolf. These games are usually played in moderately large groups with a referee. There are many variations, but here's the version I grew up playing.[1] At the beginning of Werewolf, the players all put their heads down. The referee moves silently among the players, tapping a few on the shoulder. The tapped players are now the werewolves; all other players are villagers. The werewolves are on one team, and the villagers are on another. The villagers far outnumber the werewolves. But the werewolves will know who is on which team, while the villagers have no idea who is who. The villagers must live in a constant state of uncertainty and dread. The game is played over a set of "day" and "night" rounds. Each day, all the players—including the hidden werewolves—will talk to each other. Then all the players will vote, choosing one person to lynch. That person will be knocked out of the game. At night, the werewolves will awaken and silently decide which of the villagers to murder. Then the cycle repeats, until either all the werewolves are eliminated, or the werewolves win by outnumbering the villagers.

Most of the game happens in the daytime discussion about who will be lynched. The villager players are trying to figure out who can be trusted and who is really a werewolf. The werewolves are trying to survive; they dissemble, they manipulate, they sow confusion. They are trying to get the villagers to mistakenly lynch one of their own. Play proceeds through careful

---

[1] Recently, there have been commercial releases of specified rule sets of these games, such as *Ultimate Werewolf*, and some nearby variants, such as *The Resistance: Avalon*. I will admit that several of these, especially *One Night Ultimate Werewolf*, are vast improvements on the versions I grew up playing, distilling the interesting parts of the game and removing much of the tedium.

epistemic manipulation. The werewolf players know exactly who their enemy is. But if they simply murder whichever villagers are closest to figuring out the truth, they'll give themselves away. They must proceed through careful misdirection, casting doubt on the credentials of different villagers. During the day, they must hide their allegiance to one another. They must feint and dissemble, pretending to lack the certainty they, in fact, have. They must sow discord and confusion. And the villager players must decode all this action, and sort the good information from the bad.

The game is elemental. The world of the game is composed entirely of particular social and epistemic relationships, brought into being by the rules. It is a game made entirely of simplified agencies, handed out at random to players. The challenges and experiences arise from wholly the emergent interactions of those agencies. Werewolf uses the medium of agency to create a set of social relationships, which in turn drive the activity and create the character of the game. The design of Werewolf takes advantage of what we might call nested mediums. Werewolf uses the medium of agency to work in the medium of sociality. The designated agencies imply a complicated network of social relationships. And the game uses those social relationships to create an experience of social uncertainty—of a war between sowers of informational chaos and detectives fighting that chaos.

In this chapter, I look at some of the different ways games can work in the medium of sociality, and how games can transform our social experience. I look at particular designed cooperative structures in games, and at the capacity for games to function as engines for the moral transformation. And I argue that, given the aims of avant-garde social art, it should look to the techniques of game designers and their masterful use of the mediums of agency and sociality.

On Cooperation in Games

In multiplayer games, game designers create particular practical relationships between players by manipulating the players' agency of and their practical environment. They are socially transformative in a literal sense. In playing such games, one transforms one's social relationships with others. Often, the game creates cooperation, by designating specific practical relationships between the players. You may not be friends with this person before the game, or after the game—but during the game, you are teammates. The precise delineation of practical relationships is particularly clear in modern team-based computer games. Take, for example, team-based multiplayer shooters and battle arena games, such as *Team Fortress* and *Defense of the Ancients*, in which teammates take on agentially diverse roles, each with its own distinctive special powers. One player is a lightly armored sniper; another, the engineer who can build turrets; another, a heavily armored tank character; and another, a medic capable of healing fellow characters. The complementary design of these agencies pushes the players toward specific forms of cooperation inside their team.

There's also been a recent surge of fully cooperative games—titles like *Pandemic, Lord of the Rings*, and *Arkham Horror*, and many others in which the players take on different complementary roles, and cooperate to accomplish some collective task (Zagal, Rick, and Hsi 2006). Let's consider some recent examples from the innovative world of cooperative and semi-cooperative tabletop gaming. First, there's the cooperative deduction game *Hanabi*, which is about the social distribution of information. Players are dealt a hand of cards from a deck of twenty-five cards. The cards come in five ranks and five colors. The goal of the game is quite simple. The players want to organize the cards into five rows, one for each color, and lay the cards into their proper row in the correct sequence. You want the red cards ordered from one to five, and the blue cards ordered the same, and so on. Sounds easy, right? Of course, there's a most excellent catch. Players are never allowed to look at the fronts of their own cards. You must hold their own cards facing away from you, so that all the other players can see which cards you hold, but you yourself cannot. When it's your turn, you must give one other player a single hint about the cards in their hand, and then you must play down one of your own cards, having never looked at its face.

Players must deduce what cards they are holding from the narrow tidbits of information they've been given. The contents of the hints are strictly limited by the rules, which permit only the barest trickle of information. At first, the game seems impossible—there simply isn't enough information to go around. Slowly, players figure out the real depth of the problem. First, you need to remember and assemble the hints you've been given. But the game makes it impossible to give out enough information explicitly in the hints to do the job. You also must think about the information that is implicit in the hints—you must deduce things, not only from what other players said, but from what they didn't say. You must think about what other players would have told you if you needed to know it, and also how what they didn't tell you says something about what must be in your hand.

Hanabi is a crystallized version of a basic epistemic dilemma of our social lives: how we can assess each other's informational needs, manage an entire group's informational needs, and cooperate within limited communicational capacities. It is an experience tightly focused on our trust in each other. A slight detour into the philosophy of trust will help to illuminate this. Karen Jones offers a very useful distinction between finding somebody reliable and finding them trustworthy. Clocks are reliable; they do the same thing every day, and we can depend on them to do it. But the trustworthy person isn't just reliable. Trustworthy people actively take into account that others rely on them, and modify their activities because of those dependencies. The trustworthy person *anticipates* others' needs, and responds to them without being asked (Jones 2012). *Hanabi* is a constructed social interaction that calls our attention precisely to the degree to which trustworthiness is reflective and anticipatory. And it doesn't do so by representing a particular real-world system. Instead, it creates a novel practical activity that focuses us on the delicate network of interdependence. To play it well, I must anticipate what information you need and give it to you. And you must count on me to have anticipated it, and use not only the information that I gave you, but also the information that I didn't give you. *Hanabi* offers us a heightened, concentrated experience of epistemic dependency. It is a frame put around our active trustworthiness.

Consider, also, the delightful *Space Alert*—a board game where we play as astronauts on a damaged space station, trying to work together to save the day. The players must run around the space station dealing with various emergencies. What's more, the emergencies require all sorts of complicated, coordinated actions. These actions are chosen during a programming phase, when the players must decide their particular character's next few actions several moves in advance: move to the next room, pull this lever, leave the room, enter the elevator. And the players must do all their programming simultaneously. The programming phase is also timed and excessively short, so all the players end up screaming at each other, desperately trying to figure out what needs doing and the best way to do it, trying to coordinate and program their actions all at once. *Space Alert* is, in a sense, very much like *Hanabi*. It is a game about assessing and managing our informational needs, and cooperating given limited communicational capacity. But *Hanabi* gives the players unlimited time; it challenges the limits of their memory, deductive capacity, and cleverness at efficiently passing information. *Space Alert*, on the other hand, challenges their speed, efficiency, and ability to communicate in a situation of extreme chaos. It crystallizes the experience of coordination in an emergency. (It is also very, very funny.)

The game designer not only designs individual interactions with a practical environment. Game designers can also design social structures. This is not always the case, even in multiplayer games. Sometimes, games simply give players a collective goal and leave the circumstances of cooperation largely up to the players. Many online role-playing games and group crafting games, such as *Minecraft*, offer relatively unstructured spaces for communication and cooperation. Players are for the most part free to create their society as they please. But in many other games, such as *Hanabi* and *Space Alert*, the game design offers a tightly restricted communicational and cooperative environment, with tightly delineated social relationships. In these cases, the designers are creating a particular social structure and relationship pattern by creating an interlocking network of the players' abilities, needs, and blind spots. By working the medium of agency, designers can also work in the medium of sociality.

Games as Morally Transformative Technologies

Hanabi and *Space Alert* are not simply representations of alternate social arrangements. They actually change how we interact with each other during the game. The game itself is a social transformation. But the socially transformative powers of games will be even clearer if we leave wholly cooperative games behind, and start thinking about competitive games.

Let's take a bit of a detour, which will help us come to grips with the power games have over our social relationships. Let's think about one of the most basic facts about games—something where lifelong familiarity may have masked a genuine philosophical oddity. Games have a peculiar social property. Sometimes we have to compete extremely hard against each other to try to have a good time.[2] Playing games can involve a rather profound sort of social and moral transformation. My spouse and I make a pleasant dinner

---

[2] This section contains ideas I originally developed in Nguyen and Zagal (2016) and Nguyen (2017b, 2017c). Those articles contain more detailed treatments of the surrounding literature. The present version has been revised to incorporate an improved understanding of the agential mechanisms involved in game playing. It is my preferred statement of my positive account.

together, chat about our respective days over the food, and put our child to bed. Then we haul out a favorite board game and proceed, for an hour or so, to try to thwart, undercut, and destroy each other. During the game, I am doing all I can to win. I am trying to wreck her plans and block her actions, and she is doing the same to me. Afterward, we put the box away and talk about whether the game was fun, interesting, or even beautiful. During the game, my spouse and I are competing with each other. But even though, locally speaking, we are competing, in a more global sense, we are actually cooperating. We are helping each other to have the wonderful experience of struggle that we both desire. This is not the only relationship people have with each other when they play games. Professional chess players and professional boxers may, in fact, have thoroughly competitive relationships; they may have no interest in showing their competitors a good time. But it seems that, for many sorts of game playing, the competition is limited to inside the game. By competing in the game, the players are, on a larger scale, cooperating to have an interesting time. Some games have an almost magical power. When the situation is right, they can transform competition into cooperation.

This perplexing phenomenon is quite easy to explain with the analysis of disposable ends and temporary agencies. For a striving player, the desire to win is a disposable end. A striving player takes on the desire to win for the sake of the struggle. When striving players oppose one another in a game, they are impeding only one another's attempts to achieve their disposable ends. In terms of their enduring ends, they actually support one another. By opposing a striving players in a game, you are actually helping them get what they really want in life—a particular sort of valuable struggle. Here's another way to put it. For striving players, it's only the temporary in-game agencies that are competing. Their full agencies are cooperating in creating a struggle. But they are cooperating by submerging themselves into temporary opposed agencies.

Some have argued that competitive game playing is a zero-sum activity. If the value of playing a game comes from winning, the argument goes, then the positive value of game playing for the winner will be precisely counterbalanced by the negative value of game playing for the loser.[3] But this line of thinking neglects the possibility of striving play. Striving players

---

[3] A variety of such zero-sum accusations, and some standard responses, are usefully surveyed in Kretchmar (2012).

don't really care about winning; they only take up a disposable and temporary interest in winning for the sake of having a struggle. Striving players
thus are not locked into a zero-sum activity. Game playing can be quite productive for them. If we all enjoy a good struggle, then a competition between
striving players can function as an engine of transformation, turning competitive actions into valuable experiences for all. For that reason, we can
think of games as *morally transformative technologies*. They take an action
that is normally negatively valenced—brutal competition—and turn it into
something good. We can all get what we truly want out of playing a game,
if we are striving players. For pure achievement players, on the other hand,
competitive play might be an entirely zero-sum proposition. When achievement players are competing, they are actually blocking each other's attempts
to achieve their enduring ends.

However, the transformation I've described here—turning competition
into cooperation—depends on the successful alignment of many factors. To
see this, let's compare my account with some other accounts of the transformative power of games. First, some have tried to explain the transformational power of games in terms of contracts. Steven Weimer argues that
sports can morally transform competitive and even seemingly violent acts,
such as punches in boxing. But for Weimer, the prime mover is not anything
like the complex motivational structure I've described. Instead, for Weimer,
the primary engine of moral transformation is something very simple and
familiar: consent. According to Weimer, when you and I agree to a boxing
match, what we have actually done is formed a contract, whereby you agree to
attempt to strike me in return for my attempting to strike you. We each enter
into that contract to have an opportunity to develop our own excellences.
Games, in other words, are an exchange of services. We are agreeing to be
something like biological gym equipment for each other. Thus, when I strike
you, I am doing something actively good—I am fulfilling my contractual
obligations to you (Weimer 2012).

Notice that Weimer offers us a picture of an entirely binary transformation,
and a notably unfinicky one at that. Either we have consented to a contract, in
which case all our in-game attacks are good, or we have not, in which case all
our in-game attacks are bad. But this view misses out on many of the moral
intricacies of gaming. Suppose that I thoroughly enjoy humiliating novices.
I like to find particularly cocky ones, get them to consent to having a game,
and then publically crush and humiliate them. I know ahead of time that they
won't enjoy this, but I pick the ones who are arrogant enough (or insecure

enough) that they won't be willing to resist my challenge. Or, imagine that I know my spouse despises any game that involves lying and manipulation. I am in a nasty and spiteful mood, and I propose a game of *Diplomacy*, which involves precisely those hated forms of social manipulations. I do so knowing that she will never back down from a challenge. The game proceeds to make her miserable for the rest of the night. Under Weimer's view, in both cases I am doing something good when I play the game. The players have created contracts through consent, and now I am fulfilling my contractual obligations. But it seems clear to me that I am doing something wrong in both cases, despite having obtained my opponent's consent.

In my account of moral transformation, the value of oppositional striving games does not reduce to the mere fulfillment of our contractual obligations. Rather, it comes from players *actually attaining the kind of activity they value*. Players need to actually have a good time or an interesting struggle, or obtain whatever else it is they desire, for the moral transformation to come off. And achieving that desirable struggle is often a delicate affair. It is not guaranteed merely by the players' having consented to the game. First, it often involves matching skill levels. In most games, striving is only desirable when the challenge is of appropriate difficulty. There is very little of interest for most people in crushing a newbie or in being utterly destroyed by a vastly superior opponent. Second, it requires a psychological fit between player and game. Each of us has different reasons to want striving activities and different sorts of striving activities that we value and enjoy. I find the incredibly fast speeds of serious *Starcraft 2* play quite unpleasant, but I find the analysis of decision trees in Chess quite delicious. My spouse despises games in which one lies to the face of another player; I find them quite amusing.

Third, the design of the game itself matters. The transformation is importantly *technological*. That is, it is the game that does much of the transformative work, not only the player's intent or psychological framing. Various forms of game design can be better or worse at achieving specific types of struggling. Chess, basketball, *Magic: The Gathering, Starcraft 2*, and *Team Fortress 2* are designed so that in-game competition tends to create very interesting or satisfying sorts of challenges. Dribbling around a guard in basketball, escaping from a diabolical fork in chess, dodging gunfire and lobbing a grenade at just the right moment in *Team Fortress 2*—these are the sorts of challenges and struggles that many of us value and enjoy. At the same time, we can imagine any number of game designs that are very bad for moral transformation: an insult contest where we try to insult one another until one of us cries; a whipping contest where we whip each other until one of us passes out. (Perhaps there are a small number of people psychologically constituted to enjoy such games, but most of us are not.)

Thus the transformation of competition into a valuable struggle isn't guaranteed by our merely having consensually entered into a game. Rather, the positive value is achieved only when all these other factors go right: when the game design is good, when the game fits the players' psychology, and when the players fit each other in skill. Whereas Weimer's view puts the entire responsibility for moral transformation in a contractual transaction between the players, I suggest that the responsibility is *distributed*. The player's motivational state—that they are engaging in striving play—does makes the moral transformation possible; but the details of game design and player fit are what actualize that possibility. Games are morally active, and game designers are thereby partially morally implicated, for good or ill, in the moral functioning of their designs.

Next, consider Robert Simon's account of cooperation in sports. The apparent competition in games, says Simon, is actually a kind of cooperation; the players are helping to develop each other's excellences. The point isn't to win; winning is merely a signal that one is properly developing one's excellences (Simon 2014, 36). Simon's account, to my mind, gets something quite wrong about the phenomenology of oppositional play. Simon's account requires an intention to cooperate, through and through. It requires that we *keep in mind* our goal of helping another to develop their excellence. And I think we do sometimes have such interactions, where we constantly focus on the development of the other players. But we call those interactions "training," not actually playing the game. Game playing is something quite different. What Simon is missing is the motivational two-step that is possible in striving play. In striving play, I don't need to keep my opponent's well-being in mind. I can simply give myself over to trying to thwart their in-game plans, within the limits of the game, and trust to the game design and the player fit to transform those in-game violences into something good. I can submerge myself in a temporary in-game agency, and go all out to compete.

What's interesting is why this works. Such submersion in wholly competitive agencies is morally permissible when we know that it will yield desirable experiences for all involved. Thus, we can *psychically offload* our interest in cooperation to the game itself and to the gaming environment. When we do so, we are trusting the externalities of the system to do the transformation for us. We may enter into the game for the sake of each other's well-being, but we don't need to keep each others' well-being in mind during the game. We can trust to the game itself, and to the appropriate match we have found, to convert our opposition into something valuable. Thus, the layered, transformational nature of this account allows for something that Simon's straightforwardly cooperative model does not. It shows how games can let us indulge our impulses toward aggression, lose ourselves temporarily in the predatory delights of competition, and do so in a morally acceptable way. But we are also responsible for choosing the right game and the right gaming context in the first place.

On Magic Circles and Willpower

We might call Simon's and Weimer's views ones of voluntarism about moral transformation in games—that is, the transformation depends solely on the mental acts of the players. Another branch of voluntarism about games has arisen in various debates over what's called the "magic circle" of play. This debate takes off from Johan Huizinga's suggestion that there is a specially bounded space of play that is morally separated from normal life (Huizinga 1955).[4] Katie Salen and Eric Zimmerman made Huizinga's magic circle a central concept in their extremely influential game-design textbook, *Rules of Play*. There, they offered a more explicit and robust account of the magic circle. A magic circle, for them, is

1. A bounded space for play, formally separated from everyday life
2. Precisely defined in space and time
3. Players crossing this boundary enter an alternate world, such that new rules have authority, and actions and objects acquire new meanings. (Salen and Zimmerman 2004, 95–97)

Most writers have attributed to Salen and Zimmerman the more radical view that the magic circle is entirely impermeable for morality, meaning, or consequences. Cruel acts in the game could not, by this theory, have any moral weight outside of the game context.[5] The view that game play is

---

[4] I offer a fuller survey of the history of the magic-circle debate in Nguyen (2017c).
[5] Zimmerman himself has since repudiated this reading, and claimed that it is something of a straw man (Zimmerman 2012).

radically impermeable has come under significant criticism. For example, Thomas Malaby argues that the boundary is highly permeable, pointing to such socially embedded practices as gambling. In gambling, money enters and leaves the arena of play. There are also social stakes—in many communities, success in sports grants social status and renown (Malaby 2007). T. L. Taylor argues for the permeability of game play by pointing to the existence of online game communities, particularly around massively multiplayer online games such as *World of Warcraft,* where online chatter on external discussion forums significantly shapes in-game play (Taylor 2009, 2007). Mia Consalvo points to gold farming in online games—that is, laboriously leveling up a character or earning in-game items, and then trading it to other players for real-world cash (Consalvo 2009, 408–409). For all these reasons, the radical version of the magic-circle theory seems dead in the water.

But some theorists have recently suggested an amended and significantly more plausible version of a magic-circle theory. Jaakko Stenros has argued that the magic circle is best conceived of as an explicitly negotiated social contract—as an agreement to treat the in-game events as separated from the world (Stenros 2012, 15). Similarly, Annika Waern suggests that game play occurs in a social frame in which actions are resignified—that is, the frame changes the meaning of the actions inside (Waern 2012, 5–9). Both of their accounts are useful, and they are in many respects compatible with my structural account. But they are also both voluntarist, putting the entire burden of moral transformation on an interpretive mental act of the players. In these voluntarist accounts, we achieve moral transformation through an effort of will. Hostile acts are turned into pleasant ones through the player's mental reinterpretation of the meanings of in-game actions.

I do not think that voluntarism can fully account for the moral transformation of games. Voluntarist accounts do not adequately capture the way in which the agency of moral transformation is distributed across players, game design, and community structure. We can now see how different the account I've offered is from voluntarist accounts. In my account, structural features of the game-playing environment—features of game design, community structure, and player alignment—are crucial to the moral transformation. In other words, it's not just the player, it's the game.

Imagine that I have a belligerent work colleague. He viciously attacks my character and my work at every opportunity, but I am obliged to take lunch breaks with him. I come up with a clever plan: I suggest that we play some pick-up basketball during our lunch breaks. His aggression and hostility will then be transformed into something much more pleasant for me—not by his intention or his agreement, but simply by the design of the game itself. He need not agree to any norms of impermeability, nor does he need to participate in some mutual attempt to re-signify. Probably, he's just playing the game as just another opportunity to humiliate me.

Crucially, Stenros's account depends on the psychic effort of the player. I must, through force of will, maintain this impermeability, and refuse to let what happens in the game matter to me outside the game. But what explains the limits of that moral transformation? Suppose my nasty colleague aggressively blocks my shots while, at the same time, viciously trash-talking me about all my character failings. His intentions may be equally nasty in both sorts of actions, and I have equal motivation to re-signify all of his actions. But my motive, by itself, is insufficient. If moral transformation occurred through a simple act of will—through a decision to re-signify—then I ought to be able to re-signify any of his actions. But often, I cannot. His harangue may wound me, and I may be able to do nothing about it, despite my best wishes. But his physical efforts to defeat me are transformed by the game itself. Basketball transforms the basic form of his actions, by channeling them along new lines. He moves in order to steal the ball from me, and that action is a pleasurable one for me to deal with. The moral transformation of shot-blocking comes, not from an act of my will, but from the particular arrangement of rules about dribbling, shooting, and guarding. The change here is not an internal resignification, but an external transformation of action.

Compare the significant morally transformative powers of basketball with the rather paltry transformative powers of dodgeball. Here is how we played dodgeball in my elementary school: a circle forms, and the people on the outside hurl balls at the people on the inside. If anybody on the inside gets hit, they're out, and they must join the outer circle. At least on my playground, all the unpopular kids dreaded dodgeball because of the game design. The bullies would point out their targets, scream insults, and then bury us in a vicious hail of rubber. There's no significant moral transformation here. It's just as humiliating and painful to be hit in the head with a rubber ball inside the game as outside of it. Compare this to how my vicious co-worker is forced to behave toward me in basketball. He must engage in movements of guarding, blocking, dodging, all of which are much more entertaining to me than what he would be doing if we left his viciousness unchanneled.

I may wish for transformation, and try to re-signify the meanings of actions, just as much in both games, but that won't help me with the humiliation of being hit in the face with a dodgeball. It is the rules of basketball, and not just a mental effort of resignification by the players, that makes basketball such a potent instrument of moral transformation. If moral transformation were simply up to me, as an act of interpretation—of just taking up a playful *attitude*—then I should have been able to enact that transformation just as well in either game, and I should have no reason to prefer basketball. But I vastly preferred basketball to dodgeball, and I did so because it is a better game design for moral transformation. What we've stumbled across here is a natural version of the philosopher's controlled-variable thought experiment. My intentions and psychological framing, and those of the bullies, are the same throughout dodgeball and basketball. The only thing that varies is the game design. Thus, any increased efficacy of moral transformation between the two cannot come from the player's mental acts alone; it must also arise from the design of the game.

What Stenros, Waern, Simon, and Weiner all leave out is the moral importance of game design. None of these theories can cope particularly well with the fact that different game designs are variably effective at supporting the morally transformative effects. By focusing on the mental acts of the players to re-signify in game actions, voluntaristic accounts leave out the moral contribution of the game designer. The motivational state of striving is, indeed, a mental state that is a necessary prerequisite for moral transformation. But though it is necessary, it is not sufficient. The design of the game and embedded social features of the community of play are also crucial.

Games as Socially Active Artifacts

We've now learned something significant from our detour into the morally transformative powers of games. Multiplayer games, it turns out, are a kind of social technology. They reconfigure their players' social relationships temporarily for the sake of some overall effect. This isn't some special sauce that's been introduced in avant-garde gaming practice, nor is it some novel resonance between gaming practices and contemporary art practices. It is baked into the very essence of multiplayer game play. Multiplayer game design is a manipulation of the medium of agency, which produces, among other things, particular designed relationships and emergent social and interpersonal practical structures. Sometimes, those are explicitly cooperative endeavors; other times, those arrangements can lead to morally transformed competitive behaviors.

To generalize, then: I suggest that multiplayer games are social technologies and that they can rearrange our social relationships to some end. In some games, that end is creating productive, enjoyable activity out of structured competition. But that is not the only end, as we shall soon see. More importantly, the social engineering is exactly that: engineering. It arises from regulated, structural aspects of game design. Game designers specify agencies, and through them shape the social structures of those agents. I am suggesting here that we move past a player-centric view of gaming. The pattern of social relationships in a game is not entirely attributable to the contribution of the players. Such patterns are often produced, or at least profoundly shaped, by game design.

The precision of social design is not simply confined to the cooperative aspects of games. Games can arrange competitors into astoundingly precise and intricate social structures. Take, for example, Cole Wehrle's remarkable game design for the board game *Root: A Game of Woodland Might and Right*. *Root* is a simulation of political and economic warfare—of a struggle for the hearts and minds of the people. Crucially, the game is radically asymmetric. Each side plays by different rules and aims at different goals; they virtually play different games. *Root* is based on the COIN series of war games—a series of extremely complex simulations of counterinsurgency warfare. For example, the COIN game *Fire in the Lake* is set in Vietnam during the Vietnam War, with the United States, the South Vietnamese army, the North Vietnamese army, and the Vietcong all involved in radically asymmetrical warfare. Another COIN game simulates the United States' attempts to root out the Taliban. These are massive, complex, and grueling simulations that take hours to learn and many more hours to play. *Root* takes that system and boils it down into an easily learnable, crisp, and utterly delightful little game, while retaining much of the fascinating asymmetry. It also gives the whole thing an adorable woodland critters theme, while keeping the series' attempt to model the politics and economics of counterinsurgency warfare.

One side in *Root* is the Marquise de Cats—a bourgeois industrialist who rules the forest, and who is literally a fat cat. Another side is the Eyrie, a society of brittle, rule-bound, and warlike old aristocrats, who are also birds. Another side is the Woodland Alliance, a loose collection of (literally) underground critters, like squirrels and mice, who are trying to win the hearts of the people over to their cause and start a revolution.

The Marquise de Cats plays an infrastructure and troop-movement game. They build buildings, collect resources, make troops, and brutally suppress any opponents. They're wealthy and powerful, and they have a ton of troops. Playing them feels like playing a classic German economic game. They are the status quo, and they get a steady stream of easy points.

The Eyrie plays a planning and programming game. They have to program all their moves in advance, building a complex plan and adding new elements to it on every turn. Once they have a plan in place, they get to execute the whole thing every turn, so they can get an enormous number of actions. But they also are forced to execute the whole plan every turn, and they can never remove or modify any element that's already in their plan. And if they can't execute one tiny bit of their plan on a turn, then they fall into turmoil. Their whole plan falls apart; they lose lots of points; and they have to start planning again from scratch. This simulates a turbulent society with constant regime changes, with inflexibly dogmatic regimes and massive leadership instability.

The Woodland Alliance starts with no troops or bases on the board. They slowly start building the people's sympathy, creeping it across the board, while the Marquise and the Eyrie ruthlessly try to use their troops to stamp out that sympathy. But if the Woodland Alliance can get enough resources together, they can create mini-revolutions, which eliminate all nearby enemy troops and create Alliance bases. And then those bases can pump out Alliance warriors who can scamper off to other spots and then melt away into the woods, to foster more sympathy from the people.

The game is astonishing in its ability to plunge players into a complex network of relationships. The Marquise de Cats starts in a dominating position, and can win simply by maintaining the status quo and suppressing change. The Woodland Alliance is extremely weak at first, but they are slippery and hard to evict. If they can get enough of a base of sympathy among the people, they can just explode and take over everything, so the other players have to stomp on them constantly to keep them from gaining a foothold. The Eyrie is hysterically fun to play; in order to get anything done, they must commit to insanely complex plans, which only grow more convoluted with time. Their plans are, at first, extremely powerful. But as the situation progresses, the Eyrie is still stuck with their inflexible plan, and they're forced to perform all sorts of nonsensical actions just to keep their regime from collapsing.

The game creates a little society that elegantly simulate all manner of political, economic, and social relationships. The Marquise de Cats and the Eyrie must maintain an uneasy alliance, cooperating to stomp out any toeholds from the Woodland Alliance. But they must also jockey for power as they cooperate, looking for any moments of weakness in the other. The Woodland Alliance sneaks around, hoping to create opportunities to get the Marquise de Cats and the Eyrie at each other's throats, so that they can exploit the chaos of war and slip into new opportunities. The game exquisitely creates an oppositional set of social relationships, and plunges players into a society made of radically asymmetric abilities and interests. It creates a set of social relationships, albeit sharply opposed ones. The game designers have not only created independent agencies—they have created a society, using the building blocks of agencies.

Social Art and Social Transformation

So, might these manipulations of sociality fit within the world of art? Let's return to the realm of avant-garde social art. We've already seen some examples from relational aesthetics, including Tiravanija's dinner works. Tom Finkelpearl offers some more representative examples, like Paul Ramirez Jones's *Key to the City*. In this social artwork, audience members fill out a passport-size booklet with personal information and then award each other a "key to the city," which is an actual, physical key. Over the next few weeks, participants may visit different locations around the city, as indicated in the booklet. At each location, they find that that their key unlocks some door: perhaps to a special hidden room in a museum, or to a downstairs kitchen at a tortilleria, where they receive a lesson in taco making and help operate a tortilla kitchen for twenty minutes (Finkelpearl 2012, 1–4).

Many of the early-stage social arts were explicitly friendly and communal. Claire Bishop argues for the importance of more antagonistic forms of social art, such as Tania Bruguera's *Tatlin's Whisper #5*. In that work, unsuspecting audiences entering a museum gallery are confronted with apparent authority figures—policemen on horses—who proceed to give directions to the audience members, herding them into arbitrary places. This gives the audience members a sense of what it would be like to be subject to an arbitrary authority, says Bishop (2004, 55–58, 67).

Finally, consider Hit Guyenn's work, *Le pont des amies*, as reviewed in *Artfoundry*:

> Audience members are conducted to a prepared room, where they are seated at a square table. At each table, exactly one audience member occupies each side. The reference is to Marina Abramovic's direct, eye-to-eye confrontations with her audience, except in this case artist has chosen to absent himself entirely from the proceeding. Participants are left to gaze at each other, or not, as they wish. One might think that this is a more radical upending of the artist-audience relationship than Abramovic's, but participants are then confronted with a set of instructions, whereby the artist instructs them in a set of exercises. Facing participants are paired in a numerical task, which involve exchanges of various numbered placards. They must cooperate, but they cannot speak directly of the matter of their cooperation. These instructions challenge the new "norms" of museum performance art. They must, instead, imply their interests through a provided code. The work forces its participants to connect through the most tenuous of means; it emphasizes the fragility of language, and yet the tenacity of the human communicative capacity. One suspects a Lacanian influence; the process of learning the code, and coding one's wishes in an arbitrary and arcane communicative system, recapitulates what one might call a social mirror stage in the life of a community. The work also extends the motion to dislocates and rupture the divide between performer and audience. We have already moved from the celebrity performer to the nameless unprofessional performer, following the directions of the artist. Now, Huytens has removed the divide between the unprofessional performer and the audience, directing the audience themselves to enter into and become the artwork. (Keune 2003)

This sort of socially oriented art practice has gone by many names lately, including "relational aesthetics," "participatory art," "community art," "social art," and "social practice art." Let's refer to this body of practices as *social art*, with the understanding that the term refers to a cluster of related practices without an obvious definition. Artworks in this vein typically consist of interactive, participatory events. What was the point of these new social events, from the point of view of avant-garde art practice? The art world, explains Bourriaud, is now involved in a new project—of "learning to inhabit the world in a better way." And art—insofar as it involves objects which we encounter together, in a social space—is better at doing this than, say, television or literature. Art creates a specific kind of social encounter. Art "tightens the space of relations," says Bourriaud. "Art is the place that produces a specific sociability" (Bourriaud 2002, 13–16).

Cities do this also, but they do it for bad ends, says Bourriaud. The urban landscape creates specific socialities, but those specifies are tuned to functional, mechanistic, and capitalist ends. Cities mechanize us, says Bourriaud; they reduce the relationships between people. Art can create different social relationships. And art need not be confined to critiquing or reflecting on the rest of the world. Art can effect change directly. Art can create real micro-utopias right now, for us to inhabit. For that reason, Bourriaud favors the creation of convivial spaces, of little oases of friendliness, like Tiravanija's cooking installations (Bourriaud 2002, 13–18, 30–31; Bishop 2004, 54).[6] Art, especially relational art, imposes specific socialities, says Bourriad. Those socialities can carry with them values. And we can export those values back into normal life. That social imposition is what makes works of relational aesthetics special: they encourage such specific socialities.

But multiplayer games, I've argued, can do exactly that, and they have been doing that for ages. Game designers work not only in the medium of agency; they can, in multiplayer games, work in the medium of sociality. By configuring agencies, they can bring into being a particular agential network—a set of relationships—be they cooperative or competitive. *Hanabi, Space Alert, Pandemic, Defense of the Ancients*, basketball—each of these creates forms of sociality, by specifying forms of agency. The degree of control exerted by the game designer over the social pattern varies widely between games. Basketball, for example, only loosely suggests certain patterns of sociality. Nothing in the rules of basketball requires, say, zone defense, or man-to-man defense, but the possibilities emerge from the strategic requirements of the game, and the agential restrictions—the dribbling and passing rules. *Hanabi*, on the other hand, specifies the social relationships with tremendous precision—its agential specifications sculpt, directly, the social relationships of its players.

Incidentally, Guyenn's *Le pont des amies* does not exist, at least not as an institutionally recognized artwork. I fabricated the *Artfoundry* review, along

---

[6] For a useful criticism of Bourriaud's approach, see Bishop's discussion of the social and transformative potential of antagonistic social art (55–70).

with the artist, for the purposes of this chapter. What I've described is actually the game of contract bridge.

Games, then, can be social works. Let's say, for the moment, that a social work is a work in which social relationships are part of the medium of the work.[7] Clearly, Tiravanija's dinner works and Bruguera's police crowd-control works are social works. In Tiravanija's dinner works and Bruguera's crowd-control works, the audience members act as themselves. I enter the space and have dinner with others, I am confronted with a policeman on a mounted horse, and I react as I naturally would. But multiplayer games are also clearly social works. And they incorporate social relationships in a particular way—by sculpting specific agencies for their participants. Games offer us a designed experience where we are, in an important way, not our selves—at least, not our habitual and usual selves. Avant-garde social art, as it is usually practiced, often creates settings in which social relationships arise spontaneously. Games, instead, force us into specific social relationships, by designated agencies that imply forms of relationship. Games may seem more intrusive than other social arts, since players are required to adopt a specified agency. But that intrusiveness is actually a way for the artist to exert greater artistic control—while making a space for the agency of the player.

Can games also model social values that can be exported out of the game? Certainly, they can. But notice the different types of values which we might model. The sorts of relational aesthetic artworks favored by Bourriaud often convey desirable social values, in a particular and colloquial sense of "social"—values of friendliness, chattiness, etc. The values modeled in Tiravanija's dinner works are most exportable to situations like dinner parties, hanging out with friends, and the like. The values modeled by games are, instead, often the values of epistemic and practical communities. The values modeled by *Hanabi* are more likely to be exportable to, say, working as part of a science lab, or partaking in a group epistemic effort like academic publishing.

Finally, can games help us "learn to inhabit the world in a better way"? Surely, if one believes that a relational artwork can, then games can too. As I argued, games put more types of agency in our agential quivers. But they also let us experience a new agency, as might occur within a new form of

[7] The terms *social work* and *social art* are used in many ways. The designator "social" has come to mean an extraordinary range of things, from relational and participatory works, to any art with a social-political purpose (Jackson 2011, 11–16). I am focusing on one important aspect of this range—but I do not suppose my stipulated definition here exhausts the whole range.

sociality. *Hanabi* lets me experience what it's like to be razor-focused on communicating with limited means, but as part of a group that is wholly oriented toward cooperation, and wholly attuned to overcoming those limitations together. *Root* lets me experience what it might be like to be, say, a wealthy member of the status quo, but as part of a live and active struggle against revolutionaries and old-guard war hawks. *Root* also lets me experience that same interlocked struggle from the perspective of a desperate, resourceless insurgent, trying to find some breathing room between the clashing economic titans.

Games give me access to new forms of sociality. They show me what it might be like to inhabit new and different communities of agents. And they can show me those new forms of sociality from different agential perspectives. Games don't just offer us access to a wide variety of agencies in isolation. They offer us access to a wide variety of social arrangements, and show us what it might be like to inhabit those different social arrangements from different roles. They give us perspectives on different socialities, and also let us view those socialites from different agential angles.

In Chapter 4, I argued that games can offer us a variety of agencies—that they support our individual autonomy. And giving ourselves over to short-term restrictions and specified agencies, when done in the right way, can actually help to develop our autonomy. We can now extend that account. Games can also offer us a variety of socialities, and show us how particular agencies give rise to particular social relationships and patterns. They can offer us experiences of alternative agencies organized within different social structures. They offer experiences of being nested within a cooperating team, or within a shifting set of alliances, or within an epistemically unstable social space. If games can offer us a library of agencies, then multiplayer games can offer us a *library of socialities*. They enhance our autonomy, not only by showing us more options about how we might inhabit our own agency, but also over how we might construct different forms of society from all these various agencies.

John Stuart Mill suggests that, to make social progress, we need to explore what life would be like as lived under different conceptions of the good. And we need to do this through empirical investigation. We need, says Mill, to conduct "experiments in living"—to try out alternative forms of life which explore alternative conceptions of the good. In practice, this means conducting small-scale experiments with radically different social arrangements. Small communes conducted by American citizens living under large-scale capitalism would count (Mill [1859] 1999; Anderson 1991; Muldoon 2015). Games, I am suggesting, are another form of experiment in living; they are quickest rough-sketch version. When we interact under an disposable end, we are exploring how social life will go under an alternative conception of the good.

Perhaps this sounds all like a wild overreach. But let me remind the reader: most of us think that human artifacts can create particular experiences, and that through those experiences we can develop ourselves— they can help us learn how to be in this world. It is not such a strange thing to think, as Nussbaum suggests, that narratives offer us emotional training and show us new emotional possibilities. Reading, watching, and listening widely can help us develop into fuller and better people: through narratives, we can receive experiences from other people. Those experiences can infiltrate the rest of our lives; they can shape our experience of, and our way of being in, the world. Why is it so strange to also think that games—the human art form in which we play with agencies, take on alternate practical identities, take up different abilities and goals, and take up new social arrangements—can also do such a thing? So many of our other constructed artifacts—books, movies, music—give us access to a wider range of experiences than we could experience directly. It is not so strange to think that games would also widen our range of experiences in their own special way.

Games are one of the oldest artifactual practices we have. When we play games, we take on a wide range of alternate agencies. Games help us to understand new forms of agency, and to understand those new forms from the inside. And if we accept all that, then it is not so strange to think that games can help us develop, change, and transform our social structures, by helping us to explore, from the inside, alternate social structures. Such explorations can help us get a handle on our own social structure, and show us what it might be like to operate within a new one.

9

Gamification and Value Capture

So far, I've sung the praises of games as the art of agency. I've explored how the medium of agency can be used to shape aesthetic experiences of practicality, and thus help develop our autonomy. A game designer sculpts a form of agency by manipulating goals, rules, and an environment, and inscribes it into the game. And in playing a game, we adopt that form of agency. We take on a different agential posture.

In this chapter, I'll consider some of the dangers of games—specifically, those that arise from the use of the agential medium. I will also explore the dangers of game-like systems in the world, which can goad us into game-like shifts in agency—sometimes without our awareness or consent. I am particularly interested in gamification, which is the introduction of game-like elements into practical life. This includes *intentional gamification*, where we use design lessons from games to change our motivations in non-game activities. The FitBit, for example, is designed to give users game-like rewards for exercising, to make the project of fitness more like a game. I am also thinking of *accidental gamification*, which introduces game-like features into our lives for other reasons, but can also come to motivate us in game-like ways. For example, academic life has recently come to be ruled by quantified metrics for research quality—like citation rates and impact factors. These metrics may not have explicitly been designed to produce gamification among researchers. Conceivably, they arose from the bureaucratic need to collate information, or in university administrators' quest to make more objective-sounding decisions about faculty hiring and promotion. But the clear, simple, and quantified nature of such metrics can also foster game-like motivations. Metrics, after all, look a lot like points. They offer some of the pleasures of games when we pursue them wholeheartedly. And if we are too eager to recapture the pleasures of games in ordinary life, we may be excessively drawn to using such simplified measures in our practical reasoning. We could be drawn to redefine our notion of success in the newly clear terms specified by those metrics, in order to get more game-like pleasures from our work. This is not all for the good. I will argue that exactly those features that are crucial

Games. C. Thi Nguyen, Oxford University Press (2020). © Oxford University Press.
DOI: 10.1093/oso/9780190052089.001.0001

to the agential fluidity of games, when exported clumsily to our non-game life, can lead to moral and social disaster.

The agential fluidity involved in game play raises its own distinctive set of dangers. They are dangers that threaten players of all kinds of games—sports, card games, board games, and video games alike. These dangers have been mostly overlooked in the rush to chart the dangers of violent and sexual representational content. But the issues of graphic violence arise only around a relatively narrow range of representational video games (and perhaps a few combat sports). The risks of the agential medium arise from any game that specifies clear goals. They are risks that attach to the players of Chess, Bridge, *Imperial, Civilization 2*, and soccer, just as much as to the players of violent video games.

Those agential risks are particularly important to understand, because they will accompany the gamification of practical life. When Amazon gamifies its work environment, giving points and rankings to its workers in order to maximize productivity, the moral threat here is not from any representation of violence. The dangers arise from that peculiarly powerful motivational pull of clear goals and quantified scoring. The purpose of this chapter is to do a bit of reorientation with respect to our worries about games. Discussions of the ethical importance and social dangers of games have largely focused on how they might represent violence or sexual content.[1] I am far more worried that games and game-like systems will encourage the spread of the unthinking pursuit of simplified and quantified goals. I am more worried about games breeding Wall Street profiteers than I am about their breeding serial killers.

Recall that narrative, according to Nussbaum, can contribute to our moral development, because narrative can transmit practical wisdom through the expression of well-tuned emotions. But that very capacity can also make narrative quite dangerous. Narratives can be used to transmit simplified, errant, or vicious emotions. Their emotional power makes them good both for moral development and for malicious propaganda. I suggest that games are similarly double-edged—but their special potency arises from how they work with agency, rather than with emotion.

One proviso: many of the provisional conclusions of this chapter depend on empirical claims about our psychology. I make no claims at empirical conclusiveness here. Rather, I will outline certain dangers that my theory

[1] For recent example from the philosophical literature, see Luck (2009); Patridge (2011); and Bartel (2012).

suggests, and offer, from anecdotes and observation, some hypotheses. I do not think my observations here are enough; we need more empirical work. The dangers of the agential medium are serious but relatively underexplored.

Total Instrumentalization

What attitudes and tendencies do we export from inside the game to the outside world? We can look, for a start, to discussions of the possible psychological after-effects from video-game violence. In *Ethics in the Virtual World*, Garry Young provides a thorough survey of that research; he concludes that the representation of violence in video games is less harmful than has sometimes been thought. Most importantly, awareness of the fictional status of game events seems to block most of the psychological after-effects—just as awareness of the fictional status of events in film and television seems to block most of the psychological after-effects of viewing the violence in those media. For the few people who cannot recognize the fictional status of video game events, playing violent video games may indeed increase the likelihood of violent behavior in real life. But for the rest of us, there is little risk (Young 2014). I'll presume that this is right for the moment—with the proviso that research into the consequences of violent video games is ongoing, and its outcomes complex.

Notice, however, that, if Young is right, then those protections from after-effects only apply to the fictional aspects of games. But how much of game playing is actually fictional? Juul reminds us, usefully, that video games are half fictional and half real (Juul 2005). Suppose we are playing an online shooter, and I shoot you. Fictionally, I have shot you and killed you. But nonfictionally, I have really scored points against you. It is not fictional at all that I outwitted you, that I was faster than you, that I was *better* than you at this game. My victory in the game is real. Suppose that most players understand that the violence in video games is merely a fiction. This will serve to screen off the habituating effects of only the fictional content. We will still be in danger of habituating from the nonfictional content of game play.

What could be dangerous in the nonfictional part of game playing? Consider the peculiar practical attitude cultivated by most Suitsian games. In ordinary life, we have to balance values. First, each of us must balance our own different and competing values, goals, and ends, which is already a difficult enough task. Then, even more torturously, we must balance our interests with the interests of others. But in games, we are permitted a brief respite from the pains of plurality. For a little while, we get to act as though only one thing matters—to lose ourselves in the pursuit of that thing. Our values simplify. We need only chase our own goal, in all its simplicity and selfishness—and that goal is usually put in simple, clear, and utterly stark terms. We need not balance our needs with the needs of others, or even with our own other complex desires. This practical clarity is, as I've said, the basis for many of the attractions of games.

We can separate the characteristic practical attitude of game playing into several distinct elements. First, game play involves taking on an all-consumingly instrumental mode of practical reasoning. In so many games, we throw ourselves into the wholehearted pursuit of a goal. We instrumentalize everything else in the game. Every resource, every competitor, is used and manipulated in our single-minded pursuit of victory.[2] As I argued in Chapter 8, this total and single-minded instrumentalization is morally permissible when the right conditions obtain. In games, we are permitted to temporarily inhabit a motivational state where only one thing is valuable. Crucially, this means that we don't need to treat others' interests as valuable. We need not treat them with, as the Kantians might put it, dignity and respect. We are permitted to manipulate, use, and destroy. This attitude is permissible in some games because our opponent's ends in the game are disposable, because our opponents have consented to the struggle, and because the design of the game can convert our purely selfish attacks into a delightful struggle for our opponents.

There is a significant danger, however, if these attitudes leak out and infect one's life outside the game. When we leave the gaming context, treating every other resource and person in the world as a mere instrument would be, obviously, morally terrible. Games have been specifically designed and carefully maintained to make it possible to unleash the all-consuming instrumental attitude for the mutual enjoyment of all. And in striving play, we are only pursuing disposable ends. Attacking another's pursuit of disposable ends does not actually harm their enduring interests. But in the rest of life, these factors

---

[2] It is important to note, however, that the all-consuming instrumental attitude is not the same as the egoistic attitude. One ought not think that one is free of the danger of such an attitude when one is, for example, a crusader for justice. One could take an all-consuming instrumental attitude toward an apparently unselfish end. For example, I might have an all-consuming instrumental attitude toward, say, the preservation of the rainforest, or the protection of my community's heritage. The problem, in the familiar language of Kant, is that the all-consuming instrumental attitude leads to treating other people as mere means to our end—no matter how good or bad the end.

do not usually obtain. Outside the game, people are usually not pursuing disposable ends. By treating others' plans as unimportant, I am genuinely interfering with them. And life is not usually engineered to convert antagonism into anything good. A mature game-player should have the capacity to adopt the all-consuming instrumentalizing attitude as part of a temporary agency during game play, and then set it aside afterward. But if they fail to—if that attitude lingers—then they invite moral catastrophe.

How is possible for us to take up, and then set aside, this all-consuming instrumentalizing attitude? The account of striving play and agential layering tells us how. Striving players take up an interest in winning for the sake of the game. By devoting themselves to winning, they are implicitly taking up the instrumentalizing attitude. But if the instrumentalizing attitude is simply part of the temporary agency for striving play, then the attitude should also disposable. We should be able to set it aside when we set aside our total devotion to the win.

Can we actually do so? A full answer is, I think, the domain of psychologists and other empirical researchers. I suspect, though, that many people can confine the all-instrumental attitude to the game context, though it seems to be a complex and sophisticated skill. We have evidence that this is psychologically possible, for some at least. Think of the paradigmatic good sport. A good sport is somebody who play hard to win during the game, but does not actually care, outside the game, whether they have won or lost. They are interested in everybody having had a good time, an interesting match, or a worthwhile struggle. They are people who celebrate an interesting loss, or are happy to lose if their friends all had a good time. For them, the all-out instrumental attitude is itself merely a temporary means to some social, aesthetic, or moral end.

The existence of such paragons of play indicates that, for at least some people, that the all-out instrumental attitude is psychologically confinable to the game. But we might also worry that the all-consuming attitude is a little sneakier than the other disposable elements of play. The fictions of the game are obvious and easy to set aside. Our interest in the win, as it is specified by the rules of the game, is also clearly an artifact of the game. But the all-consuming instrumental attitude isn't specified explicitly in the game rules. It is usually merely implied by the nature of game goals. It may be slightly harder to notice, and thus to intentionally set aside. But all these are all empirical claims, in need of further investigation.

The Fantasy of Value Clarity

There is another element to the practical attitude, beyond the all-consuming instrumental attitude I've just described, which is even more subtle and thus likely even more difficult to manage.

In game life, our temporary agency's values are usually extremely clear. That clarity is encoded into a game's specification of its goals. The values we take on in games are clearer, easier to apply, and easier to evaluate than our enduring values. The second danger, then, is that the experience of motivational clarity that we have inside games might influence our expectations outside games. The value clarity of games might bring about an expectation for value clarity outside the game, and attract players to those real-world systems that present values with game-like simplicity. And in many cases, that attraction may lead us astray. For, in much of life, the right values to have may not be the clearest values.[3] Games can present us with a fantasy of value clarity. And if we are too seduced by that fantasy, we may be moved to oversimplify our own values.

What do I mean by clear values? In the majority of Suitsian games, the goals have the following characteristics: First, their *application* is obvious. In ordinary life, my values might be for such intangible abstractions as happiness, thoughtfulness, and wisdom. Even if I know the consequences of my efforts, figuring out how those outcomes should be evaluated in those terms isn't easy. Suppose that I give up my vacation to meet an important deadline, and the result is a small promotion. Is that a net increase in my happiness? This is not an easy question to answer. When I give my students weekly pop quizzes, they come out of my classes being able to perform better on tests and essay assignments, and can spit back lecture material with more facility. Are they thereby more thoughtful and wiser? Rich, subtle values are often quite hard to apply.

It is, however, usually incredibly easy to evaluate my in-game outcomes in terms of a game's stated goals. Usually, the goals of a game are expressed in terms of points or binary victory conditions. Furthermore, the criteria for points and victory are clearly delineated. A checkmate, in chess, is a logically determinable state. In basketball, there is little fuzziness about whether the ball fell on the inside, or the outside, of the hoop. And the scope of the affairs

---

[3] An excellent discussion of why this may be so is Elijah Millgram's account of how we must refine our values by attending to the subtleties of our life experience (Millgram 1997).

that we are to evaluate in games is also tidily circumscribed. We just count up the points we made during the game, at the end. Not so with life, where my labors may not bear full fruit until long after I'm dead, and where their effects may sprawl in every direction, far beyond my ability to track.

Second, game goals are typically *easily commensurable*. Commensurability here means the capacity for different objects to be measured in terms of some common scale.[4] Dry goods and groceries, for example, are usually thought to be economically commensurable. We can determine, with mathematical precision that, say, a new copy of John Rawls's book *Political Liberalism* is worth precisely 25.7 oranges. But this sort of commensurability does not seem to hold for our deeper values—at the very least, not so easily. Our fuller values are plural and usually quite difficult to commensurate. I must often make choices between pursuing my children's happiness, my professional success, my students' development, and the progress of various large-scale social projects and institutions that I care about. How do I compare the worth of my child's happiness, were I were to take the day off and take him to the zoo, against the value of spending that day on my research? And how do I compare those against the importance of joining a protest march against the unjust detention of immigrants? The values I place in family, in philosophy, and in various political causes are all extremely difficult to compare.

In games, there is usually no such difficulty in commensurating plural values. In many games, there is a single goal. In some games, the goal is expressed in terms of a binary win condition, like producing a checkmate in chess. In other games, that single goal is expressed in a single point scale, like basketball, soccer, and poker. In all single-goal games, the value of any action can be assessed in terms of its relationship to that goal. There is only one scale for value, because there is only one value. In some other sorts of games, there can seem to be multiple goals. For example, it is a common for recent Eurogames to be praised for providing "multiple paths to victory." This means that there are distinct scoring mechanisms, which provide victory points for very different sorts of actions. For example, in Reiner Knizia's board game *Taj Mahal*, players can win by collecting sets of goods, by forming long chains of palaces on the board, or by collecting bonus tiles from the board. You can

---

[4] Ruth Chang distinguishes between incommensurability and incomparability, which is the capacity for different objects to be given a rank ordering (Chang 1997, 1–2). Though the distinction is important for more fine-grained work in this terrain, it is unimportant for my purposes. Though I will speak in terms of commensurability for brevity's sake, everything I say is also applicable to incomparability.

win by pursuing one of these goals exclusively, or by pursuing some combination of these goals. However, the game provides a commensurating currency for these different goals, in terms of "victory points." Most such games
offer clear rates of exchange between the various in-game goals. A farming
game might tell you, for example, that sheep are worth four victory points
each, that cows are worth five victory points each, and that fields of wheat
worth ten victory points each. In much of game life, values are evidently and
easily commensurable— either because there is only one form of value or because there is an explicitly and quantifiably set rate of exchange between the
values.[5] It is not so with our larger values. Even if those values are in principle
commensurable, that commensuration is often a difficult, painful procedure.

Third, when game results are commensurable, they are also *rankable*. Even
when our efforts are dedicated to a single value, the relative worth of their
outcomes is hard to compare. Suppose, for example, that I value getting at the
philosophical truth. Even if I focus, for the moment, on just that one value,
it will still be hard to rank the relative importance of different achievements.
How do I compare a paper that achieves a small insight with perfect rigor,
against another paper that offers a grand and sweeping insight based on a
looser and more slapdash argument? Philosophical success is hard to rank.
Games results are, in contrast, usually easy to rank. In many cases, commensurability and rankability are achieved by overt quantification.

Note that quantification and rankability are not necessary features of
games. For example, imagine an alternate version of *Super Mario Brothers*,
which provides no quantified point scoring. The goal would be to get to the
end of the game, past the obstacles of those chasms and enemies. This im-
aginary game—*Scoreless Super Mario Brothers*—would still be a comprehensible activity, and it would still count as a Suitsian game. And it would
still be a wonderful playing experience. But it would be difficult to rank different performances of *SSMB* against each other. I might know that you and
I had failed in approximately the same place, or that we had both finished
the game, but it would be difficult to compare our performances with any
precision. We might have to argue over the relative worth of stomping on
goombas and koopa troopas, or whether it was worth more to kill them or

---

[5] This is an observation about games in general, and not a necessary claim about all games. In
some modern computer role-playing games, for example, there may be several goals without an obvious mode of commensuration. For example, the game may track your experience points and your
money; you may also care about your guild's relative success against another guild. Note, however,
that even in these cases, it is rare that the various candidate game goals are in tension. The pursuits of
experience points, money, and victory over other guilds tend to go hand in hand.

elegantly bypass them. We might have to reach for intangibles, like style and finesse, and then argue about how various features of performance should be ranked against each other. But *Super Mario Brothers*, as it was actually published, does offer a scoring mechanism, which creates a quantitative measure of various game achievements along a single value scale. It offers an accessible, easily applicable, and quite precise method of ranking different performances in the game. This lets us create high score lists, compare our relative achievements without ambiguity, and declare with some finality who the "greatest player of all time" is. Of course, we could generate alternate scoring methods or goals, as with speedrunning. We could also start comparing the stylishness and beauty of our runs—a small handful of players do. But most players seem happy to evaluate their performances entirely with that built-in, off-the-rack value system, and accept the rankings it delivers. Games offer clear and usable modes of ranking because most players seem to want such clear rankings.

Let's call these various features—the applicability and commensurability of game goals, and rankability of game achievements—the *value clarity* of games. Value clarity isn't a necessary feature of games. We can easily imagine a game without any particular value clarity at all. For example, we could play a survival game, in which we are all thrown naked into the woods for a month, where the goal of the game is to emerge having cooked the most delicious gourmet meals, having created the most comfortable and elegant shelter and the most fashionable handmade clothes. This is clearly a Suitsian game: there are voluntary constraints and obstacles, taken on for the sake of the activity they make possible. But the goals are unclear in their application; they are plural and their values aren't easily commensurable; and successes aren't easily rankable. Let's call such games *subtle value games*.

There are, I think, a few such subtle value games. I tend to think that skateboarding is, in its informal practice, usually played as a subtle value game. Skateboarders usually pursue the goals of stylishness and increased difficulty of tricks, but those goals aren't easily assessed or commensurated. Improv comedy may be another such game, since the goal of "being funny" isn't easily assessed or ranked. In general, informal competitions where an aesthetic element is among the in-game goals are often subtle value games. Such value-unclear gaming practices often work because there is no need to declare a winner. Skateboarders can spend an afternoon competing to come up with the coolest tricks, and go home satisfied without ever having had to definitively settle on who actually won. However, when these sorts are activities are formalized into competition, we usually see changes in the nature of the activity. Sometimes, we try to settle the matter by deploying supposedly sensitive judges, as we find in Olympic figure skating. As the competitive element of such practices becomes formalized, the practices themselves often change to emphasize clear goals over subtle goals. Thus, as skateboarding was professionalized and skateboarding competitions became more formal, the emphasis shifted from its aesthetic elements to clearer and more quantifiable goals, such as jump height and number of spins (Peralta 2001).

Why, then, do the vast majority of games have such value clarity? Games are not required to have value clarity in order to be games—at least, not by the Suitsian definition. But the agential manipulation of games makes it possible to have value clarity. And since we seem to find such clarity extremely satisfying, we usually seem keen to take advantage of the opportunity. We've already uncovered a number of the reasons why value clarity is so satisfying. Value clarity offers us relief from the evaluative complexities of life, a shelter from the difficulties of assessment and commensuration. Value clarity boosts our experiences of functional beauty, because the functional beauty of an action is clearer when the action's goals are clearer. Value clarity plays a crucial role in communicating different agencies, and thus a role in developing autonomy. Goals are part of the specification of alternate agencies, and it is easier for us to find our way into a novel form of agency when its ends are specified clearly and precisely. Most games have value clarity, I suggest, because games are one of the easiest places for us to obtain the satisfactions of value clarity, and because many of the developmental goods of games are aided by value clarity.[6]

Exporting an expectation of value clarity outside the game, however, brings its own dangers—and they are subtler dangers than those of the all-out instrumental attitude. That very subtlety may increase the risk. It seems plausible to think that disposing of game ends, after the game is through, requires

---

[6] Gonzolo Frasca has said that games are activities in which performance is quantified, and Veli-Matti Karhulahti has defined video games as things that evaluate performance (Frasca 2007, 73; Karhulahti 2015). The examples I've given here run contrary to those accounts. I suggest, instead, that the barer Suitsian notion—that games involve voluntary obstacles—is closer to the heart of the matter, and that the evaluation of performance against those obstacles is a common feature of modern games, but not an essential one. Of course, the matter might be simply a semantic one. The world can handle many ways of cutting up the conceptual space. Still, I can easily imagine stripping the points from tabletop or online role-playing games, and it would still be natural for me to think of them as games, provided there were still goals and obstacles. The live-action role-playing game *Sign* serves as an excellent example. And we could easily imagine a computer implementation of such a game.

some reflective awareness of the ends as something that ought to be disposed of. The goal of committing acts of fictional violence in games' violence seems the easiest to put away. Almost all players know that killing in games is only a fiction, and that they should not export pro-killing attitudes outside the game. And many players probably also understand that the all-consuming instrumental attitude is a temporary artifact of the game. The need to confine that attitude to the game context also seems relatively clear. But value clarity is a subtler feature of games. It is easy to miss that it is a special feature of the constructed agential environment of games. This makes it easier to accidentally export the expectation for value clarity out to non-game life. Games can present a fantasy of value clarity, but many players may not realize they are indulging in a fantasy at all.

So what are the dangers of exporting an expectation of value clarity from games into non-game life? For one, it may infect the choices we make as to which enduring values and goals we should take on. After all, our values are not preestablished and we do not merely discover them. We have a hand in deciding our values and articulating them to ourselves. If we expect value clarity, we may be drawn to those social milieus and institutions that present values as artificially clear. We may be drawn to take on value systems and theories of values that provide the same satisfactions as we get from games. We might start to expect our value systems to be applicable, easily commensurable, and rankable—and so avoid the use of subtler value systems. In other words, we will be drawn to systems, institutions, social practices, and activities that closely resemble games, and we may be tempted to adjust our own goals to make our lives more closely resemble game-play. We will be attracted to whatever systems can give us game-like levels of value clarity in our non-game lives.

Is that such a bad thing? Jane McGonigal and other gamification activists have suggested not. According to McGonigal, we should gamify our lives, to harness our incredible powers of absorption in game play. By gamifying work, education, and fitness, we not only increase our motivation to perform the activities; we will also make the activities fun.[7] But I am not nearly as optimistic as McGonigal. What McGonigal and other gamifiers neglect,

---

[7] Ground zero for popular interest in positive theories of gamification is likely McGonigal (2011). For a look at techniques applied by intentional gamifiers and social engineers, see the influential gamification manual by Chou (2014). For an encyclopedic anthology of academic work on gamification, see *The Gameful World: Approaches, Issues, Application*, edited by Steffan P. Walz and Sebastian Deterding (2014). I take my discussion of value capture to concern a larger phenomenon than the explicit gamifications discussed in these texts.

I think, is the degree to which gamification changes the nature of the target. Gamification can amplify our motivation to act, but in order to do so, it needs to alter the goal. Trying to export the value of clarity we find in games to the rest of life, I will argue, can quietly undermine our aims and our autonomy. Many kinds of gamification are quite pernicious. And one of the dangers of indulging, unreflectively, in the value clarity of games is that it may encourage us to design and use excessively gamified systems in non-game life.

Gamification and Value Capture

First, consider the active and intentional gamification of non-game life. *Gamification*, as most people use the term, is the intentional application of various elements of game design to non-game life in order to alter motivational states. A typical use of gamification is to increase motivation in productive behavior. For example, fitness trackers like FitBit and Strava introduce quantification, game-like achievements, rewards, and competition to fitness routines. Such fitness trackers offer quantified reports on, say, the number of steps you took in a day, as well as leaderboards, where your daily steps are compared against the steps of other people. The car-hire apps Lyft and Uber offer their drivers badges and achievements for driving more miles. Disney, famously, gamified its hospitality workforce. Disney introduced real-time worker productivity tracking of their laundry staff, keeping track of how many comforters, sheets, and towels individual workers were washing and folding, and posting individual productivity statistics in public, on brightly lit scoreboards. Workers' names were displayed in green, yellow, or red depending on whether they were "meeting" productivity standards, "slipping," or "failing." Color-coded signals also flashed at the workers, providing real-time feedback about where they stood in the productivity rankings.

Once the system was in place, workers began to compete with each other. Productivity soared. At the same time, they began to suffer more injuries at work. They also started skipping bathroom breaks. The workers said they had a hard time ignoring the motivational pull of the game-like elements. They found themselves deeply motivated by the game-like goals, even as they actively resented being so motivated. They took to calling the system "the electronic whip." Similar explicitly gamified systems have been incorporated into other workplaces, such as Amazon's, and into social-media platforms like Facebook and Twitter. And, argues Vincent Gabrielle, such gamification represents malicious control mechanisms, imposed on us from the outside. It is a way for powerful institutions to force motivations into their workers, to the advantage of those institutions (Gabrielle 2018).

But I think explicit and self-conscious gamification is only one part of a larger phenomenon. Simple and clear statements of values or goals can take over our motivation and decision-making processes without the intentional introduction of game-design elements. And not all such game-like elements and motivations are introduced intentionally, nor do they always come from outside forces. We can gamify ourselves, and gamify by accident.

The use of the term *gamification* has become extremely diffuse, and has come to cover the adaptation of all sorts of game-design techniques, including some features that are only superficially game-like.[8] I'm going to step back from the term, because I want to focus on just one specific aspect: the motivational draw of value clarity.

Consider a phenomenon, which I'll call *value capture*. Value capture occurs when:

1. Our values are, at first, rich and subtle.
2. We encounter simplified (often quantified) versions of those values.
3. Those simplified versions take the place of our richer values in our reasoning and motivation.
4. Our lives get worse.[9]

Instances of value capture abound. Value capture includes cases of explicit gamification, but it also includes effects from other sorts measures and metrics. You might start to use a fitness tracker like FitBit, which measures the number of steps you take per day, for the sake of your health but, over time, come to chase only high step counts. Or you might go into academia for the love of wisdom and truth, but come out of graduate school valuing only publication in high-status journals and measurable research impact factors. Or you might get onto Twitter for the sake of communication and connection,

---

[8] A very good discussion of relatively ambiguous uses of the term can be found in Deterding (2014). See also Bogost's argument that the term *gamification* is bullshit (in Frankfurt's technical sense), a buzzword used by consultants to generate business (Bogost 2014).

[9] The argument, as stated, presumes that values are naturally rich and inchoate, and are better because they are so. This seems quite plausible to me; for an account, see Nussbaum (1986, esp. 51–82 and 290–317). If anyone does not accept that human values are best when they are rich and subtle, then the argument I've provided can be adapted in the following way: value capture involves a tendency to add an additional simplifying element to our process of forming values and representing them to ourselves.

but come to value high numbers of likes and retweets. Crucially, in all these cases, using the simplified version of the value can profoundly change the nature and direction of the activity. If I am on Twitter for the sake of fostering public discourse and understanding, I might try to tweet thoughtful things. If I am on Twitter for the sake of maximizing my likes and retweets, I would aim at tweeting the sorts of things that might go viral—like clear statements of moral outrage.[10]

Note that the notion of value capture is different from the notion of perverse incentives. A perverse incentive is an incentive that has an unintended consequence, which undercuts the intended purpose of the incentive's creators. Perverse incentives can operate without being internalized by the people being incentivized. Suppose we wish to improve the quality of writing across the country, and try to do so by offering high school teachers a salary bonus based on how well their students do on the standardized writing test. Suppose, then, that the teachers begin to devote significant amounts of time to teaching strategies specific to doing well on the test, but that this does not translate to writing in other contexts. The long-term effect of the policy is that the actual quality of students' writing worsens, though they do become significantly better at gaming standardized writing tests. This is a perverse incentive, but it doesn't necessarily operate by changing the teachers' values. The teachers, like any sensible modern citizen, have valued a higher salary all along; the perverse incentive is just applying a malformed lever to a preexisting value.

In value capture, on the other hand, the simplified value *takes over* as the primary guide in my practical reasoning. My values—or at least, the ways that I represent my values to myself—change. I come to immediately value high daily step counts on my FitBit, or to think about my health in terms of high step counts. The worry here is not that I can be incentivized in counterproductive directions, but that my values are transformed by the seductive clarity of simplified values.[11]

If we increase motivation by simplifying the specification of the target, we may bring ourselves to pursue, with ever more fervor and ferocity, the wrong target. And I think that we have the tools now to explain exactly why that might bring about. Value capture will turn out to be a case of the

[10] Recent research has shown that tweets expressing moral outrage get substantially greater diffusion—though diffusion between ideological bubbles actually drops (Brady et al. 2017).

[11] This section owes a significant intellectual debt to Miguel Sicart's very insightful discussion of games and value simplification (Sicart 2009).

inappropriate use of game-like motivations and designs in a non-game context. The pleasures of games can give us a motivation to simplify our values in potentially problematic ways. The worry is that value capture can push around our agential fluidity, and that we might get stuck like that.

Why Are There Simplified Values?

First, why might simplified values exist in the world? They may arise for many reasons. Vincent Gabrielle, for example, worries that the tools of gamification are used to further various forms of oppression and control. Companies and other powerful institutions, he says, deploy these techniques to control the motivations of their workers, for the sake of power and profit, and at the expense of worker health. William Davies offers a similar criticism of the field of positive psychology, which promises to deliver greater personal control over happiness and well-being. One of the most important methodologies of positive psychology is providing immediate and quantified feedback of one's own state of happiness. By offering measurements of happiness—typically in terms of increased energy and drive for increased productivity—and making these measurements motivationally powerful, positive psychology offers a means for capitalist interests to intrude on our motivational states (Davies 2015).

Davies and Gabrielle are surely on to something. Powerful institutions and groups certainly use, as one of their tools of oppression, the manufacture of seductively simple values. Furthermore, such oppression-based forms of alienation are also the clearest cases for the harm of value capture. When we uptake values that were manufactured by some external force, for the sake of getting us to act against our interests, then it's easy to see that we've been harmed, and our autonomy reduced by outside interests.[12]

But the oppressive use of value capture by powerful institutions is not the end of the story. I am also worried that we might induce value capture in ourselves, or that we might be accidentally captured by quantified systems set up for other purposes. If simplified values are problematically seductive just in virtue of their being clear, then value capture need not only be the product of

---

[12] A relevant account of how one can be harmed by outside influences on one's motivational set can be found in the feminist literature on deformed desire and adaptive preference formation. See Nussbaum (1986) and Superson (2005).

some intentional and malicious design. Our values can be captured by any instance of a simplified value—and there are many reasons why such simplified presentations of value might come into being. For one, someone might introduce game-like goals and systems into their life in an independent effort to amplify their motivation. Many people, for example, attempt to quantify their daily exercise for the sake of increasing their fitness. I myself have tried to implement a simple mechanism, which I acquired from a self-help book: I create a daily to-do list, and then give myself a score at the end of the day for how many items I checked off.[13]

But simplified values can be introduced into our lives for other reasons entirely—some of them having nothing to do with any intentional effort to modify motivation. For one, large-scale institutions often need quantified measures of their various functionings for management purposes. High-level administrators in large institutions needs to be able to compare, say, productivity, customer satisfaction, and worker satisfaction across various departments. This requires quantified representations of values. An administrator might first need to aggregate productivity numbers across different departments in, say, their Tokyo and Los Angeles locations, or aggregate productivity numbers from all locations to compare institutional productivity over years (Perrow 1972, 6–14). In general, quantified measures offer some significant advantages.

Theodore Porter suggests that, in general, quantification trades informational richness for usability (Porter 1995, 1–72). Quantified measures strip away context. On the one hand, context-stripping reduces the rich informational content at hand. On the other, it makes the information that does remain easily comprehensible and usable across many contexts. And it makes the information easy to aggregate. Take, for instance, the assessment of student performance. We could assess student performance in qualitative terms—for example, a teacher could write a brief essay about each student's learning potential, habits, skills, and intellectual character. Such a qualitative assessment would record a rich amount of information and detail. But it would be quite hard to average many such qualitative assessments into a single number. It would be difficult for an administrator to assess the performance of students over time, or to create any sort of aggregate assessment of the ability of different schools to increase student performance. Grades, on

---

[13] This is part of David Allen's "Get Things Done" methodology, which, I will admit, is by and large a useful form of gamification for many of its users.

the other hand, are quantified representations of success, and that quantification enables a variety of mathematical manipulations. We can aggregate a student's many grades into a Grade Point Average. We can compare the average GPA of different departments and universities. And we can transmit grades and GPAs across contexts. A richly qualitative assessment by, say, a fine arts teacher of a student's artistic success might be hard for a distant administrator to understand. But a grade is an evaluation that has been force fit into a portable and context-free informational package. Of course, as Porter notes, it is precisely because of this context-stripping that such quantified measures appear more objective than they actually are. GPA presents itself as an objective measure, but it is typically generated through a complex and frequently subjective processes of evaluation—but those processes are hidden in the final numerical product. For this reason, Porter suggests, quantified measures are often used by administrators to disclaim decision-making, or at least to claim that some action was taken on the basis of some external and objective evidence (Porter 1995, 6–8).

Quantified measures also enable easy rankings, which we might want for all sorts of reasons. Consider the indicator. An indicator, says Sally Engle Merry, is a simple and quantitative representation of a complex state of affairs. Indicators are produced by complex processes of negotiation, compromise, and processing—but they hide that complexity (Merry 2016, 9–38). Sample indicators include, for example, the *US News and World Report*'s numerical ranking of colleges by quality; the US State Department's *Trafficking in Persons Report*, which numerically ranks countries in terms of their participation in sex trafficking; and the UN Development Programme's Human Development Index (HDI). The HDI is a particularly clear examplar of an indicator. The HDI provides a single numerical score and a ranking based on that score, which is supposed to provide an aggregate evaluation of a country's quality of human development. The number is an aggregate of a variety of other measures, including life expectancy, education quality, and standard of living. (The scores for 2018: First place went to Norway, at 0.953; Hong Kong scored 0.933; and the United States, 0.924. Last place went to Niger, at 0.354.) Such indicators are politically useful. The United Nations can use indicators to issue rankings of nations for their success in preserving human rights and stopping domestic violence. Low rankings often serve to shame countries into action.

Notice that many of the forces at play here have little to do with the intentional gamification of motivation. But they can still lead to value capture.

A university administrator steps into the job for the sake of promoting student learning, but comes, over time, to instead be primarily motivated by increasing the school's standing in the *US News and World Report* college rankings. Students goes to school for the sake of gaining knowledge, and come out focused on maximizing their GPA. Politicians go into politics for the sake of helping the people of their nations, and come to be focused on increasing their standing in the various UN indices. And these sorts of value capture can occur without any malicious attempt by an outside force to manipulate agents' values. Rather, clear and simple measures of value can arise to serve any number of comprehensible institutional and bureaucratic functions—but, in virtue of their simplicity, they can also become lures for value capture.

In fact, we have a term for when people make choices that are aimed, not at the actual goal of an activity, but at manipulating the external measures of that activity's success. The colloquial term is "gaming the system." For example: the *US News and World Report* strongly weights retention rates. But retention rates can be gamed—for example, by refusing to admit high-risk students, who might have benefited the most from education.[14] Students can game their GPAs by choosing easy courses, rather than courses that might provide the most educational benefit. But value capture is something more than just gaming the system. Gaming the system occurs when people intentionally exploit the gap between the measure and the value, usually for their own ends. Value capture occurs when they internalize that imperfect measure and so transforms their ends.

So here's a first pass at why value capture is often bad, even when it is not an intentional tool of oppression. In some cases, the quantification of a value might happen for sound reasons—or, at least, not overtly malicious and oppressive ones. Quantified measures are more usable, portable, and aggregable. They enable large-scale data collection and analysis. But they accomplish this by simplifying. Such measures are useful, but we must always recall that they are merely abbreviations—usefully portable simplifications of something larger and subtler. But when our values are captured, we are motivationally caught by a simplified measure.[15] Value capture causes us to lose touch with the richness of our values.

[14] For disheartening surveys of the actual techniques used by colleges to game the rankings, see Pérez-Peña and Slotnik (2012) and Espeland and Sauder (2016).

[15] Some may be reminded of Goodhart's Law: When a measure becomes a target, it ceases to be a good measure. This is a good principle for thinking about gaming the system, but the problems that Goodhart's Law focuses on are when incentives miss their larger purpose. It is a problem of getting

What's more, when the quantifications in question arise from institutional procedures, and from mass produced technologies, the values they encode are not adapted to us. When we internalize those values, we are internalizing something off the rack. For the values that we will rule ourselves by, we'll usually be better off if we can do some significant tailoring. As Millgram puts it, it's not always obvious what the right values are, and especially what the right value for *you* to have is. And the right value depends on so many conditions—your personality, the culture you find yourself in, your professional roles. We need to adjust our values finely and sensitively, by paying careful attention to how our life goes when we follow those values (Millgram 1997). But when our values are captured by an institutional expression of value, they come to resist such personalized tailoring. Their external and public nature puts those values beyond our immediate control. And insofar as we are drawn to their prepackaged explicitness, and their wide adoption, then we will be motivated to stick with the off-the-rack version.

Off-the-rack, prepackaged, simplified values are easy to use. They have, first of all, all the pleasures of any kind of simplified value—the game-like pleasures of value clarity. But their very publicity adds another set of attractions. When we succeed in those terms, our successes are so easily comprehensible to others. If I chase a better income or more Twitter followers, then my successes come in clear terms, in some common currency of value. But the cost for centering our lives around such off-the-rack values is deep, for we cannot tailor them to fit our psychology and situation with any degree of delicacy.

Instrumentalizing Our Ends

Value capture, as I've defined it, involves a value shift that is harmful. Two questions now loom. First, what could the mechanism for a value shift be? And second, would such a value shift actually be harmful, or bad for your life? You might think that your values are just your values. If you change them, then the new values will simply be your new values. Thus, you can never be harmed by changing your values. If I go from being a person who hates sushi to a person who loves sushi, I lose nothing. Perhaps I've gone through some

people to do the right thing. Value capture is, I think, even more insidious—since it involves, not only errant incentives, but also internalized oversimplifications.

form of personal transformation, but I'm none the worse for wear. Where's the harm, then, in value capture?

Much depends on our account of value. Suppose that what constitutes our well-being is an objective matter. Suppose that our internal values are simply representations of that objective well-being. Our values are not simply up to us; they need to fit the objective facts of the matter. We are supposed to value what is really good. It is easy, under such a theory, to show why value capture is problematic. Consider, for example, Thomas Hurka's Aristotelian account of human well-being. According to Hurka, there is an objective list of the features that make for a good life, derived from human nature. Those features include our rationality, our autonomy, and our various physical capacities (Hurka 1996). Note that the various human goods are subtle—they are hard to assess, difficult to commensurate, and their achievements are often hard to rank. And since the list is objective, somebody could just value the wrong things. Game-like motives offer us rewards for oversimplifying our representations of the good. We can fill our life with game-like pleasures if we represent the goods of human life to ourselves as being simpler than they really are. It is easy, under such an account, to explain the wrong of value capture. Value capture is a form of belief in bad faith. For Hurka, our values should track what's really important. But value capture pressures our values to change, not in light of what is really good, but for reasons of pleasure, ease, and aesthetic satisfaction. It permits irrelevant factors to bear on our belief formation about what's really important.

Here's another way to put it: when we engage in striving play, we push around what we value to maximize the pleasures of the struggle. The striving attitude asks us to instrumentalize our ends, for aesthetic and hedonic reasons. Instrumentalizing our temporary ends inside a game is fine, because those ends are disposable. But our enduring ends aren't disposable. In basketball, it's fine to value making baskets for the pleasures of the struggle, because making baskets doesn't have any value that is independent of the activity of basketball. But outside of the game, we should value other people because they are genuinely valuable. Life is not a game. Game ends are free-floating, but our enduring ends should be grounded in genuine value in the world—at least according to such objective theories of values. And if that's true, then instrumentalizing our ends for our own satisfaction turns out to be a kind of bad faith reasoning.

Similar concerns arise for desire-based theories of human well-being. Suppose you think that the good of a person is getting what that person desires. Such a theory would say that you promote your own well-being by fulfilling your desires, and promote well-being in general by helping to fulfill others' desires. But you can be wrong about what you desire,[16] and you can, obviously, be wrong about what others desire. If what we are supposed to value is the fulfillment of desires, then the harm of value capture is still easy to understand. It is the adoption of oversimplified representations of whatever the relevant desires are. It might run something like this: I want to fulfill my desires. I treat my income as a measurement of my capacity to satisfy my desire; then I begin to value my income as an expression of my own good, and do whatever I can to increase it. Or: we treat a country's Gross Domestic Product as a measure of its capacity to satisfy its citizens' desires. And then we begin to value GDP itself, and try to increase it in whatever way we can. But, of course, GDP is not the same as the satisfaction of human desires, and my income is not the same as the actual fulfillment of my desires.

Autonomous Values and Heuristic Drift

The foregoing arguments depend on a view that what's important is, in some sense, an objective feature of the world, and that the job of my values is just to get those objective features right. But suppose, instead, we think that our values are up to us—that we have autonomy with respect to our values. Suppose we think that we can choose and change our values—and that exercising this power is an essential part of those values actually being ours. Furthermore, we can have very good reason to change our values. For example, I might wish to make my values more coherent. Suppose that I value both my family and my work. I come to find that these values conflict too much—that I am always in a state of tension—and resolve to care about work less, in order to bring myself into greater harmony. Alternately, I could change my values to become more like the person I wish to be. I could, for example, work to become kinder and gentler, and to transform my values in that direction. So long as my value transformation arises from and is directed by my own values, it will be autonomous.[17]

---

[16] Some resist this claim, by claiming that what you desire is whatever you think you desire. This seems patently false. For a brisk counterargument, see Ashwell (2012). For a diagnosis of that resistance, see Moran (2001, 1–35).

[17] Agnes Callard has recently offered an excellent account of the latter sort of self-development, which surmounts some of the apparent puzzles of autonomous self-transformation—particularly the puzzle of how one could be directed by a value that one does not yet fully have (Callard 2018).

We also often attempt to improve the motivational grip our values have on us. In graduate school, for example, I valued becoming a philosopher far more than I valued playing addictive computer games. But I found myself perpetually weak of will, and constantly returned to those computer games instead of reading philosophy. I resolved to be more motivated by my philosophical values, which involved developing all sorts of habits and capacities for making and fulfilling resolutions. (First among them: delete and destroy all my copies of *Civilization II.*)

In all these cases, bringing about some change in my values, or their motivational force, is simply a way of improving myself. It is not a barrier to my autonomy. Rather, such self-remaking is a core expression of autonomy. And, crucially, many forms of gamification are pitched as tools for such self-improvement. Self-gamification is supposed to be a way of fixing weakness of the will. Suppose I want to learn Chinese. I find myself unable to motivate myself to do that work. The language learning program Duolingo promises to use gamified elements to help me to motivate myself. It offers points for progress, clear targets, and gamified rewards, which are all supposed to motivate me to do the actions that are required for me to actually pursue what I value. Perhaps it is not the simplified values themselves that matter, but the source. Simplifications pressed on us from the outside, like Disney's gamification of worker productivity, undermine our autonomy, while self-chosen simplifications improve it.

But this leaves out a way in which we can, through our own decisions, undermine our autonomy. Clearly, gamification can sometimes be a tool for getting around weakness of the will, and so enhancing our autonomy. A system like Duolingo is a particularly good case of an autonomy-enhancing gamification, because the target of the system—learning a language—is a relatively clear goal. Learning a language is, by its nature, a clear and simple target, and is easily translated into a set of game-like goals with little loss of content. The gamification of language learning seems to leave the goal largely in place. But even intentional self-gamification can lead to a loss of autonomy, when we gamify a subtler value.

Consider what we might call *heuristic drift*. Our values are many and complex. Most of us value our own happiness, our various projects, the flourishing of various communities and institutions we are involved in, and more. The individual values are often subtle to apply, and the mass of them is even more difficult. In order to cope with this, we often use *heuristic principles of action* or *heuristic expression of value*—simple principles and representations, which can be readily applied in situations.[18] We need such heuristics to manage in everyday life. If we always had to reason keeping in mind our full range of values, in all their richness and complexity, we would never be able to act. Thinking and deciding are resource-intensive activities. We use heuristics to cope with the complexity of our value system and the complexity of the world. The choice of heuristics should be governed by two considerations: accuracy and usability. The ideal heuristic for a value would be a usable representation of the value that, when followed in the long term, would lead to the greatest fulfillment of that value. Suppose I need to get myself exercising for the sake of my health, but often become lost in the decision-making process of how and when I will exercise each day. So I formulate a simple plan: I will do 30 minutes of exercise every morning before breakfast. That plan is a heuristic principle of action for the target value of my health. Most of the time, I simply do it because it is my plan. However, given my larger purposes, I should evaluate my plan and tweak it, now and again, by stepping back and considering whether the heuristic is actually helping me to achieve what I really value.

Of course, it should be clear that this structure of reasoning bears some resemblance to a temporary gaming agency. And game-like considerations can take hold in the formation and evaluation of my heuristic principles. Suppose I start wearing a FitBit for the sake of my health. I set up a competition with my friends for the sake of amping up our motivation. Who can get the most steps per day? Then I become obsessed with beating my friends at the FitBit measure. Suppose that, in fact, taking a lot of steps per day turns out to not be a good path to health for me. Perhaps, given my physical history, I would have actually been far better off with a balanced program of running, yoga, and weight training. But since yoga and weight training aren't counted by FitBit, I'm not motivated to do them. My value heuristic has been captured by the game-like value clarity of FitBit. The measures provided by FitBit turn out, in this case, not to be a good heuristic representation of health, but I am drawn to keep them as my heuristic for the game-like rewards of doing so. The value clarity that FitBit provides is seductive. It distracts me from my goal; it provides an undermining pressure on the ways in which I form,

---

[18] Various accounts of such heuristics show up in many accounts of practical reasoning, including Michael Bratman's notion of a policy, Richard Holton's notion of an intention, especially the special subtype of resolutions, and Chrisoula Andreou's discussion of intentions. See Bratman (1999, 56–91); Holton (2009); and Andreou (2009). The account that follows draws upon the general outlines of their discussions, while trying to avoid commitments to controversial details.

evaluate, and adjust my heuristics. In that way, value clarity can undermine my autonomy, since it runs against my attempt to form a good heuristic for my value, and so stands in the way of my bringing myself to act in the pursuit of my values.

This is not the only way things could go. I could also gamify on purpose, specifically to achieve game-like pleasures, and so successfully achieve them. I might, for example, be interested in engaging in an activity that fulfills the twin values of providing me with health and with the aesthetic joys of striving. One might easily, for example, imagine somebody signing on for rock climbing, or marathons, or any other competitive activity for the sake of such twin goals. In that case, the game pleasures, as long as they are held in the proportion intended by the agent, are simply part of an agent's autonomous plan. That isn't the case with value capture. Value capture happens when the pressure of the game-like pleasures has an unintended effect on our values. Value capture happens when I shape a heuristic in pursuit of reasons other than achieving the pleasures of games, but game-like pleasures insinuate themselves into my motivational system, and exert an untoward pull on the formation of my heuristics.

And this seems a plausible account of many real-world cases of value capture. I don't think somebody who was captured by their FitBit would actually say, on reflection, that they *value*, in any deep sense, high FitBit numbers. They value physical health, fitness, well-being, and longevity. But they treat the FitBit numbers as their easy-to-use daily proxy. And the worry is that the FitBit, in virtue of its game-like clarity, is slightly too sticky a proxy. It displaces the use of subtler and richer proxies. And when the system is so accessible and ready-made—when it is packaged in an easy-to-use product—the ease of use may seduce me away from the complex process of carefully updating and maintaining my heuristic. FitBit's value clarity, and the pleasures that proceed from it, make it possible for its measures to loom motivationally larger in an agent's motivational psychology than they ought to.

The problem here is, I think, a cousin of weakness of the will. Perhaps we can call it a *seduction of the will*. Importantly, the methods of heuristic formation are actually a technique of willpower, designed to overcome weakness of the will and other cognitive limitations. But in the case of heuristic drift, those efforts are seduced down a different path by the game-like pleasures of value clarity. The capacities I usually exert as a form of exerting my will are diverted to another purpose. In heuristic drift, my values don't change. Rather, the way I represent my values to myself, in some daily and usable form, is captured, pulled away from my actual values. Heuristic drift undermines my autonomy by diverting my efforts of self-control toward a more game-like target.

Self-Transformation and Coarse-Grained Values

Another way in which value capture might undermine autonomy is by shrinking the space of my values. The seductions of game-like pleasures, exported to non-game life, can bring me to give up some of the richness of my own vocabulary for thinking about my own values, and so narrow my capacity to value.

Let me draw here on Richard Moran's very rich analysis of self-knowledge. This will have to be a quick sketch of a very complex account. We have a very special relationship to many of our own attitudes, says Moran. First, we have a special authority over our attitudes. I do not simply discover that I am happy, as another discovers that I am happy, by reading the signs. On the other hand, we can be wrong about what attitudes we have, as when we unearth, through therapy or self-reflection, hidden loves, hates, and desires. My relationship to my attitudes, then, isn't completely self-constituting and voluntary, since I can be wrong about them. But my relationship is also quite special, because I have more authority over the content of my attitudes than another person could ever have. The right explanation of these two features, says Moran, is that many of our attitudes are the result of *self-interpretation*. The attitude of pride, for example, has two elements. First, it needs to have the right phenomenal base. I can't have an attitude of pride if I don't have the right sort of positive self-oriented feelings. Thus, I might be wrong in believing that I am proud, if I don't have the right phenomenal base. But the mere presence of those phenomena isn't enough, since I might discount them or I might embrace them. In order to actually have pride, I need to decide that pride is the appropriate feeling for me to have. The attitude of pride is partially constituted by certain felt mental phenomena, and partially constituted by my own deliberation on those phenomena. Part of what it is to have pride is to interpret these various sensations as pride. I have pride, in part, because I think pride is the appropriate attitude to take.

This account entails that I play a self-consciously participatory role in the creation of my attitudes. Many of my attitudes are partially self-constituted, in that I need to interpret myself as have those attitudes, in order to actually have them. But this means that what attitudes I can have depend on what attitudes I can understand myself as having. For me to have pride, I must possess the concept of pride, and be ready and willing to deploy it in my process of self-interpretation. And surely, attitudes of valuing are partially self-constituted in this way. To value something, as Samuel Scheffler points out, involves both having the right affective responses to the thing, but also deciding that it is right to value the thing (Scheffler 2011).

But notice that the seductions of value clarity can work to reduce my ready vocabulary of value. Thus, they can reduce the range of valuational stances I can take toward the world. Here's another way to put it. The account of heuristic drift I have just offered wouldn't, by itself, change my actual values. But if we think in terms of self-interpretation, we can see how the simplification of my heuristics could also, eventually, effect a change in my values. For if the constant use of simplified heuristics leads to a reduction of my active conceptual vocabulary for describing my own valuing attitudes, then my actual range of functional valuing attitudes will shrink. If I am drawn to use the narrower category heuristically, and the seductiveness leaves me to think largely in those terms, I will lose facility and readiness with my subtler value concepts. They may leave my ready inventory of self-descriptive concepts. And if I stop thinking of myself as having those attitudes when I perform my self-interpretation, then I will no longer have them. And that is, quite plausibly, a path to a loss of autonomy. It is a long-term decrease in the flexibility and variety of my valuing responses to the world. And notice, furthermore, that it is one that can happen even if I have autonomously self-gamified my life. The process of self-gamification may have been autonomous, but the result may be a narrowing of my range of values. We are making our values more *coarse-grained*, and blunting our capacity for sensitive and subtly varied evaluative responses to the world.

This self-interpretation story is only one single mechanism by which we might coarsen our own values. There are, I suspect, many other mechanisms by which the constant use of simplified value heuristics might lead to long-term changes in my values—simple habituation, for one. But the general story will be something like this: the game-like pleasures of value clarity press on my motivational structure in a distinctive manner. My daily efforts of being—my acting, deciding, and doing—will give me the pleasures of value clarity if they are conducted under the auspices of simplified values. I will have a reason to replace, in my daily practice, richer values with simpler ones, and to replace richer sets of values with narrower ones. I could

gain the pleasures of value clarity if I actually shift my values in this direction, or if I shift my heuristic representations of my values toward the simpler
and fewer. But even if the process is conducted autonomously, the consequence is a loss of autonomy. For I now have an impoverished variety of valuing attitudes to respond to the world with. And that is, by itself, a loss of
autonomy.

The Call of Oversimplification

So here is the picture. Life is a confusing welter of subtle values, in a vast and
confusing plurality. Living our lives, as fully sensitive valuing agents, involves
making painful judgments, tough decision calls, and agonizing comparisons.
As practical agents pursuing values, we must struggle and fight to make sense
of our place and our purpose in that confusing value landscape.

But the experience of games is one of a cleaned and simplified landscape
of values. Games offer us value clarity. This supports any number of aesthetic
pleasures and psychic reliefs. And such simplifications and clarifications
aren't necessarily a bad thing. The arts, Dewey suggested, reach into the welter
of practical life and create crystallized versions of practical experience. The
arts create little unities. The value clarity and harmonious agency of game life
is, in a sense, no worse than the unnatural harmoniousness of music, or the
narrative clarity and unity of fictions. But value clarity becomes problematic
when we export a need for it outside the game. In the game, that clarity can
be extremely therapeutic, satisfying, useful, and even beautiful—but we must
resist the temptation to export the fantasy of value clarity outside the game.

Of course, the danger of value capture is independent of games. One can
be seduced by a simplified value system without ever having played a game.
But the existence of games heightens the danger of value capture from simplified value systems. If we fail to manage our expectations across the transition from game life to ordinary life, we can come out with an expectation
of the clarity of value. And that will provide more reasons to seek out such
simplified value systems.

10

The Value of Striving

Is there any way out of these worries about gamification and value capture? I think there is some relief to be found, deep in the very nature of game play itself. Gamification and value capture occur when that narrowly instrumental attitude threatens to expand beyond the gaming context. We make value capture more likely when we mismanage the transition from games back into non-game life—when we fail to put away the expectation for value capture. But the motivational structure of striving play also offers us some very good tools to resist value capture. Striving play can help give us the tools to step back from the narrowness of games, and to reflect on our practical absorption from a wider perspective.

The motivational structure of striving play encourages a particular form of reflection about the value of a gaming experience. In striving play, winning isn't the ultimate purpose. We take up an interest in winning as a means to a very different end. And that odd kink in the motivational structure calls out for reflection, for stepping back and asking questions like "Was chasing that goal worth it? Was it beautiful, fun, or worthwhile?" The mental shift involved in stepping back is particularly distinctive in aesthetic striving play. This is because the aesthetic attitude is, in many ways, opposed to the narrowed in-game state of practical absorption in the pursuit of clear goals. Aesthetic appreciation is open-ended and subtle. We do not engage in aesthetic appreciation by applying simple and determinate rules. In aesthetic appreciation, we open ourselves to surprise and subtlety; we sensitively grapple with the complexities and nuances of experience. Aesthetic striving play, then, encourages players to alternate between two very distinctive mental states. We must shift from the tightly practical attitude of games to the subtle and sensitive attitude of aesthetic appreciation. Aesthetic striving play fosters a special form of agential fluidity, where we enter into, and then step back from, the narrowly practical state.

In this brief coda, I will sum up what we've learned about the value of games. And I will make a case that striving play—especially aesthetic striving play—has a special role in developing our agential fluidity, and in our

Games. C. Thi Nguyen, Oxford University Press (2020). © Oxford University Press.
DOI: 10.1093/oso/9780190052089.001.0001

capacity to manage that fluidity. I will suggest that this management capacity is, among other things, a way of fighting against the creep of the narrowed in-game state. In a well-managed agential fluidity, we can deploy temporary agencies and agential modes without losing ourselves to them. And aesthetic striving play, I will claim, is a potent tool for learning how to manage our agential fluidity well.

I don't mean to claim that striving play is only valuable as a developmental exercise. I am a pluralist about the value of games; I think games can provide aesthetic values and, at the same time, develop our capacities and abilities. But it should be unsurprising that the activity that involves playing around with our own agency should yield both aesthetic wonder and developmental value, and that these different forms of value should emerge from the way games play with agency.

Striving Play and Reflection

Here's what we've learned so far. The in-game mental state is usually narrowed and focused. We are absorbed in the practical pursuit of a clearly specified goal. There are many goods that arise from that narrowed state. Narrowing makes it easier to experience functional beauties. The beauty of an action is crisper when the action's goal is clear. Narrowing helps us to acquire and add new agential modes to our inventory. Agencies are easier to find our way into when they are clearly specified, and when we are permitted to throw ourselves wholeheartedly into them. And the narrowing is itself a pleasure and a balm—a relief from the painful and difficult deliberations of life against a landscape of rich, subtle, and conflicting values.

The danger is that these narrowed agential states of games might leak out of the game and shape the player's non-game motivations. Games expose us to a fantasy of value clarity. They encourage us to associate various pleasures and satisfactions with the narrowed state. With pleasure and satisfaction comes the danger of habituation. We may be tempted to take on values that aren't good ones to have—to lose ourselves in proxies that fail to capture our full values. Players need to learn to resist that habituation, somehow. We need to develop the capacity to manage and distance ourselves from that narrowed state. This is especially important because narrowed agential states aren't unique to games. They also occur in the wild—in our professional roles, in moments of practical focus—where they possess much of the same motivational stickiness. And those narrowed agential states are very handy to have around. We get a lot done when we submerge ourselves in a subagency and pursue a well-defined goal. When the practical going gets tough enough, deploying a series of narrowed agential modes may be the only way to get anything done. But we need to develop the capacity to manage those narrowed states, to deploy them under our control, and to extract ourselves from them.

Achievement play doesn't contain any inherent protections against the spread of that narrowed state. In fact, achievement play may encourage the creep of the narrowed state. An achievement player values the win either for its own sake or for what follows from it. If they value the win intrinsically, then they are directly attached to the value of winning. If they value the win extrinsically, then winning is linked, in a linear relationship, to what the player really values. Achievement play never asks the players to step back from their dedication to winning on the game's terms. On the contrary: in achievement play, winning is constitutive of, or linearly attached to, one's enduring ends. Consequently, the evaluation of the value of achievement play is usually quite simple: the more winning, the better. Success in a game's narrowed terms is success, period. Achievement play reinforces the validity of the pursuit of victory in the game's own terms.

Striving play, on the other hand, involves a much more complex justificatory relationship. Taking on an interest in winning is merely an instrument of the value of the struggle. Striving play encourages us to evaluate our interest in winning in terms that have nothing to do with the value of winning. It asks us to step back from a goal we are pursuing, and to ask questions about the deeper value of the whole activity. It encourages us to ask the question: Is this a good goal to have? Is pursuing this goal a good form of life for me to inhabit?

Striving play puts motivational distance between winning and value. It asks us to abandon the sharp-edged terms of victory, as specified within the game. We set aside our absorption in a particular specified goal and ask ourselves, "Was it worth it? Was that activity a good way to spend my time?" And that notion of "worth" must be worked out in terms other than what the game provides. The fully self-aware and reflective achievement player does not need to negotiate any such right-angle turn in motivation. But the fully self-aware and reflective striving player must change the terms of their evaluation. The value of striving play is not linearly connected to the winning itself. The value of striving play turns a corner.

Aesthetic Striving Play and Subtle Valuation

But striving play, in and of itself, does not guarantee that we will reflect in subtler terms on the simplified goals of gaming. The terms in which we evaluate striving may also be simplified. Suppose, for instance, that I had an interest in fitness, which I expressed to myself in terms of lowering my Body Mass Index. I might take on game goals for that purpose, competing in marathons for the sake of lowering my BMI. In that case, we have a clear, quantified game goal—achieving a good ranking in a marathon—nested inside a distinct, but also clear and quantified extragame purpose—lowering my BMI.

But aesthetic striving play is different. Aesthetic qualities are subtle. Aesthetic evaluation, by its very nature, resists simplification. There are various way to hash out why this is, exactly. Frank Sibley's account is something of a touchstone here. It seems clear, says Sibley, that aesthetic judgments are essentially nonmechanical. Their application is not determined by simple rules or principles. Why? Aesthetic properties, says Sibley, are epistemically peculiar. Aesthetic properties depend on nonaesthetic properties, but there are no necessary or sufficient conditions by which we could determine which aesthetic concepts apply to nonaesthetic properties. The fact that a line is graceful depends on simple nonaesthetic features of the line—its physical placement—but there is no way to determinately specify which nonaesthetic features will necessarily lead to gracefulness (Sibley 1959). The application of aesthetic concepts is crucially mysterious. We can never reliably infer, from the nonaesthetic qualities of something, what its aesthetic qualities will be; we have to look and see for ourselves. And notably, since aesthetic concepts are partially evaluative, this means that our aesthetic evaluations are crucially mysterious.

Mary Mothersill makes a closely allied point. There are, says Mothersill, no principles of taste. We cannot infer, from any description of an object, whether we render a positive aesthetic verdict.[1] Or, as Arnold Isenberg puts it:

---

[1] For the initial statement of the claim, see Mothersill (1984, 84–86; for the defense of the claim, see 100–144). Though she attributes the claim she is defending to Kant, I take her argument to be widely convincing—especially to those who do not share the Kantian framework.

There is not in all the world's criticisms a single purely descriptive statement concerning which one is prepared to say beforehand, "If it is true, I shall like that work so much the better." (Isenberg 1949)

Notice, says Mothersill, the historical failure of all attempts to formulate any principles of taste. Obviously, any attempt to do so based on very simple and accessible features fails. There is no principle along the lines of, "Everything that is symmetrical is beautiful." Furthermore, every attempt to formulate a more complex principle of taste has found some eventual refutation. There are always new and unexpected artworks that compel a positive judgment, despite their failing to fit the purported rules.[2] To put it in my terms, aesthetic evaluations lack value clarity; they involve the application of more subtle values.

There are many variations on this line of thinking; I don't want to dwell on the details here. What matters is that the cognitive attitude that lies under aesthetic evaluation is, in some crucial way, distinctive from the narrowed state of game play. Game playing usually involves taking on an instrumentally absorbed state, in which we bend all our efforts to achieve some clearly defined goal. Our in-game judgments occur against the background of value clarity. And aesthetic evaluation involves getting onto qualities and making evaluations against a background of subtle values. When we shift from trying to win the game to reflecting on the aesthetic qualities of our gaming experience, we must abandon evaluative narrowness. We must pivot, and reflect on our experience of acting under clear values from the standpoint of subtler ones.

Managing Narrowness

Aesthetic striving play is valuable on its own, for strictly aesthetic reasons. But it can also offer another useful outcome. Aesthetic striving play can help

---

[2] This is only a small part of Mothersill's argument. Readers familiar with this terrain will recognize this territory; in the recent literature variations on these claims have emerged in the discussion of noninferentialism and particularism in aesthetics. Obviously, I favor the noninferentialist and particularist sides of the debate. There have been some recent defenses of inferentialism (Dorsch 2013; Cavendon-Taylor 2017). I think, however, even if one accepts the mild form of inferentialism defended there, some version of my claim can still be salvaged. I need only claim that aesthetic judgment be significantly more subtle in its operation than evaluating success by specified game conditions.

develop our capacities to be fluid, self-managing agents. As a byproduct of our pursuit of the aesthetic experience of striving, we also end up practicing a mental transition between more and less narrowed forms of evaluation.

Obviously, playing specific games can have a clear function in the development of specific skills and capacities. Rock climbing develops balance and physical control, and chess develops one's calculative capacities. I've already suggested that playing a broad variety of games may offer another developmental bonus: by shifting between so many different forms of agency, we practice our agential fluidity. I am now suggesting that aesthetic striving play, in particular, offers us a further developmental bonus. Engaging in aesthetic striving play could plausibly train us to *reflect on* our agential fluidity, and to reflect in a way unburdened by the narrowed evaluative attitude of a particular agential mode. Aesthetic striving play asks us first to absorb ourselves in a narrow goal, and then to step back and think about the value of the whole activity in an open-ended, sensitive way.

Aesthetic striving play, then, brings us to practice a pair of crucial, and opposed, human capacities. First, any kind of striving play builds the capacity to submerge ourselves in narrowed agential modes. Second, aesthetic striving play builds the capacity to step back and reflect on the value of these narrower states from a wider, less artificially clarified perspective. And this second, reflective capacity may turn out to be protective against the stickiness of narrowed agential modes.

A yoga teacher once told me that we all needed to develop a pair of opposing capacities. We need to be flexible, but we also need to be strong, to control that flexibility. More flexibility, by itself, would just make it easier the world to push us around and hurt us. This, she said, is why we need to have a yoga practice that builds strength and power, along with flexibility. Freedom comes from a balance of flexibility and control.

Aesthetic striving play, I'm suggesting, offers a way to build an analogous pair of capacities. First, it develops the capacity to submerge ourselves in temporary agencies. But it also helps to develop the capacity to manage and control that submersion. It helps us assert our own values and interests against the pull of the temporary agencies, with their compartmentalized and clear experiences of value. Aesthetic striving play builds both the agential fluidity, and the capacity to manage that fluidity.

One might wonder: if games can offer us only a chancy protection against a danger raised by games themselves, why even bother in the first place? But it is not only games that expose us to sticky and seductive agential modes. Our professional roles and institutions do it, too. And we have reason to construct and inhabit narrow agential modes without games or institutions, in order to cope with our cognitive finitude. But such modes are, in virtue of their very narrowness, psychologically appealing. The trap of sticky agential modes arises from the very nature of our capacity for agential fluidity. We submerge ourselves in temporary narrowed agencies for practical reasons—but those narrowed agencies offer us seductive experiences of value clarity. They are pleasurably sticky. What grounds do we have to leave such a narrowed agency, once we have entered it? We need to have built up some kind of reflexive habit of distancing, of pulling back from any sticky and seductive subagencies and stepping back from the world of value clarity.

Games let us flirt with such seductive little agencies in a protected context. Here is the hope: if you spend a lot of time engaged in aesthetic striving play, you will have plenty of practice losing yourself in, and then drawing back from, the pleasures of value clarity. You will be used to wearing your submersion a little lightly. Then when life hands you far more pressing agential modes, and value clarities with more seriousness and force behind them—when you face the calls of the crisp and clear value systems inherent in money, grades, Twitter likes, and research impact factors—you will have developed the right habits of lightness and control with your agency.

Games, Play, Life

When we play games, we adopt new goals, values, and practical focuses. We play around with different ways of being a practical agent in the world. And we do so in a guided, structured way. We make artifacts to record these agencies, to pass them around. Games work in the medium of agency. So it is unsurprising that they will play a role in the development of our agency. Games are a way for us to learn to expand and control our agency—to practice submerging ourselves in narrowed agencies, but also to practice stepping back and managing that submersion. And they are where we can find sculpted aesthetic experiences of our own agency and practicality. The value of games is to be found in the flowering possibilities of the art of agency.

Discussion of the value of games has been haunted by the tension between the aesthetic and the practical. There seemed to be something at odds between the unnarrowed, defocused, open-ended nature of aesthetic engagement, and the focused, purposeful, closed-end nature of practical engagement. I have suggested that we resolve that tension by positing that both practical engagement and aesthetic engagement in games happen at different agential layers. At the inner layer of agency, in the temporary gaming agency, our attitude is entirely practical. At the outer layer of agency, our attitude is aesthetic. This resolution, as it turns out, is not just a clever way to answer a theoretical challenge. It is at the heart of what makes aesthetic striving play special. Aesthetic striving play asks us to pivot agencies, to alternate between profoundly opposing modes. And it asks us to evaluate narrowed agential modes from a widened perspective.

The danger of narrowed agential modes would have threatened us even if we had never invented games. The pressure to take up agential modes is a natural one; it arises from the demands of being a finite practical agent in an overwhelming practical world. All cognitively finite agents sometimes need to narrow their attention to certain abilities and approaches. Those agential modes also simplify our experience of value and success; they narrow our practical being. And agential modes, just like games, are seductive. Agential modes give us some form of value clarity. When they are paired with quantified expressions of value, when they become institutionalized, prearranged niches for us, they become especially seductive.

But aesthetic striving play asks us to make the opposing motion with our agency. It asks us to step back from a narrowed agency, to give up that value clarity, to ask ourselves difficult and subtle questions of worth. In aesthetic striving play, we are asked to synthesize two opposing attitudes. We do so by nesting them and by transitioning between those layers. Aesthetic striving play encourages us to dip into agential modes, but not be caught by them. It encourages us to develop the capacity to step back, to abandon the seductions and pleasures of value clarity, to return to subtlety. And aesthetic striving play asks us to do that over and over again—to dip in and out, to narrow and to widen, to clarify and then to complicate.

Games are, then, a danger and an opportunity. They offer us thinned out values, but they also offer a mode of play in which we step into and out of those thinned out values. They are inscriptions of agency, but they make it possible to practice shifting between agencies. They ask us to conform to a particular agency—but by playing many games, we may gain the more profound control over how we inhabit our own agency, and how we evaluate that inhabitation. Games let us muck around with the shape of our own agency, to flit between its different expressions.

Often associated with the notion of "play" are the qualities of lightness, unseriousness, and changeability. And there is a sense in which the suggestions I've made about striving play fit with that notion. When we are involved in striving play, especially aesthetic striving play, we are learning to wear our agency lightly. We are learning not to be too stuck in a certain practical frame of mind, not too attached to certain clear goals. We learning to dip in and out, to devote ourselves and then to pull back. We are learning to play around with our own practical attitudes. We are learning to be more light-footed with our way of being in the practical world.

Acknowledgments

Writing this book has been an enormous journey; I could not have done it without an enormous number of people. First and foremost, I'd like to thank Melissa Hughs. Not only did she talk through every idea in this book with me, but almost every game in this book I played with her.

I'd also like to think, for their support and intellectual contributions, David Agraz, Kara Barnette, Christopher Bartel, Romain Bige, Aili Bresnahan, Thomas Bretz, Tim Brown, Noel Carroll, Renee Conroy, Anthony Cross, Adrian Currie, Eva Dadlez, John Dyck, David Ebrey, David Egan, David Friedell, Kristina Gerhman, Javier Gomez-Lavin, Andrew Grace, Andreas Gregersen, Laura Guerrero, Matt Haber, Sherwood Hachtman, Barbara Herman, Brittany Hoffman, Tom Hurka, Andrew Kania, Veli-Matti Karlahti, Alex King, Pierre Lamarche, Kevin Lande, Anita Leifall, Olli Tapio Leino, Sarah Lennon, Dominic McIver Lopes, Samantha Matherne, Kris McClain, Aaron Meskin, Michaela McSweeney, Sebastian Moring, William Morgan, Shelby Moser, Shannon Mussett, Jonathan Neufeld, Ryan Nichols, Stephanie Patridge, Jacqueline Radigan-Hoffman, Nancy Radigan-Hoffman, Chelsea Ratcliffe, Michael Ridge, Nick Riggle, Jon Robson, Derek Ross, Mike Shaw, Grant Tavinor, Katherine Thomson-Jones, Regina Rini, Jon Robson, Guy Rorbaugh, Stephanie Ross, Brock Rough, John Sageng, Nick Schwieterman, Ezgi Setzler, Roy Shea, Alexis Shotwell, Mark Silcox, Eric Stencil, Matt Strohl, Brandon Towl, Christopher Yorke, Servaas van der Berg, Daniel Vella, Chris Weigel, Mary Beth Willard, Adam Wilson, Jessica Wilson, Jose Zagal, and Elliot Zans. I'd also like to thank the students who attended the University of Utah Kaffeeklatsch, all my students who worked through the games material with me in my various classes, and all the members of the audiences for the various versions of this material I've presented, who've helped me think all this through in so many ways.

This project started long ago from two seeds—Calvin Normore handed me Suits's *The Grasshopper*; and Jonathan Gingerich and I began talking about the philosophical aspects of games on a climbing trip—a conversation that has continued for years, and sprawled out into long-term projects for both of us. Thanks to Peter Ohlin and the Oxford University Press team for all their efforts with the book. And special thanks to Elijah Millgram, who provided endless intellectual camaraderie and support, and who believed that this was real philosophy even when I had my suspicions.

References

Aarseth, Espen J. 1997. *Cybertext: Perspectives on Ergodic Literature*. Baltimore: Johns Hopkins University Press.

Alexander, Christopher. 1977. *A Pattern Language*. New York: Oxford University Press.

Anderson, Elizabeth. 1991. "John Stuart Mill and Experiments in Living." *Ethics* 102 (1): 4–26.

Andreou, Chrisoula. 2009. "Taking on Intentions." *Ratio* 22 (2): 157–169.

Annas, Julia. 2008. "Virtue Ethics and the Charge of Egoism." In *Morality and Self-Interest*, edited by Paul Bloomfield, 205–224. Oxford: Oxford University Press.

Arjonta, Jonne. 2015. "Real-Time Hermeneutics: Meaning-Making in Ludonarrative Digital Games." PhD thesis, University of Jyvaskyla.

Ashwell, Lauren. 2012. "Deep, Dark . . . or Transparent? Knowing Our Desires." *Philosophical Studies* 165 (1): 245–256.

Bacharach, Sondra, and Deborah Tollefsen. 2010. "We Did It: From Mere Contributors to Coauthors." *Journal of Aesthetics and Art Criticism* 68 (1): 23–32.

Baker, Chris. 2013. "Playing This Board Game Is Agony. That's the Point." *Wired*, December 23.

Barandiaran, Xabier E., Ezequiel Di Paolo, and Marieke Rohde. 2009. "Defining Agency: Individuality, Normativity, Asymmetry, and Spatio-Temporality in Action." *Adaptive Behavior* 17 (5): 367–386.

Bartel, Christopher. 2012. "Resolving the Gamers Dilemma." *Ethics and Information Technology* 14 (1): 11–16.

Best, David. 1974. "The Aesthetic in Sport." *British Journal of Aesthetics* 14 (3): 197–213.

Best, David. 1985. "Sport Is Not Art." *Journal of the Philosophy of Sport* 12 (1): 25–40.

Bird, Alexander. 2014. "When Is There a Group That Knows? Distributed Cognition, Scientific Knowledge, and the Social Epistemic Subject." In *Essays in Collective Epistemology*, edited by Jennifer Lackey, 42–63. New York: Oxford University Press.

Bishop, Claire. 2004. "Antagonism and Relational Aesthetics." *October* 110: 51–79.

Bogost, Ian. 2010. *Persuasive Games: The Expressive Power of Videogames*. Cambridge, MA: MIT Press.

Bourriaud, Nicolas. 2002. *Relational Aesthetics*. Translated by Mathieu Copeland, Fronza Woods, and Simon Pleasance. Dijon: Les presses du réel.

Bradford, Gwen. 2015. *Achievement*. New York: Oxford University Press.

Brady, William J., Julian A. Wills, John T. Jost, Joshua A. Tucker, and Jay J. Van Bavel. 2017. "Emotion Shapes the Diffusion of Moralized Content in Social Networks." *PNAS* 114 (28): 7313–7318.

Bratman, Michael. 1979. "Practical Reasoning and Weakness of the Will." *Nous* 13 (2): 153–171.

Bratman, Michael. 1999. *Intention, Plans, and Practical Reason*. Cambridge, MA: Harvard University Press.

Bratman, Michael. 2014. *Shared Agency: A Planning Theory of Acting Together.* New York: Oxford University Press.

Browne, Pierson. 2017. "Engineering Evolution: What Self-Determination Theory Can Tell Us about Magic: The Gathering's Metagame." *First Person Scholar*, February 15.

Budd, Malcolm. 2003. "The Acquaintance Principle." *British Journal of Aesthetics* 43 (4): 386–392.

Bunnell, Peter. 1992. "Pictorial Photography." *Record of the Art Museum, Princeton University* 51 (2): 11–15.

Burge, Tyler. 1993. "Content Preservation." *Philosophical Review* 102 (4): 457–488.

Burge, Tyler. 2007. *Foundations of Mind.* Oxford: Clarendon Press.

Buss, Sarah. 2012. "Autonomous Action: Self-Determination in the Passive Mode." *Ethics* 122 (4): 647–691.

Buss, Sarah. 2013. "Personal Autonomy." In *Stanford Encyclopedia of Philosophy* (Winter 2016 edition), edited by Edward Zalta. https://plato.stanford.edu/archives/win2016/entries/personal-autonomy/.

Callard, Agnes. 2018. *Aspiration.* Oxford: Oxford University Press.

Cardona-Rivera, Rogelio E., and R. Michael Young. 2014. "A Cognitivist Theory of Affordances for Games." *DiGRA '13—Proceedings of the 2013 DiGRA International Conference: DeFragging Game Studies.* http://www.digra.org/digital-library/publications/a-cognitivist-theory-of-affordances-for-games/

Carroll, Noël. 2003. *The Philosophy of Horror: Or, Paradoxes of the Heart.* New York: Routledge.

Carter, Marcus, Martin Gibbs, and Mitchell Harrop. 2012. "Metagames, Paragames and Orthogames: A New Vocabulary." In *FDG '12 Proceedings of the International Conference on the Foundations of Digital Games.* https://dl.acm.org/citation.cfm?id=2282346.

Cavendon-Taylor, Dan. 2017. "Reasoned and Unreasoned Judgment: On Inference, Acquaintance and Aesthetic Normativity." *British Journal of Aesthetics* 57 (1): 1–17.

Chalkey, Dave. 2008. "Reiner Knizia: 'Creation of a Successful Game.'" *Critical Hits* (blog), July 3. http://www.critical-hits.com/blog/2008/07/03/reiner-knizia-creation-of-a-successful-game/.

Chang, Ruth. 1997. *Incommensurability, Incomparability, and Practical Reason.* Cambridge, MA: Harvard University Press.

Chou, Yu-Kai. 2014. *Actionable Gamification: Beyond Points, Badges, and Leaderboards.* Milpitas, CA: Octalysis Media.

Collingwood, R. G. 1938. *The Principles of Art.* London: Oxford University Press.

Consalvo, Mia. 2009. "There Is No Magic Circle." *Games and Culture* 4 (4): 408–417.

Cordner, C. D. 1984. "Grace and Functionality." *British Journal of Aesthetics* 24 (4): 301–313.

Crowther, Paul. 2008. "Ontology and Aesthetics of Digital Art." *Journal of Aesthetics and Art Criticism* 66 (2): 161–170.

Darley, Andrew. 2000. *Visual Digital Culture: Surface Play and Spectacle in New Media Genres.* London: Routledge.

Davies, David. 2003. "Medium in Art." In *The Oxford Handbook of Aesthetics*, edited by Jerrold Levinson, 181–191. Oxford: Oxford University Press.

Davies, David. 2004. *Art as Performance.* Cambridge: Cambridge University Press.

Davies, William. 2015. *The Happiness Industry: How the Government and Big Business Sold Us Well Being.* London: Verso, 2016.

Deterding, Sebastian. 2014. "The Ambiguity of Games: Histories and Discourses of a Gameful World." In *The Gameful World: Approaches, Issues, Applications*, edited by Steffan P. Walz and Sebastian Deterding, 23–64. Cambridge, MA: MIT Press.

Dewey, John. [1934] 2005. *Art As Experience*. New York: Perigree-Penguin.

Dickie, George. 1964. "The Myth of the Aesthetic Attitude." *American Philosophical Quarterly* 1 (1): 56–65.

Dickie, George. 1974. *Art and the Aesthetic: An Institutional Analysis*. Ithaca, NY: Cornell University Press.

Dor, Simon. 2014. "The Heuristic Circle of Real-Time Strategy Process: A Starcraft: Brood War Case Study." *Game Studies* 14 (1). http://gamestudies.org/1401/articles/dor

Dorsch, Fabian. 2013. "Non-inferentialism about Justification: The Case of Aesthetic Judgments." *Philosophical Quarterly* 63 (253): 660–682.

Elster, Jon. 1977. "Ulysses and the Sirens: A Theory of Imperfect Rationality." *Information (International Social Science Council)* 16 (5): 469–526.

Eskelinen, Markku. 2001. "The Gaming Situation." *Game Studies* 1 (1): 68. http://www.gamestudies.org/0101/eskelinen/.

Espeland, Wendy and Michael Sauder. 2016. *Engines of Anxiety: Academic Rankings, Reputation, and Accountability*. New York: Russell Sage Foundation.

Finkelpearl, Tom. 2012. *What We Made: Conversations on Art and Social Cooperation*. Durham, NC: Duke University Press.

Fischer, J., and M. Ravizza. 1998. *Responsibility and Control: A Theory of Moral Responsibiltiy*. Cambridge: Cambridge University Press.

Flanagan, Mary. 2013. *Critical Play: Radical Game Design*. Cambridge, MA: MIT Press.

Frankfurt, Harry G. 1971. "Freedom of the Will and the Concept of a Person." *Journal of Philosophy* 68 (1): 5–20.

Frankfurt, Harry G. 2009. *On Bullshit*. Princeton, NJ: Princeton University Press.

Frasca, Gonzalo. 1999. "Ludology Meets Narratology: Similitude and Differences between (Video)Games and Narrative." *Parnasso* 3:365–371.

Frasca, Gonzalo. 2003. "Simulation versus Narrative." In *The Video Game Theory Reader*, edited by Mark J. P. Wolf and Bernard Perron, 221–236. New York: Routledge.

Frasca, Gonzolo. 2007. "Play the Message: Play, Game and Videogame Rhetoric." PhD diss. IT of University Copenhagen.

Gabrielle, Vincent. 2018. "Gamified Life." *Aeon Magazine*, October 10.

Gaut, Berys. 2010. *A Philosophy of Cinematic Art*. Cambridge: Cambridge University Press.

Gilbert, Margaret. 2013. *Joint Commitment: How We Make the Social World*. Oxford: Oxford University Press.

Goldman, Alan H. 2006. "The Experiential Account of Aesthetic Value." *Journal of Aesthetics and Art Criticism* 64 (3): 333–342.

Hardwig, John. 1985. "Epistemic Dependence." *Journal of Philosophy* 82 (7): 335–349.

Hardwig, John. 1991. "The Role of Trust in Knowledge." *Journal of Philosophy* 88 (12): 693–708.

Holton, Richard. 2009. *Willing, Wanting, Waiting*. Oxford: Oxford University Press.

Hopkins, Robert. 2011. "How to Be a Pessimist about Aesthetic Testimony." *Journal of Philosophy* 108 (3): 138–157.

Huizinga, Johan. 1955. *Homo Ludens: A Study of the Play-Element in Culture*. Boston: Beacon Press.

Humphreys, Christmas. 1999. *Concentration and Meditation: A Manual of Mind Development*. Boston: Element Books.

Hurka, Thomas. 1996. *Perfectionism*. Oxford: Oxford University Press.

Hurka, Thomas. 2000. *Virtue, Vice, and Value*. Oxford: Oxford University Press.

Hurka, Thomas. 2006. "Games and the Good." *Proceedings of the Aristotelian Society, Supplementary Volumes* 80 (1): 217–235.

Irvin, Sherri. 2005. "The Artist's Sanction in Contemporary Art." *Journal of Aesthetics and Art Criticism* 63 (4): 315–326.

Iseminger, Gary. 2004. *The Aesthetic Function of Art*. Ithaca, NY: Cornell University Press.

Isenberg, Arnold. 1949. "Critical Communication." *Philosophical Review* 54 (4): 330–344.

Jackson, Shannon. 2011. *Social Works: Performing Art, Supporting Publics*. New York: Routledge.

James, Aaron. 2014. *Assholes: A Theory*. New York: Anchor Books.

Johansson, Stefan J. 2009. "What Makes Online Collectible Card Games Fun to Play?" In *DiGRA Conference*, West London, UK.

Jones, Karen. 1999. "Second-Hand Moral Knowledge." *Journal of Philosophy* 96 (2): 55–78.

Jones, Karen. 2012. "Trustworthiness." *Ethics* 123 (1): 61–85.

Juul, Jesper. 2005. *Half-Real: Video Games between Real Rules and Fictional Worlds*. Cambridge, MA: MIT Press.

Juul, Jesper. 2013. *The Art of Failure: An Essay on the Pain of Playing Video Games*. Cambridge, MA: MIT Press.

Kageyama, Toshiro. 2007. *Lessons in the Fundamentals of Go*. San Francisco: Kiseido.

Kania, Andrew. 2018. "Why Gamers Are Not Performers." *Journal of Aesthetics and Art Criticism* 76 (2): 187–199.

Karhulahti, Veli-Matti. 2015. "Defining the Videogame." *Game Studies* 15 (2). http://gamestudies.org/1502/articles/karhulahti.

Keller, Simon. 2007. "Virtue Ethics Is Self-Effacing." *Australasian Journal of Philosophy* 85 (2): 221–231.

Kemp, Gary. 1999. "The Aesthetic Attitude." *British Journal of Aesthetics* 39 (4): 392–399.

Keune, Stan. 2003. "Hit Guyenn's Bridge-Building Social Art Masterpiece." *Artfoundry* 42 (1): 25–28.

Kirkpatrick, Graeme. 2011. *Aesthetic Theory and the Video Game*. Manchester, UK: Manchester University Press.

Konzack, Lars. 2009. "Philosophical Game Design." In *The Video Game Theory Reader 2*, edited by Bernard Perron and Mark Wolf, 33–44. New York: Routledge.

Kretchmar, Scott. 2012. "Competition, Redemption, and Hope." *Journal of the Philosophy of Sport* 39 (1): 101–116.

Kwon, Miwon. 1997. "One Place after Another: Notes on Site Specificity." *October* 80, 85–110.

Leino, Olli Tapio. 2012. "Death Loop as a Feature." *Game Studies* 12 (2). http://gamestudies.org/1202/articles/death_loop_as_a_feature

List, Christian, and Philip Pettit. 2011. *Group Agency: The Possibility, Design, and Status of Corporate Agents*. Oxford: Oxford University Press.

Livingston, Paisley. 2003. "On an Apparent Truism in Aesthetics." *British Journal of Aesthetics* 43 (3): 260–278.

Lopes, Dominic McIver. 2010. *A Philosophy of Computer Art*. New York: Routledge.

Lopes, Dominic McIver. 2014. *Beyond Art*. Oxford: Oxford University Press.

Lopes, Dominic McIver. 2018. *Being for Beauty: Aesthetic Agency and Value*. New York: Oxford University Press.

Luck, Morgan. 2009. "The Gamers Dilemma: An Analysis of the Arguments for the Moral Distinction between Virtual Murder and Virtual Paedophilia." *Ethics and Information Technology* 11 (1): 31–36.

Majewski, Krystian. 2014. "Android Netrunner: The Game Designer's Game." *Game Design Scrapbook*. http://gamedesignreviews.com/scrapbook/android-netrunner-the-game-designers-game/.

Malaby, T. M. 2007. "Beyond Play: A New Approach to Games." *Games and Culture* 2 (2): 95–113.

Margolis, Joseph. 1980. *Art and Philosophy*. Atlantic Heights, NJ: Humanities Press.

McElroy, Justin. 2014. "Octodad: Dadliest Catch Review: Father Knows Best." *Polygon*, January 30.

McGonigal, Jane. 2011. *Reality Is Broken: Why Games Make Us Better and How They Can Change the World*. New York: Penguin Books.

Meier, Sid. 2012. "Interesting Decisions." Conference presentation, Game Developers Conference 2012, March 1–6, San Francisco. http://www.gdcvault.com/play/1015756/Interesting.

Merry, Sally Engle. 2016. *The Seductions of Quantification: Measuring Human Rights, Gender Violence, and Sex Trafficking*. Chicago: University of Chicago Press.

Mill, John Stuart. [1859] 1999. *On Liberty*, edited by Edward Alexander. Peterborough, CAN: Broadview Press.

Millgram, Elijah. 1997. *Practical Induction*. Oxford: Oxford University.

Millgram, Elijah. 2004. "On Being Bored Out of Your Mind." *Proceedings of the Aristotelian Society* 104:165–186.

Millgram, Elijah. 2015. *The Great Endarkenment: Philosophy for an Age of Hyperspecialization*. Oxford: Oxford University Press.

Montero, Barbara. 2006. "Proprioception as an Aesthetic Sense." *Journal of Aesthetics and Art Criticism* 64 (2): 231–242.

Moore, Marianne. 1961. *A Marianne Moore Reader*. New York: Viking Press.

Moran, Richard. 2001. *Authority and Estrangement: An Essay on Self-Knowledge*. Princeton, NJ: Princeton University Press.

Moser, Shelby. 2017. "Digitally Interactive Works and Video Games: A Philosophical Exploration." PhD diss., University of Kent.

Mothersill, Mary. 1984. *Beauty Restored*. New York: Adams Bannister Cox, 1991.

Muldoon, Ryan. 2015. "Expanding the Justifactory Framework of Mill's Experiments in Living." *Utilitas* 27 (2): 179–194.

Mumford, Stephen. 2012. "Emotions and Aesthetics: An Inevitable Trade-Off?" *Journal of the Philosophy of Sport* 39 (2): 267–279.

Mumford, Stephen. 2013. *Watching Sport: Aesthetics, Ethics and Emotion*. New York: Routledge.

Murakami, Haruki. 2009. *What I Talk about When I Talk about Running*. New York: Random House.

Nanay, Bence. 2016. *Aesthetics as Philosophy of Perception*. Oxford: Oxford University Press.

National Public Radio. 2014. "Stuck in the Machine Zone: Your Sweet Tooth for 'Candy Crush.'" All Tech Considered, NPR, June 7. https://www.npr.org/sections/alltechconsidered/2014/06/07/319560646/stuck-in-the-machine-zone-your-sweet-tooth-for-candy-crush.

Nguyen, C. Thi. 2010. "Autonomy, Understanding, and Moral Disagreement." *Philosophical Topics* 38 (2): 111–129.

Nguyen, C. Thi. 2011. "An Ethics of Uncertainty." PhD diss., University of California, Los Angeles. Retrieved from ProQuest Dissertations and Theses database. UMI No. 3532448.

Nguyen, C. Thi. 2017a. "The Aesthetics of Rock Climbing." *Philosopher's Magazine*, no. 78 (3rd Quarter): 37–43.

Nguyen, C. Thi. 2017b. "Competition as Cooperation." *Journal of the Philosophy of Sport* 44 (1): 123–137.

Nguyen, C. Thi. 2017c. "Philosophy of Games." *Philosophy Compass* 12 (8): 1–18.

Nguyen, C. Thi. 2017d. "The Uses of Aesthetic Testimony." *British Journal of Aesthetics* 57 (1): 19–36.

Nguyen, C. Thi. 2018a. "Cognitive Islands and Runaway Echo Chambers: Problems for Expert Dependence." *Synthese*. https://doi.org/10.1007/s11229-018-1692-0.

Nguyen, C. Thi. 2018b. "Echo Chambers and Epistemic Bubbles." *Episteme*. https://doi.org/10.1017/epi.2018.32.

Nguyen, C. Thi. 2018c. "Expertise and the Fragmentation of Intellectual Autonomy." *Philosophical Inquiries* 6 (2): 107–124.

Nguyen, C. Thi. 2018d. "Games and the Moral Transformation of Violence." In *The Aesthetics of Videogames*, edited by Grant Tavinor and Jon Jobson, 181–197. New York: Routledge.

Nguyen, C. Thi. 2019a. "The Right Way to Play a Game." *Game Studies* 19 (1). http://gamestudies.org/1901/articles/nguyen

Nguyen, C. Thi. 2019b. "The Forms and Fluidity of Game Play." In *Suits and Games*, edited by Thomas Hurka, 54–73. Oxford: Oxford University Press.

Nguyen, C. Thi. 2019c. "Autonomy and Aesthetic Engagement." *Mind*. https://doi.org/10.1093/mind/fzz054

Nguyen, C. Thi. 2019d. "Games and the Art of Agency." *Philosophical Review* 128 (4): 423–462.

Nguyen, C. Thi, and Jose Zagal. 2016. "Good Violence, Bad Violence: The Ethics of Competition in Multiplayer Games." DiGRA/FDG '16–Proceedings of the First International Joint Conference of DiGRA and FDG. http://www.digra.org/digital-library/publications/good-violence-bad-violence-the-ethics-of-competition-in-multiplayer-games/.

Nussbaum, Martha C. (1986) 2001. *The Fragility of Goodness: Luck and Ethics in Greek Tragedy and Philosophy*. Rev. ed. Cambridge: Cambridge University Press.

Nussbaum, Martha C.. 1992. *Love's Knowledge: Essays on Philosophy and Literature*. New York: Oxford University Press.

Osborne, Harold. 1964. "Notes on the Aesthetics of Chess and the Concept of Intellectual Beauty." *British Journal of Aesthetics* 4 (2): 160–163.

Parfit, Derek. 1984. *Reasons and Persons*. Oxford: Oxford University Press.

Parsons, Glenn, and Allen Carlson. 2008. *Functional Beauty*. Oxford: Oxford University Press.

Patridge, Stephanie. 2011. "The Incorrigible Social Meaning of Video Game Imagery." *Ethics and Information Technology* 13 (4): 303–312.

Peralta, Stacy, dir. 2001. *Dogtown and Z-Boys*. New York: Sony Pictures Classics.

Pérez-Peña, Richard and Daniel E. Slotnik. 2012. "Gaming the College Rankings." *New York Times*, Jan 31. https://www.nytimes.com/2012/02/01/education/gaming-the-college-rankings.html.

Perrow, Charles. (1972) 2014. *Complex Organizations: A Critical Essay*. 3rd ed. Brattleboro, VT: Echo Point Books and Media.

Pettigrove, Glen. 2011. "Is Virtue Ethics Self-Effacing?" *Journal of Ethics* 15 (3): 191–207.

Porter, Theodore M. 1995. *Trust in Numbers: The Pursuit of Objectivity in Science and Public Life*. Princeton, NJ: Princeton University Press.

Railton, Peter. 1984. "Alienation, Consequentialism, and the Demands of Morality." *Philosophy and Public Affairs* 13 (2): 134–171.

Rawls, John. 2005. *Political Liberalism*. New York: Columbia University Press.

Riggle, Nicholas Alden. 2010. "Street Art: The Transfiguration of the Commonplaces." *Journal of Aesthetics and Art Criticism* 68 (3): 243–257.

Robson, Jon, and Aaron Meskin. 2016. "Video Games as Self-Involving Interactive Fictions." *Journal of Aesthetics and Art Criticism* 74 (2): 165–177.

Rockwell, Geoffrey M., and Kevin Kee. 2011. "The Leisure of Serious Games: A Dialogue." *Game Studies* 11 (2).

Rosewater, Mark. [2002] 2013. "Timmy, Johnny, and Spike." *Magic the Gathering*, Dec 3. https://magic.wizards.com/en/articles/archive/making-magic/timmy-johnny-and-spike-2013-12-03

Rosewater, Mark. 2006. "Timmy, Johnny, and Spike Revisited." *Magic the Gathering*, Mar 20. https://magic.wizards.com/en/articles/archive/making-magic/timmy-johnny-and-spike-revisited-2006-03-20.

Saito, Yuriko. 2010. *Everyday Aesthetics*. Oxford: Oxford University Press.

Salen, Katie, and Eric Zimmerman. 2004. *Rules of Play: Game Design Fundamentals*. Cambridge, MA: MIT Press.

Scheffler, Samuel. 2011. "Valuing." In *Reasons and Recognition: Essays on the Philosophy of T.M. Scanlon*, edited by R. Jay Wallace, Rahul Kumar, and Samuel Freeman, 25–40. Oxford: Oxford University Press.

Schellekens, Elisabeth. 2007. "The Aesthetic Value of Ideas." In *Philosophy and Conceptual Art*, edited by Peter Goldie and Elisabeth Schellekens, 71–91. Oxford: Oxford University Press.

Schmidtz, David. 2001. "Choosing Ends." In *Varieties of Practical* Reasoning, edited by Elijah Millgram, 237–257. Cambridge, MA: MIT Press.

Schüll, Natasha Dow. 2012. *Addiction by Design: Machine Gambling in Las Vegas*. Princeton, NJ: Princeton University Press.

Scully-Blaker, Rainforest. 2014. "A Practiced Practice: Speedrunning through Space with de Certeau and Virilio." *Game Studies* 14 (1). http://gamestudies.org/1401/articles/scullyblaker

Sharp, John. 2015. *Works of Game: On the Aesthetics of Games and Art*. Cambridge, MA: MIT Press.

Sibley, Frank. 1959. "Aesthetic Concepts." *Philosophical Review* 68 (4): 421–450.

Sicart, Miguel. 2009. "The Banality of Simulated Evil: Designing Ethical Gameplay." *Ethics and Information Technology* 11 (3): 191–202.

Sicart, Miguel. 2014. *Play Matters*. Cambridge, MA: MIT Press.

Sidgwick, Henry. 1907. *The Methods of Ethics*. Indianapolis, IN: Hackett.

Simon, Robert L. 2014. *Fair Play: The Ethics of Sport*. Boulder, CO: Westview Press.

Smith, Quintin. 2014. "Quinns' Favorite Drinking Games." *Shut Up & Sit Down*, December 5. https://www.shutupandsitdown.com/quinns-favourite-drinking-games/.

Smith, Quintin. 2015. "How Netrunner Took Over My Life—and Why It Should Take Over Yours Too." *The Guardian.* https://www.theguardian.com/technology/2015/may/14/netrunner-took-over-my-life-and-why-it-should-take-over-yours-too.

Smuts, Aaron. 2005. "Are Video Games Art?" *Contemporary Aesthetics* 3. https://contempaesthetics.org/newvolume/pages/article.php?articleID=299

Smuts, Aaron. 2007. "The Paradox of Painful Art." *Journal of Aesthetic Education* 41 (3): 59–76.

Smuts, Aaron. 2009. "Art and Negative Affect." *Philosophy Compass* 4 (1): 39–55.

Sripada, Chandra. 2016a. "Free Will and the Construction of Options." *Philosophical Studies* 173 (11): 2913–2933.

Sripada, Chandra. 2016b. "Self-Expression: A Deep Self Theory of Moral Responsibility." *Philosophical Studies* 173 (5): 1203–1232.

Stang, Nicholas F. 2012. "Artworks Are Not Valuable for Their Own Sake." *Journal of Aesthetics and Art Criticism* 70 (3): 271–280.

Stear, Nils-Hennes. 2017. "Sport, Make-Believe, and Volatile Attitudes. *Journal of Aesthetics and Art Criticism* 75 (3): 275–288.

Stenros, Jaakko. 2012. "In Defence of a Magic Circle: The Social and Mental Boundaries of Play." In *Proceedings of DiGRA Nordic 2012 Conference: Local and Global - Games in Culture and Society.* http://www.digra.org/wp-content/uploads/digital-library/12168.43543.pdf.

Stewart, Bart. 2011. "Personality and Play Styles: A Unified Model." Gamasutra, September 1. https://www.gamasutra.com/view/feature/134842/personality_and_play_styles_a_.php

Stocker, Michael. 1976. "The Schizophrenia of Modern Ethical Theories." *Journal of Philosophy* 73 (14): 453–466.

Stolnitz, Jerome. 1960. *Aesthetics and the Philosophy of Art Criticism.* Boston: Houghton Mifflin.

Strohl, Matthew. 2012. "Horror and Hedonic Ambivalence." *Journal of Aesthetics and Art Criticism* 70 (2): 203–212.

Strohl, Matthew. 2019. "Art and Painful Emotion." *Philosophy Compass* 14 (1): 1–12.

Suits, Bernard. [1978] 2014. *The Grasshopper: Games, Life and Utopia,* 3rd ed. Peterborough, CAN: Broadview Press.

Superson, Anita. 2005. "Deformed Desires and Informed Desire Tests." *Hypatia* 20 (4): 109–126.

Tavinor, Grant. 2009. *The Art of Videogames.* Oxford: Wiley-Blackwell.

Tavinor, Grant. 2017. "What's My Motivation? Video Games and Interpretative Performance." *Journal of Aesthetics and Art Criticism* 75 (1): 23–33.

Taylor, T. L. 2009. *Play between Worlds: Exploring Online Game Culture.* Cambridge, MA: MIT Press.

Taylor, T. L. 2007. "Pushing the Borders: Player Participation and Game Culture." In *Structures of Participation in Digital Culture,* edited by Joe Karaganis, 112–130. New York: Social Science Research Council.

Thomson-Jones, Katherine. 2016. "Movie Appreciation and the Digital Medium." In *Current Controversies in Philosophy of Film,* edited by Katherine Thomson-Jones, 36–54. New York: Routledge.

Upton, Brian. 2015. *The Aesthetic of Play.* Cambridge, MA: MIT Press.

Vella, Daniel. 2016. "The Ludic Muse: The Form of Games as Art." *CounterText* 2 (1): 66–84.

Ventre, Matt. 2016. "Netrunner Finally Has Its Magic Moment." *Medium*. https://medium.com/@mventre/netrunner-finally-has-its-magic-moment-fd81c8402a93.

Waern, Annika. 2012. "Framing Games." *DiGRA Nordic '12: Proceedings of 2012 International DiGRA Nordic Conference*.

Waller, Bruce N. 1993. "Natural Autonomy and Alternative Possibilities." *American Philosophical Quarterly* 30 (1): 73–81.

Walton, Kendall L. 1990. *Mimesis as Make-Believe: On the Foundations of the Representational Arts*. Cambridge, MA: Harvard University Press.

Walz, Steffan P., and Sebastian Deterding, eds. 2014. *The Gameful World: Approaches, Issues, Application*. Cambridge, MA: MIT Press.

Watson, Gary. 1975. "Free Agency." *Journal of Philosophy* 72 (8): 205–220.

Weimer, Steven. 2012. "Consent and Right Action in Sport." *Journal of the Philosophy of Sport* 39 (1): 11–31.

Wilson, Douglas. 2011. "Brutally Unfair Tactics Totally Ok Now: On Self-Effacing Games and Unachievements." *Game Studies* 11 (1). http://gamestudies.org/1101/articles/wilson

Wimsatt, William Kurtz, and Monroe C Beardsley. 1946. "The Intentional Fallacy." *Sewanee Review* 54 (3): 468–488.

Wolf, Susan. 1993. *Freedom within Reason*. New York: Oxford University Press.

Wollheim, Richard. 1980. *Art and Its Objects*. 2nd ed. New York: Cambridge University Press.

Wolterstorff, Nicholas. 2015. *Art Rethought: The Social Practices of Art*. New York: Oxford University Press.

Woods, Stewart. 2012. *Eurogames: The Design, Culture and Play of Modern European Board Games*. Jefferson, NC: McFarland.

Young, Garry. 2014. *Ethics in the Virtual World: The Morality and Psychology of Gaming*. New York: Routledge.

Zagal, José P., Jochen Rick, and Idris Hsi. 2006. "Collaborative Games: Lessons Learned from Board Games." *Simulation and Gaming* 37 (1): 24–40.

Zangwill, Nick. 2007. *Aesthetic Creation*. Oxford: Oxford University Press.

Zhu, Feng. 2018. "The Freedom of Alienated Reflexive Subjectivity in the Stanley Parable." *Convergence* (website). https://doi.org/10.1177/1354856517751389.

Zimmerman, Eric. 2012. "Jerked Around by the Magic Circle: Clearing the Air Ten Years Later." *Gamasutra*, February 7. https://www.gamasutra.com/view/feature/135063/jerked_around_by_the_magic_circle_.php.

Index